1,000
PHOTOGRAPHY
HINTS

1,000 PHOTOGRAPHY HINTS

Barry Monk

CONTENTS

First published in Great Britain in 1985 by
Octopus Books Limited
59 Grosvenor Street, London W1

Third impression, 1986

© 1985 Hennerwood Publications Limited

ISBN 0 86273 213 1

Printed and bound in Great Britain by Collins, Glasgow

Cameras

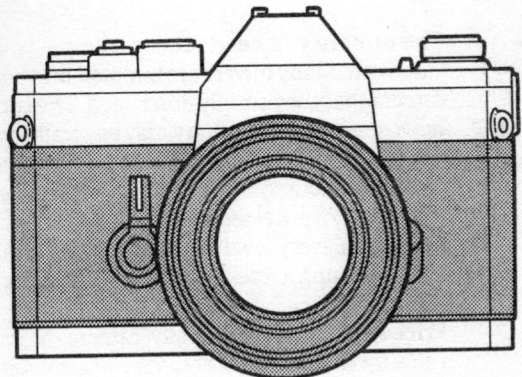

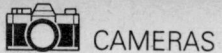

BUYING A CAMERA

Camera choice Don't be put off by the seemingly endless array of cameras when you go into a photographic store. It might seem difficult to make a choice initially, but do not worry. There is a large number of models, but only a few different *types* of camera. Once you know the type of camera you want (110, disc, 35mm, etc.) it is then a case of deciding on a particular make or model.

●Don't buy the first camera that takes your fancy. Listen to useful advice, but don't be swayed by sales jargon.

The camera you need Choose the one you feel at ease with. Many buyers are tempted into buying a camera that they simply don't need. The complete newcomer to photography may be totally baffled by an electronic-marvel 35mm camera – and then become discouraged from taking pictures because of its complexity. Remember, there is a camera on the market for every level of photography, from simple snap-shooting to tackling professional assignments.

Price and quality Generally, cameras are very good value for money. In most cases you get what you pay for, but even at the lower end of the price scale, you can find a camera which will produce acceptable results. Obviously, the more you pay the better the quality of the camera. But don't confuse this with achieving better quality results – *which depends far more on how the photographer uses the camera.*

BEFORE YOU BUY

Before you part with any money for a new camera, ask yourself a few pertinent questions. What can I realistically afford? Do I want a simple snapshot camera? Do I want a camera which will stretch my photographic ability? Do I want to be able to add a range of useful accessories later? Who can I ask for some useful informed advice? Have I read as much

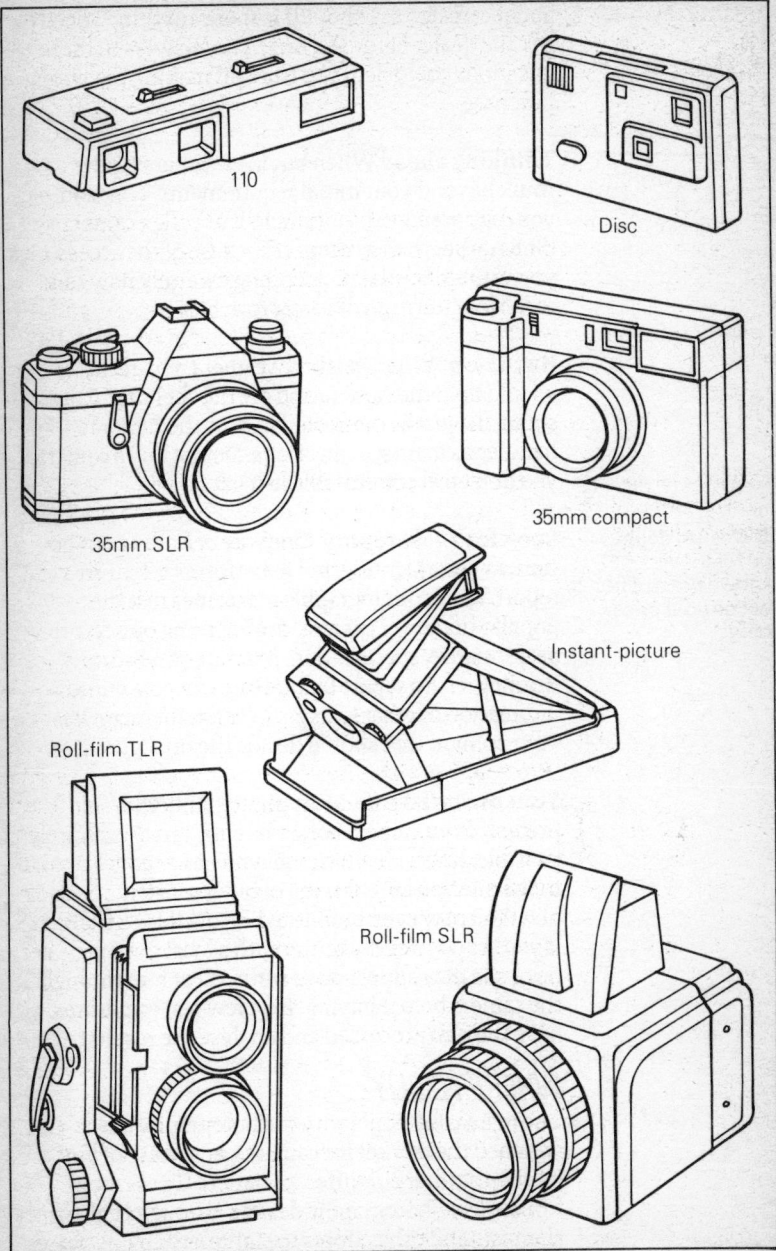

110

Disc

35mm SLR

35mm compact

Instant-picture

Roll-film TLR

Roll-film SLR

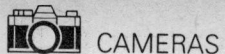

about cameras as I should? Is there anything I need to ask the dealer before buying? The answers to these questions could help you to avoid making the wrong purchase.

Thinking ahead When buying a camera it pays to think beyond your initial requirements. For example, you may prefer to buy a single-lens reflex camera (SLR) rather than a compact because of the accessories you want to buy later. Spending carefully now can make long-term goals easier to achieve.

Hands-on When you buy a camera, you really should hold the camera and get the 'feel' of it. You should be just as interested in how the camera handles as in its specifications. Do not buy a camera if you don't feel comfortable using it.

●**When in doubt,** go for a well-known brand if it is within your price range.

Look for a test report One way of finding out how a camera you are interested in performs is to read a test report. Many photographic magazines test the popular brands of camera, commenting on performance, specification, handling, and so on. Reading such a report beforehand can give you an impression of what to expect – but remember, it is *your* opinion that should decide the final purchase.

Your own trial run Most photographers would prefer to try a camera before buying, but this is rarely possible. If you have a friend who has a model similar to the one you are thinking of buying, ask his opinion of it. You may even be able to borrow it for a trial run. If you are on friendly terms with a local camera dealer, he or she may allow you to run a roll of film through the camera before buying. Do a few test exposures, have the film processed and analyse the results.

WHERE TO BUY

The increasing popularity of photography has widened the market for cameras, and you can buy them in a variety of different outlets. These range from solely photographic dealers, through High Street chemists and other stores to stationery chains. Prices

are usually fairly stable, except in certain lines or
during special sales.

Specialist dealers While cameras are available from
various sources, most keen enthusiasts buy from
specialist photographic stores. This is mainly because
of the dealer's specialist knowledge of the subject and
because good dealers will not only stock a range of
accessories but also offer camera repair and film
processing services.

Mail order Be careful when buying cameras by mail
order. While this is a simple and convenient way of
buying, particularly if there isn't a camera store
nearby, it often involves buying 'blind'. Remember, if
you are not satisfied with your purchase, most mail-
order companies offer a money-back guarantee.

About guarantees Most cameras are supplied with a
manufacturer's worldwide warranty. Read the
guarantee very carefully so that you know exactly
what is covered in case of a fault. If a shop sells a faulty
product, the onus is on them to replace or repair it.

Buying secondhand If you are looking for a camera
bargain, the secondhand market is worth considering.
Some specialist dealers offer used stock for sale and
there are also plenty of secondhand bargains to be
found in the classified sections of magazines, or even
in your local paper. There is always the risk, however,
of buying a 'dud'; so, if no guarantee is offered, follow
the rule: *buyer beware*.

Camera film speeds All films are given a numerical
rating that indicates the speed of their reaction to
light: the higher the number, the faster is the film.
Two rating systems are used: the ASA, devised by the
American Standards Association, and the ISO,
devised by the International Standards Organization;
the latter system is gradually replacing the former.
Both use identical number scales: 400 ASA, for
instance, has the same value as ISO 400. You will find
the ASA or ISO rating printed on the film carton.

●**Shop around** for
the best camera
price. The market *is*
very competitive,
so you can find a
bargain.

11

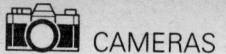

SIMPLE CAMERAS

When you buy a 110 or disc camera you are opting for simplicity. Most of these cameras are compact, easy to operate and produce acceptable snapshots. Today's simple cameras can be said to carry on the Kodak tradition of 'You press the button, we'll do the rest'. The 110 camera has been the most popular snapshot choice over recent years, but while these cameras are still widely available, they are being gradually superseded by disc cameras.

Careful framing Despite the simplicity of pocket cameras, many people still manage to end up with pictures showing subjects with heads or legs missing. This problem can easily be put right by using the camera viewfinder properly. When you look into the viewfinder you are likely to see a rectangular yellow frame. Anything included *within* the frame will be included in the picture, so take care to remember this when composing the picture.

The right distance With a pocket camera most subjects will be sharply focused at a distance of 1 metre (3ft) or more. Go any closer than 1 metre and the result is likely to be 'fuzzy'. However, when photographing people don't be afraid to go in close – many snaps are spoilt by the subject being merely a spot in the distance, rather than being the most important part of the picture.

A steady hand It is always important to hold a camera steady, particularly if the camera is small and light. If the results from your pocket camera are blurred, the chances are that either the subject moved when the picture was taken, or the photographer shook the camera. If both subject and background are blurred, it is camera shake. To avoid this, hold the camera firmly with both arms tucked into the sides of your body for extra support. Squeeze the shutter release button *gently* and wait until the shot has been taken before moving again.

Quality Pocket cameras are designed to produce reasonable results in standard enprint size 14×9cm (5.5×3.5in). Because the film is small (disc is slightly smaller than 110) there is a noticeable lack of quality when prints larger than enprint are produced. Results may be acceptable up to, say, 13×18cm (5×7in), but if you order larger prints, the colour and sharpness deteriorate.

Print sizes You will usually get standard-size enprints 9×14cm (3.5×5.5in) from 110 and disc film. Some processing houses offer special 'jumbo' sized prints, but these are often slightly more expensive.

THE 110 CAMERA

Advantages This type of camera features easy film loading – the specially designed cartridge film slots into the back of the camera. The 100 is easy to use because it has few controls. Most models feature only a shutter-release button and film advance lever. Another advantage is size: it is easy to carry a 110 in a pocket or handbag. Many keen photographers carry a 110 as a second 'snapshot' camera. A 110 film commonly has 24 exposures.

●**Don't** take portraits with the 110 held vertically. Hold it horizontally to allow more of the subject, and not the background, to be seen in the picture.

Limitations Because of its simplicity a 110 is limited to basic snapshooting, unless it is one of the advanced types offering more flexibility in focusing, exposure, etc. You can take successful pictures with a 110 as long as you accept its limitations.

Controlling exposure With many 110s this is not something which you need worry about. Exposure is fixed – that is, the camera has a single fixed shutter speed and lens aperture. Where there is some kind of adjustment for exposure, this is usually in the form of weather 'symbols'. By setting the camera to the right symbol – usually sunny, cloudy or overcast – the

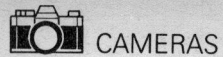

camera will adjust the exposure to the lighting conditions.

Tele-lens advantage Some 110s have the additional feature of a tele-lens attachment. This is simply a small plastic lens element which slides over the main lens and is used when greater magnification of the subject is required. The degree of magnification by the tele-lens is limited. However, it is most useful for bringing distant subjects a little nearer or for taking close-up shots of people.

● **Make sure** your fingers don't cover the built-in flash tube when taking indoor shots.

Flash photograph For taking pictures indoors, or at night, many 110s have built-in flash. This is usually electronic, powered by separate batteries inserted into the camera. Other 110 cameras without this facility use flashcubes or special 'Flipflash' which are slotted into the top of the camera.

Red eye One problem when using built-in flash is 'red eye', when the subject's eyes glow red in the picture. This is a reflection of the flash light from the retina of the eye and can be avoided by asking the subject not to stare directly at the camera.

● **Never remove** 110 or disc film until the last frame has been shot; or if you have to, press the shutter and wind the film on to the end before removing, otherwise some shots may be lost.

Film choice Most users of 110 cameras use colour print film. This is usually rated at ISO, or ASA, 100 and is suitable for most good weather conditions (ISO and ASA are designations of a film's speed and sensitivity). However, some models also take faster ISO 400 film which can be used in lower lighting conditions, or when the photographer needs to shoot movement. (Simple cameras which can take faster film have a faster fixed-shutter speed to 'freeze' action.)

110 slides It is possible to produce slides from the 110 format. The film to use is Kodachrome 64 in 110 size – the price for which includes processing by Kodak, who return the finished slides in mounts ready for viewing. Special 110 projectors are available, or you can re-mount the slides into 35mm slide mounts for use in conventional projectors.

110 SLRs For the advanced 110 enthusiast, Pentax produce a 110 single-lens-reflex (SLR) camera. This is basically a scaled-down version of a larger 35mm SLR. See information on 35mm SLRs pages 21-24. This type of camera offers far more features than a normal 110 camera, such as through-the-lens viewing and metering (for more accurate focusing and exposure) and the facility for changing lenses.

110 SLR system The Pentax 110 SLR system includes a full range of lenses (from wide angle to telephoto) as well as useful accessories such as flash, motorwind film, and so on. The camera system is designed for the committed 110 enthusiast and, apart from the disadvantages of the film format when compared to 35mm, there is a lot to be said for this very compact and useful camera system.

DISC CAMERAS

Disc films Disc cameras differ from the 110 in that they are flatter in design, though they are nonetheless pocketable. The film is incorporated into the outer edges of the film disc and is not in roll form like conventional film. The disc rotates automatically frame-by-frame as each picture is taken, so the film does not have to be advanced by hand.

Colour prints Disc cameras may suit you if you have a preference for colour prints. One difference from 110 cameras is that the film produces 15 photographs per disc. The film speed of disc film is slightly faster than standard 110 film at ISO 200. This extra speed allows for more flexibility, particularly when shooting in poor light conditions.

Special flash One advantage offered by disc camera is the special 'non-electric' flash which is built-in for indoor shots, or where a certain amount of extra fill-in light is required outdoors. Because of the size of the flash tube, the subject(s) should not be more than 3 metres (10ft) away from the camera, otherwise the results will be under-exposed. The flash does not require batteries.

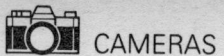

35MM COMPACT

For slightly more serious snapshooting, the 35mm non-reflex, or compact, camera is a good choice. Like many of the 110 and disc cameras, the 35mm is designed for easy use. Controls are kept to a minimum, while some models offer a few extra facilities to help the user develop his or her picture taking techniques. 35mm compacts often cost a bit more than other simple cameras, but the added advantages offered are usually worth paying for.

More shots A possible disadvantage with disc film is that it offers only 15 shots per film. The 35mm compact uses 35mm film, which comes in a loaded cassette form in lengths of 20, 24 or 36 exposures. Having so many shots on a film can take some getting used to, so make sure you are prepared to make use of the whole film if you choose a 36-exposure film – you shouldn't leave a film in the camera for too long.

Better quality A 35mm compact can undoubtedly offer better-quality images than disc or 110 film because the image area of the film is larger. This means that any enlargement made from the 35mm film will have less of a 'grainy' look than prints made from smaller format films. Good quality enlargements up to about 20×25cm (8×10in) should be possible in most cases. There are a great number of types of film available in the 35mm size, so the photographer can choose the film to suit the quality of picture required. See Film Types, page 86.

Auto exposure One feature offered by many 35mm compacts is automatic exposure control. Instead of a fixed shutter speed and lens aperture (as found in many simple cameras) a tiny photocell at the front of the camera 'reads' the amount of light reflected from the subject and automatically selects the shutter speed and/or lens aperture for a correctly exposed picture. Thus the 35mm compact user can shoot successful results in varied lighting conditions.

Setting the film speed Because films are 'rated' at different speeds (most 35mm colour-print film is rated at ISO 100), 35mm compact cameras have a film speed dial. For correct exposures, the dial must be set for the ISO (or ASA) speed of the film being used. If the film is ISO 100 (see the film carton) set the dial to 100. If you don't set the dial correctly, your pictures could be either under-exposed or over-exposed.

DX cameras Some of the newer 35mm compacts are of the DX type and there is no need to set the film speed on them because the camera automatically 'reads' the film speed from a special code on the film cassette and exposures are automatically set for this film speed.

Focusing Some of the lower-priced 35mm compacts feature fixed focusing, so no adjustment is necessary. With this type of compact, pictures should be reasonably sharp from 1 metre (3ft) onwards. For more accurate focusing, most 35mm compacts have a built-in *range-finder*.

Using a rangefinder The rangefinder in a 35mm compact enables very accurate focusing of the subject – much more accurate than the limited range offered by simple cameras. When you look through the camera viewfinder, two separate overlapping images

●**When the 35mm film is loaded,** tighten the rewind crank in the clockwise direction. Each time the film is advanced, the crank will rotate, indicating the film is going through properly.

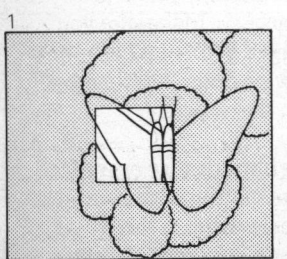 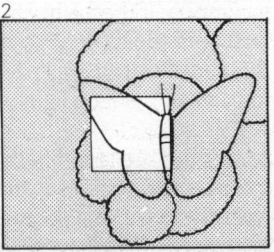

Left Focusing with a rangefinder:
(1) overlapping (unfocused) images;
(2) image in focus.

17

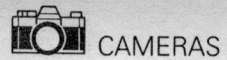

can be seen when the subject is out of focus. Adjusting the lens focusing ring in the right direction brings the two images together. When they are in exact register the subject will be in focus.

Careful framing The viewfinder in most compacts is 'bright line' – that is, it gives a bright clear viewing image and features a line frame in which the picture should be composed. This is usually a bright yellow line which covers the outer edge of the viewfinder. When taking pictures, make sure any detail you require to include does not lie outside the line.

Autofocus One of the most exciting innovations in recent years has been the introduction of automatic focusing to many makes of compact camera. On an autofocus camera, when you press the shutter button to take the picture, the camera automatically measures the distance the camera is from the subject and sets the focusing ring on the lens for a perfectly sharp picture – all in a fraction of a second. You have to ensure the subject is in the centre of the picture (since this is the area covered by the autofocus measurement), otherwise the camera could focus on something else, leaving your main subject out of focus.

Compact flash A feature on many compacts is built-in electronic flash. On some cameras this needs to be switched on when indoor or night-time shots are being taken. Sometimes the flash comes into effect automatically when there is insufficient light available for an acceptable result. A small 'flash needed' warning light may flash in the camera viewfinder if the facility is needed. Make sure you wait until the flash has charged before taking a shot – this usually takes only a few seconds. Full charge is indicated by a neon light on the camera.

●**Check any batteries** in the camera beforehand, especially when using flash or if the camera has an autowind facility. Carry a spare set if possible.

Autowind To simplify the film advance operation compacts sometimes feature motorised film wind-on. Apart from making the camera easier to use, motorised film advance allows pictures to be taken in rapid succession without moving your eye from the viewfinder – especially useful when taking a series of action shots.

Rewinding Because 35mm is loaded into a single cassette, it must be rewound into the cassette after the last shot has been taken. To rewind, press in the rewind button (usually on the base of the camera) and turn the rewind crank (usually top-left of the camera) in a clockwise direction. You should feel the film come off the take-up spool when nearly fully rewound. Make another couple of turns before opening the camera and remove the cassette.

Auto rewind Advanced 35mm compacts feature motorised film rewind, usually via a special rewind switch. This is often in addition to auto film advance.

Watch fingers! When you look through the viewfinder of a 35mm compact, bear in mind that you are not looking through the picture-taking lens. Therefore, it is easy to accidentally cover the object lens with your fingers while taking pictures. The same problem can also arise when using built-in flash – so keep your fingers away from the front of the camera when shooting.

Lens cap Where 35mm compacts are supplied with a lens cap, for protecting the lens when the camera is not in use, it is easy to forget to remove it when taking pictures. If a blank film comes back from the processors, the chances are the lens cap was on when you took the shots. A written reminder saying 'Remove lens cap' can be taped to the back of the camera – this can save valuable film and shots.

Frame counter To keep track of the number of pictures taken, compacts feature a frame counter, usually on top of the camera, which runs from 1 up to 36. Once the film has been inserted and the back of the camera closed, wind the film on to the '1' mark for the first frame. A motorised film advance should do this automatically.

●**Keep your fingers away** from the lens and flash.

●**Tie back long hair** if there is any danger that it might blow across the lens.

●**Check** that the camera strap or camera case will not fall across the lens.

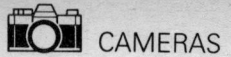

Film safety check A feature found in some compacts is a film safety indicator. This is usually on the top of the camera and shows that the film is loaded correctly. If the indicator is not visible, re-open the camera in the shade and check that the film end is inserted into the take-up spool correctly. Make sure the perforations in the film line-up with the sprockets near the take-up spool, otherwise the film will not advance properly.

Self-timer If you want to include yourself in a picture, set the camera up on a firm support (a tripod is best), focus on the spot where you will pose and compose the picture, then set the camera's self-timer mechanism. When you press the shutter release, there will be up to about eight to ten seconds delay before the exposure is made – enough time to run and pose in front of the camera.

Lens protection For crisp, clear pictures it is essential that the lens is kept clean. Make regular use of the lens cap when not using the camera. To keep the lens clean use a lens cleaning cloth or tissue, or a special blower brush for removing dust.

Accessories Various accessories are available for 35mm compact cameras. These vary from simple lens accessories, such as filters, to close-up lens attachments, cable releases (used for firing the camera shutter without touching, and possibly shaking, the camera) and other useful devices. See pages 79-83.

35MM SLR

Simple cameras are quite good enough for general photography but, if you want to be more creative, choose a 35mm SLR. This type of camera offers many useful facilities to help you take better pictures. With an SLR, you can add different lenses and other accessories, as well as make more effective use of exposure and focusing. SLRs vary from easy-to-use automatics through more sophisticated automatics to complex manual models.

Reflex viewing When you look through the viewfinder of a 35mm SLR you see the subject

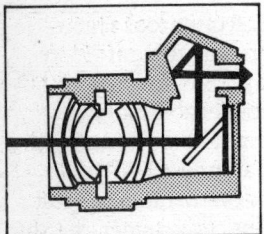

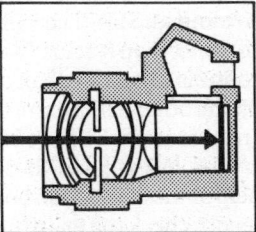

Left Drawings show passage of light through camera before, during and after shutter release.

1. Light passes through lens to viewfinder via mirror and prism.

2. Shutter-release button pressed: mirror rises, aperture closes to required stop.

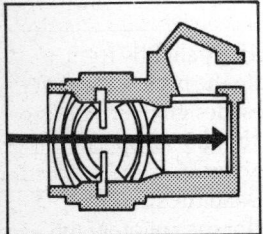

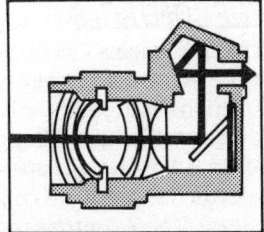

3. Shutter opens, exposing film immediately behind it.

4. Shutter closes; aperture and mirror return to original positions.

21

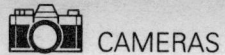

through the actual picture-taking lens (viewing is through a separate lens system in simpler 'non-reflex' cameras). The subject is seen the right way up and the correct way round, i.e., there is no reversal of the image. This is achieved with mirrors. Light enters through the lens, is reflected up from a 45 degree mirror through a focusing screen to two other angled mirrors and comes out through the viewfinder.

Reflex action When you press the shutter release on an SLR, a sequence of electronic and/or mechanical movements takes place by reflex within a fraction of a second to allow the picture to be taken. This is what happens:

The 45 degree mirror lifts
Light passes through to the shutter blind
The shutter blind opens to expose the film
The shutter closes and the 45 degree mirror drops again, allowing you to view the next shot.

●**Don't be frightened** by the complex appearance of an SLR. All of these cameras are roughly the same in operation. Just read the instruction book methodically and get used to the controls before you begin to take pictures.

Around an SLR The 35mm SLR often looks more complex than it actually is. Certainly there are more controls to operate than on, say, a 35mm compact, but on the other hand, extra facilities enable more creative control. Before you start taking pictures with an SLR, learn to find your way around it. With the help of the instruction book, or even a magazine test report, check the main functions of the camera step by step from the loading of the film onwards. Spend time familiarising yourself with your camera so as to avoid valuable pictures being spoilt later.

THE CONTROLS

The five 'basics' 35mm SLRs vary slightly from model to model, but most retain the five basic control functions used since the earliest designs. Become familiar with them. They are: the shutter-speed selector dial, the lens-aperture control, the film-speed selector dial, the focus control, and the shutter release. These controls are set for each photograph but, in some cases, settings can remain the same for an entire film. Additional 'secondary' controls include the film advance and rewind.

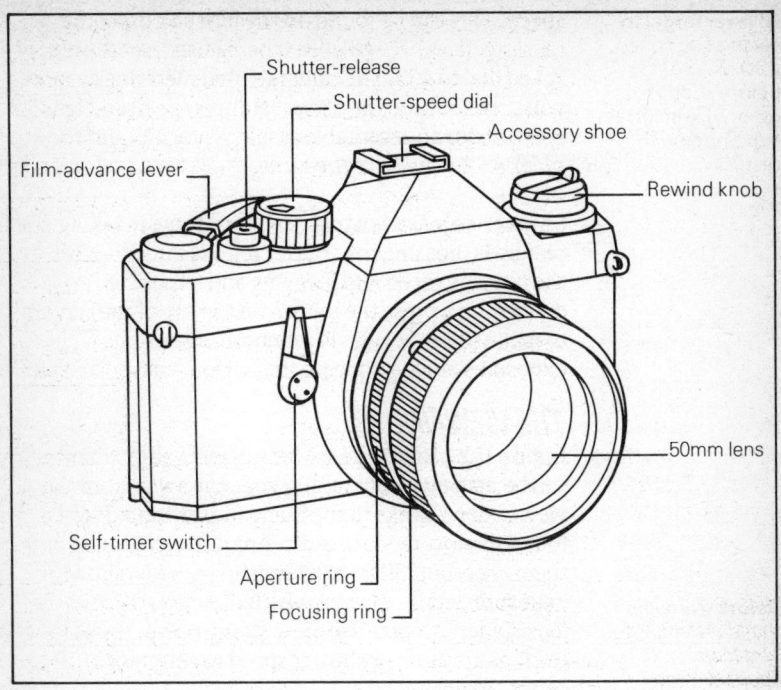

Shutter-release

Shutter-speed dial

Accessory shoe

Film-advance lever

Rewind knob

50mm lens

Self-timer switch

Aperture ring

Focusing ring

Shutter-speed dial The shutter-speed dial is used to select the amount of time the shutter remains open. This is usually marked in standard steps from around 1 second to 1/1000 second. On modern cameras the dial is replaced with a push-button facility, with the speed indicated in a readout form on the camera or in the viewfinder.

Lens-aperture control The focusing ring on the lens is used to control the aperture. This opens and closes to regulate the amount of light reaching the film. On a standard 50mm lens, the range of apertures (or f/stops) is from around f/16 (smallest aperture) to f/2.8 (largest aperture).

Film-speed dial Every film type is designed to operate best at particular light levels, and the camera film speed dial should be set to the film's ISO (or ASA)

Above The main controls and components of a 35mm SLR.

23

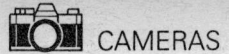

●**Never forget** to set the film speed (ISO or ASA) before shooting, otherwise incorrect exposures will result.

speed. This can be found on the film box or on the cassette. If an ISO 400 film is being used, set the film speed dial to 400. The camera's own metering system will then indicate the correct shutter speed and lens aperture for an acceptable result. *Note: ISO and the older ASA values are the same.*

Shutter-release button The final stage in taking a picture is pressing the shutter release button. With the film advanced and focusing and exposure determined, press the button on the top of the camera to make the exposure. For smooth, shake-free exposures always squeeze the button – never jab at it.

THE VIEWFINDER

Inside the viewfinder Many camera adjustments can be made without taking your eye away from the viewfinder, thanks to the many indicating aids to be found in most modern SLRs. Apart from focusing aids there are often LEDs (light emitting diodes) showing exposure details, or even which direction to focus the lens. Older cameras feature a 'swing needle' indicating the lens aperture or shutter speed to select for a correct exposure.

Below Through-the-lens metering. Left: correct aperture/speed combination is obtained when needle is in central position. Right: position of light spot on scale indicates correct shutter speed for given aperture.

Viewfinder aids Modern SLRs offer useful aids in the viewfinder for focusing, exposure, and so on. For focusing, most viewfinder screens incorporate a *split-image* surrounded by a *microprism*. Other aids commonly found in the viewfinder include exposure readout (shutter speed and lens aperture).

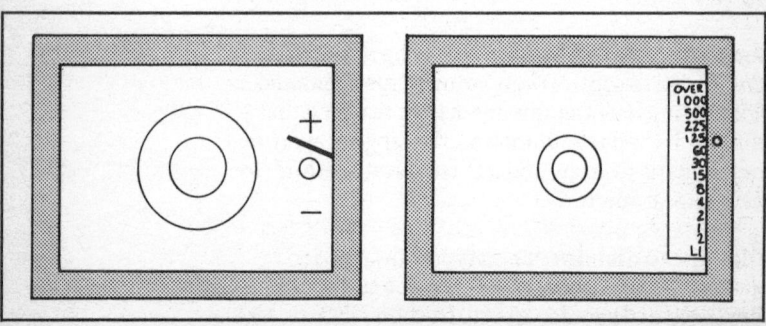

LENSES

Lens fitting The leading camera brands feature their own types of lens fittings, e.g., the Pentax 'K' mount, the Nikon bayonet fitting, and so on. Apart from design requirements, the manufacturers have their own fittings to encourage SLR users to buy the same-brand lenses. Think carefully therefore about the lenses you prefer before selecting the camera. Some lens fittings incorporate electronic connections for controlling the lens aperture automatically. Fit the lens by carefully rotating it into the camera – don't force it or you could damage both camera and lens.

Lens-focusing control One advantage of using an SLR is the through-the-lens focusing system. This allows pin-sharp accuracy over a wide focusing range – with a standard 50mm lens, for example, this range can be from about 45cm (1.5ft) to infinity and any distance in between. Turn the lens control and you can see the subject moving into and out of focus in the viewfinder.

Autofocus SLRs One innovation borrowed from 35mm compact cameras is autofocusing, by which the camera lens focuses automatically on the subject. One particular camera, the Pentax ME-F, features focusing indicators in the viewfinder which show which way to rotate the lens focusing control for a sharp picture. A camera like the Nikon F3AF offers fully automatic motorised focusing, but is very expensive compared to conventional manual focusing models.

METERING
TTL metering Through-the-lens (TTL) metering is featured in nearly all 35mm SLRs. Light entering the camera is 'read' by a small photocell inside the camera. This information is translated into an exposure

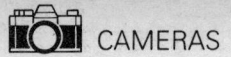

readout in the viewfinder. The photographer then sets the required shutter speed/lens aperture for a correct exposure. On an automatic camera this is done by the camera itself.

Autosettings On automatic SLRs there are two basic meter-operating modes to choose from. Some SLRs offer *aperture priority* metering, where you choose the lens aperture manually, while the camera selects the required shutter speed automatically. On a *shutter priority* camera this operation is reversed. Some more sophisticated models offer both of these priority modes.

'P' for Program For virtually problem-free automation, choose an SLR with a 'Program' mode. The Canon AE1 Program is an example. With this function, the camera is left to select both the lens aperture and shutter speed automatically, without the need for any manual setting. This obviously makes the camera a lot easier, and quicker, to use. In some cases, the camera may have an override facility to enable the settings to be made manually if required.

Complete automation Some SLRs, like the Canon T70, are designed to handle many of the normal manual functions (such as exposure control, film winding, and so on) automatically, often via sophisticated electronic circuitry. If you want an easy-to-use SLR, look for this type of camera.

Exposure override SLRs with some form of automatic exposure control often give the photographer an option to override this control manually. This is useful in certain difficult lighting conditions – for example, where the camera meter is likely to expose for a bright background, but the photographer wishes to capture detail in a shaded area of the subject's face, the override control can be set up to ±2 stops to compensate.

Spot metering The TTL metering in most SLRs can provide only a general light reading of the subject being photographed. Some SLRs offer a spot-metering facility, enabling one to measure one small part of the subject area and thereby obtain a more accurate exposure. Use this facility when exposing for areas which are either very bright or in shade.

OTHER CONTROLS

Film wind-on Once the 35mm film is loaded, use the film wind-on lever to advance the film to the next frame. This action also 'cocks' the shutter in most cameras. Don't be too aggressive when winding-on otherwise you may damage both camera and film. Practise a smooth action, making sure the lever returns to the flush position after use. In some cameras moving the wind-on lever slightly away from the camera body switches on the camera metering. Some SLRs feature motorised film advance as a built-in feature. Accessory motor winders can be added to many cameras.

Film rewind After shooting the last frame on the film, rewind into the cassette before the camera back is opened. Press in the film-rewind button (usually in the base of the camera) and turn the rewind crank (top left) clockwise until the film is released from the take-up spool. The crank can be felt to turn more easily when this happens. On a lot of SLRs, the fastenings locking the back of the camera are disengaged by pulling the crank upwards. Automatic rewinding can be found on a few of the more expensive SLRs.

Hot shoe For synchronised flash shots a hot shoe is fitted onto the top of the SLR. This is a bayonet fitting to hold a portable flash unit. Small electronic contacts in the fitting fire a compatible flash unit automatically when the shutter-release button is pressed.

X-sync If the camera or flashgun is not hot-shoe linked, connect the flash via a short lead to an X-sync (synchronization) socket on the camera. Some older cameras have an M-sync socket, but use this with *flashbulb units only.*

●**Never open** the back of the camera after finishing a film until the the film is rewound into the cassette, otherwise many frames (if not all) could be ruined.

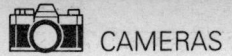 CAMERAS

Auto-flash exposure If you want trouble-free flash photography, go for an SLR which offers an auto-flash exposure mode. Linked with a compatible flashgun, the camera will calculate a correct exposure by controlling the amount of light given out by the flash. As well as ensuring the most accurate results, this flash control can also save valuable battery power, since the flashgun will only produce sufficient light for each subject.

Self-timer The self-timer on an SLR can be set to delay the exposure for around 15 seconds. This may be done by setting a mechanical lever on the front of the camera, although modern cameras do this electronically. Use the self-timer to include yourself in the shot, or where you don't wish to touch the camera at the moment of exposure and cause camera shake.

●**Don't forget** to check camera batteries before a trip – take spares if in doubt.

Battery check Because electronic SLRs rely on battery power for shutter operation and/or exposure control, it pays to check the cells regularly – certainly before taking the camera on location, for example. A battery check is common on many SLRs and the strength of the cells is often indicated by a red light on the camera, or inside the viewfinder. In some cameras you may even find the words 'battery OK' flash in the viewfinder. Always carry spare cells in your gadget bag for emergencies.

ROLL-FILM SLR

If you are looking for more professional results, but wish to retain all the advantages offered by a reflex camera, consider a roll-film SLR. This type of camera uses 120 roll film, which offers a larger image area than 35mm (up to 6×6cm compared to the 2.4×3.6cm format of 35mm). Roll-film SLRs are much bulkier than 35mm cameras so, if you are considering one of these SLRs, handle it first. Hiring one from a specialist camera dealer for a short period may save you from making an expensive mistake (see Camera hire page 35-6).

Film format Roll-film cameras use 120 film (or the longer 220 film in some cases). A camera may offer one or more formats within this film size, including 6×6, 6×4.5, 6×7 and 6×9cm. Many professionals shoot on the square 6×6cm format so that their pictures can be easily cropped for reproduction in magazines. Most amateurs find the 6×4.5cm format a better shape, particularly for landscapes. The latter also provides you with more shots per film – 15 compared to 12 on the 6×6cm format.

●**You don't need to worry** about rewinding 120 roll film. The film loads spool-to-spool. Just wind-on a few frames after the last shot has been taken, open the camera back and remove the film spool.

Quality One major reason for choosing a roll-film SLR is the quality of the results. In many cases, an enlargment made from a 120 film negative can be of higher quality than one from a 35mm negative. Similarly many magazines prefer the size of 120 transparencies to 35mm because of their higher reproduction quality. If you know someone with a roll-film SLR, compare results with 35mm and judge for yourself. If you are happy with 35mm, you'd be well advised to stick with it.

Special backs Some roll-film SLRs feature interchangeable film backs. Such a facility is useful if

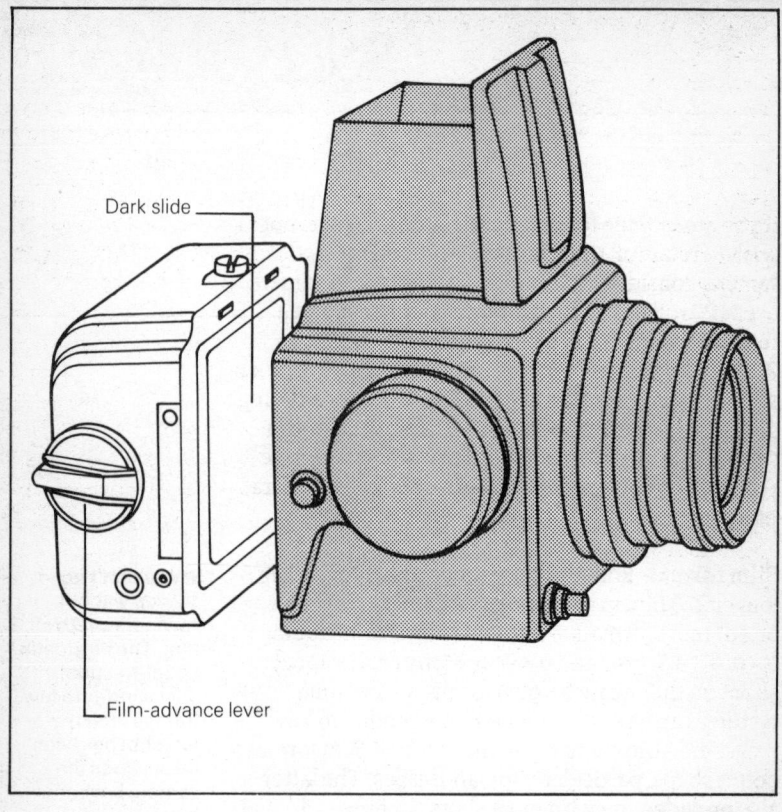

Dark slide

Film-advance lever

Above *Detachable backs on some roll-film SLRs enable rapid change from one type of film to another, even in mid-roll. When back is detached, dark slide keeps light away from film.*

you wish to carry a couple of ready-loaded film backs, or even change films (colour to black-and-white, for instance) during a shooting session. You can change format in some cases, or even switch films half-way through, using the remainder later if necessary.

Lenses and accessories As with 35mm SLRs, there is a wide selection of lenses and accessories available for roll-film cameras. Most roll-film SLRs require their own lenses, but certain accessories from your 35mm set-up may be used, e.g., tripods, filters, flash, and so on. However some accessories may have to be purchased specially, so bear this in mind when buying. Look carefully at the manufacturer's catalogue and see what items are available for the camera.

Price Consider cost when purchasing a roll-film camera. In general, these SLRs are more expensive than 35mm SLRs (see comparison chart, page 37). Lenses and accessories are also expensive, so you have to be sure that buying a roll-film SLR system is a good investment in the long run. You are getting high quality – but at a price.

TLR cameras The twin lens reflex (or TLR) camera features separate viewing and 'taking' lenses. A single focusing control is used to operate both lenses together. The TLR uses 120 (or 220) film and offers many of the advantages of the roll-film SLR, but without reflex viewing and, in some cases, the facility to change lenses or add useful accessories.

●**Remember to shoot** wisely on roll film. With an average of 12 shots per film (compared with up to 36 on 35mm film) try and make each shot count.

Below Main controls of a roll-film TLR camera.

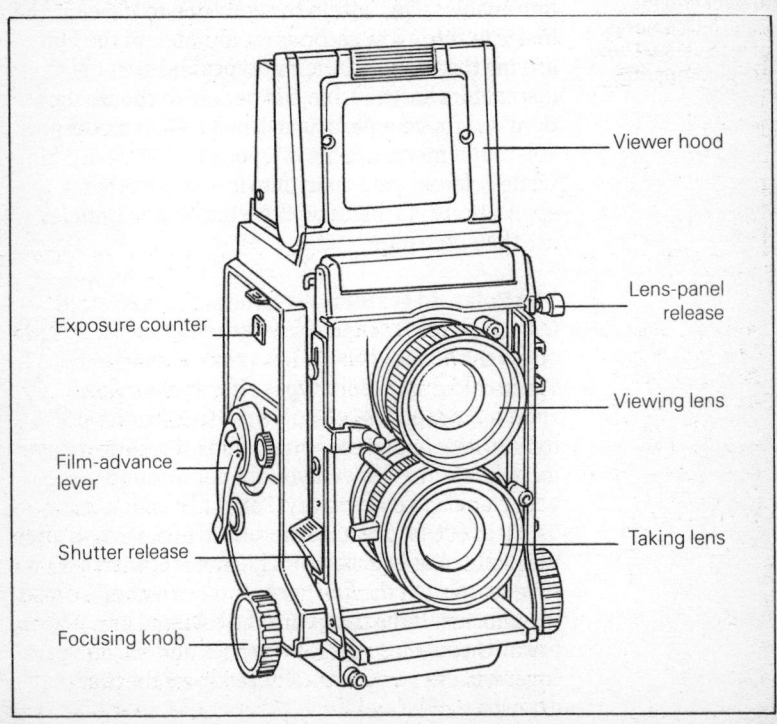

Viewer hood

Lens-panel release

Exposure counter

Viewing lens

Film-advance lever

Shutter release

Taking lens

Focusing knob

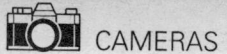

INSTANT PHOTOGRAPHY

Instant-picture cameras If you don't want to wait for your pictures to come back from the processors, buy an instant-picture camera. There are several types available and you can choose from simple point-and-shoot to more sophisticated reflex models. In recent years instant-picture cameras and films have improved greatly. Kodak and Polaroid produce their own instant systems, so choose the camera that feels most comfortable to hold.

●**Never** buy Kodak instant film for Polaroid cameras, or vice versa. They are incompatible.

Instant film The unique design of instant-picture film enables dyes within the emulsion to 'develop' the image within a few seconds (or minutes) of the film leaving the camera. Different types and sizes of instant film are available, but be sure to choose the right one for your particular camera. Most modern Polaroid cameras use the 600 Series SX-70 sealed film, while Polaroid 'peel-apart' film is used for other applications. As might be expected, Kodak cameras use their own film.

The Polaroid system With the popular Polaroid instant-picture system, use either Polaroid SX-70 film or, for the Polaroid 600 Series cameras, 600 High Speed colour film. Both types offer a colour print approx 8×8cm (3⅛ × ⅛in) with 10 exposures per film. Be sure to buy the correct film for your particular model – ask the dealer if you are not sure and take your camera in if necessary. Polaroid cameras using SX-70 or 600 film feature motorised film ejection after the picture has been taken. The motor is powered by a small battery *in the film pack*, not the camera. To load the film, insert the pack with the coloured tab towards you. Close the camera back and the film pack cover will eject automatically, ready for the first exposure.

Instant-picture Cameras

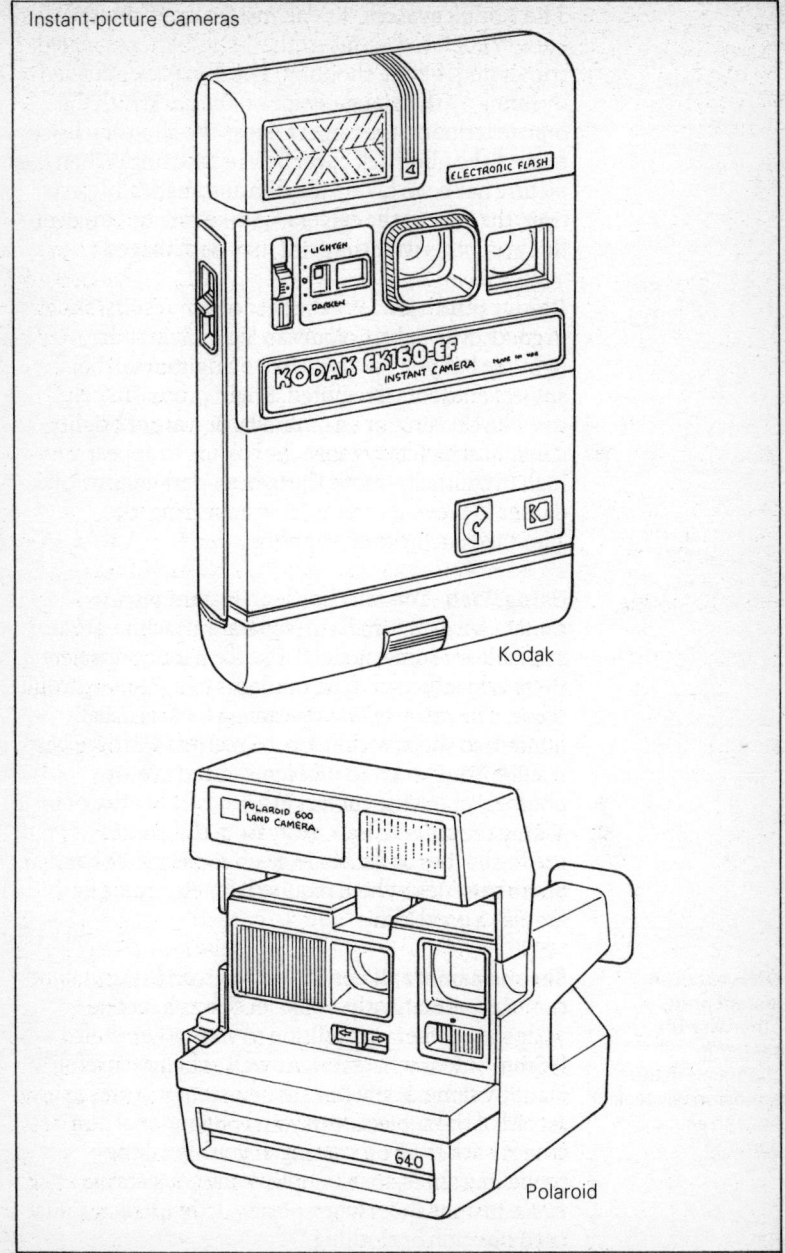

Kodak

Polaroid

33

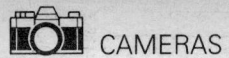

The Kodak system Kodak instant cameras are battery operated, so insert the 'J-size' battery (angled corner first) before shooting. The film pack is loaded by lining up the orange stripe on the pack with the orange stripe on the camera. Press the shutter release to eject the film-pack cover before shooting. When the picture has been taken, the film automatically ejects from the base of the camera, so take care not to cover this area otherwise the print may be damaged.

Colour rendition For the best colour results, shoot in good, even light. Colour can look flat in dull lighting, but you can use flash to brighten up the subject outdoors if required. Bright props can help too, like clothing, or an umbrella. Beware of bright sunlight which may cause the colours to appear very high in contrast – move the lighten/darken control to darker to prevent colours from appearing too 'bleached out' in strong lighting.

Using flash You can choose an instant picture camera with built-in flash (separate attachments are available for some models). Use flash indoors where there is insufficient light, outdoors to lighten-up a dull scene. The range of instant camera flash is usually limited, so shoot within 1.2-2.5 metres (4-8ft) for best results. You can avoid problems of 'red eye' by photographing the subject in a brightly lit area, or by asking the sitter to look away from the camera. If you use flashcubes or flashbars, keep some spares handy. Spare batteries (where required) for electronic flash are also a good idea.

●**Never** cut an instant print, otherwise the sealed-in chemicals in the emulsion will leak out and cause damage.

Second camera If you are not keen on using instant cameras permanently, consider one as a second 'snapshot' camera in addition to your other choice (35mm SLR or whatever). As well as being a useful standby camera, you can shoot instant pictures as a record of the subject until your conventional film comes back from processing. If you are taking modelling shots, for example, some subjects may like to see instant shots when posing, to help them adjust their position or clothing.

CAMERA CHECKLIST

Camera carrying When using a camera, make sure the carrying strap is secure. If you are likely to attach weighty accessories to the camera, choose a heavy-duty strap for extra support. An additional body strap will prevent the camera from bouncing around when you are on the move. When the camera is not in use, keep it in a camera case or gadget bag.

Camera care Remember that a camera is a precision instrument and should be looked after. To avoid mechanical and electronic problems, bear in mind that prevention is better than cure. Handle the camera carefully, don't force any of the controls during operation, and try and keep it as dry as possible. Try and keep the camera as dust-free as possible – a blower brush is a useful aid. Store the camera in its case in a damp-free place. A small bag of silica gel (usually supplied with the camera) will absorb any harmful moisture.

Camera servicing Modern cameras are designed to provide long and reliable service. You can carry out simple maintenance yourself, such as checking for loose screws, checking battery connections are clean, and so on. Many camera manufacturers can carry out routine servicing quickly, so bear this in mind; although cameras usually only need a service once every couple of years. If the camera breaks down, the manufacturer should repair or replace it if it is still under guarantee. If not get a quote for repair. There are also local repair workshops. *Do not attempt to carry out complex repairs yourself.*

● **Never** use your camera in continuous rain, or the internal electronics may be damaged. Use a special rain pouch for protection – a polythene bag with a hole cut in it for the lens will do.

Camera hire If you want to try out a particular camera before buying, or you need a specialist camera for an assignment, hiring is a good option. Many

35

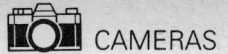

retailers offer hire services and, in 1985, it is possible to hire a camera like a Hasselblad from around £15 per day. But remember you may have to pay a returnable deposit covering the value of the equipment hired, and/or pay an insurance premium.

Camera clubs To share your interest in photography with like-minded enthusiasts, join a camera club. There are local clubs in most areas, so enquire at the library or citizens' advice bureau. The Photographic Alliance of Great Britain (PAGB) has federations throughout the country which list local clubs. The Royal Photographic Society (RPS) is also worth considering. Some camera manufacturers, such as Canon and Pentax, have their own clubs.

●**Never** buy a camera abroad which has no international guarantee or you may not be able to have guarantee work done back home.

Camera manufacturers Most camera production is in Japan, but many companies have their own UK subsidiaries. Apart from distribution and service, the manufacturers often work hard to help photographers with problems and to generate interest in photography. If you need help or advice on a camera or piece of equipment, write to the manufacturer.

Camera Comparisons

Prices are typical for early 1985

TYPE	FILM TYPE	TYPICAL ADVANTAGES	PRICE RANGE (£)
110	110 cartridge	Easy to carry Simple to use Easy film loading Auto exposure (some) Built-in flash (some)	10-30
Disc	Disc film	Pocket size Easy film loading Auto exposure Built-in flash Motorised film advance	20-40

TYPE	FILM TYPE	TYPICAL ADVANTAGES	PRICE RANGE (£)
35mm Compact	35mm cassette	Rangefinder focusing (most) Auto exposure Built-in flash Motorised film advance (some) Autofocus facility (some)	50-100
35mm SLR	35mm cassette	TTL focusing TTL metering Wide range of lenses Wide range of accessories Manual/fully auto modes (some) Motorised film advance (some) Motorised film rewind (some)	75-750
Roll-film TLR	Roll film	Separate viewing and taking lenses Coupled rangefinder Interchangeable lenses (some) Built-in meter (some)	75-250
Roll-film SLR	Roll film	TTL focusing TTL metering Wide range of lenses Wide range of accessories Interchangeable backs (some)	250-1000
Instant	Instant film	Produces developed print in minutes Easy and convenient to use Autofocusing (some)	20-100

Lenses

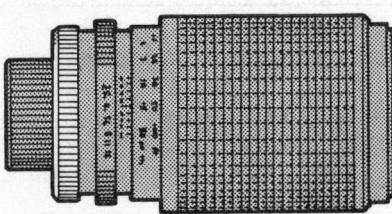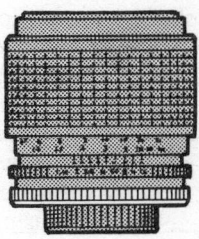

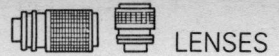
UNDERSTANDING THE LENS

What is a lens? Lenses in all cameras, from the simplest 110 to the most complex roll-film model, are designed to do just two things – to focus the image and allow light to reach the film. Light rays entering the camera are gathered together and sharply focused at the film surface.

Elementary Each lens is made up of one or more glass (or plastic) elements. A simple camera can have just one fixed element to focus the image. The standard 50mm lens on a 35mm camera might have a collection of six or seven different elements, all designed to direct and adjust the light, even improving image quality in some cases. These elements (or groups of them) move inside the lens housing when you focus.

Fixed lenses Most simple cameras have so-called 'fixed' lenses – these might be fixed mount and/or fixed focus. A fixed mount lens is there permanently – you can't replace it with another lens, as in some cameras. With a fixed-focus lens, the focusing range has been pre-determined by the manufacturer of the camera and you can't adjust it. Most shots should be reasonably sharp within a range of 1 metre (3¼ft) and infinity.

Focus control Most photographers prefer to choose a camera with some kind of focusing control. This allows you to focus precisely on the subject within a certain distance range. The focus control (or ring) is located on the lens housing and rotates for focusing. If you can't usually focus through-the-lens (as on a 35mm reflex), guess the distance from the main subject and set the lens ring indicator to that value (in feet or metres) marked on the lens.

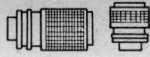
Popular Lenses

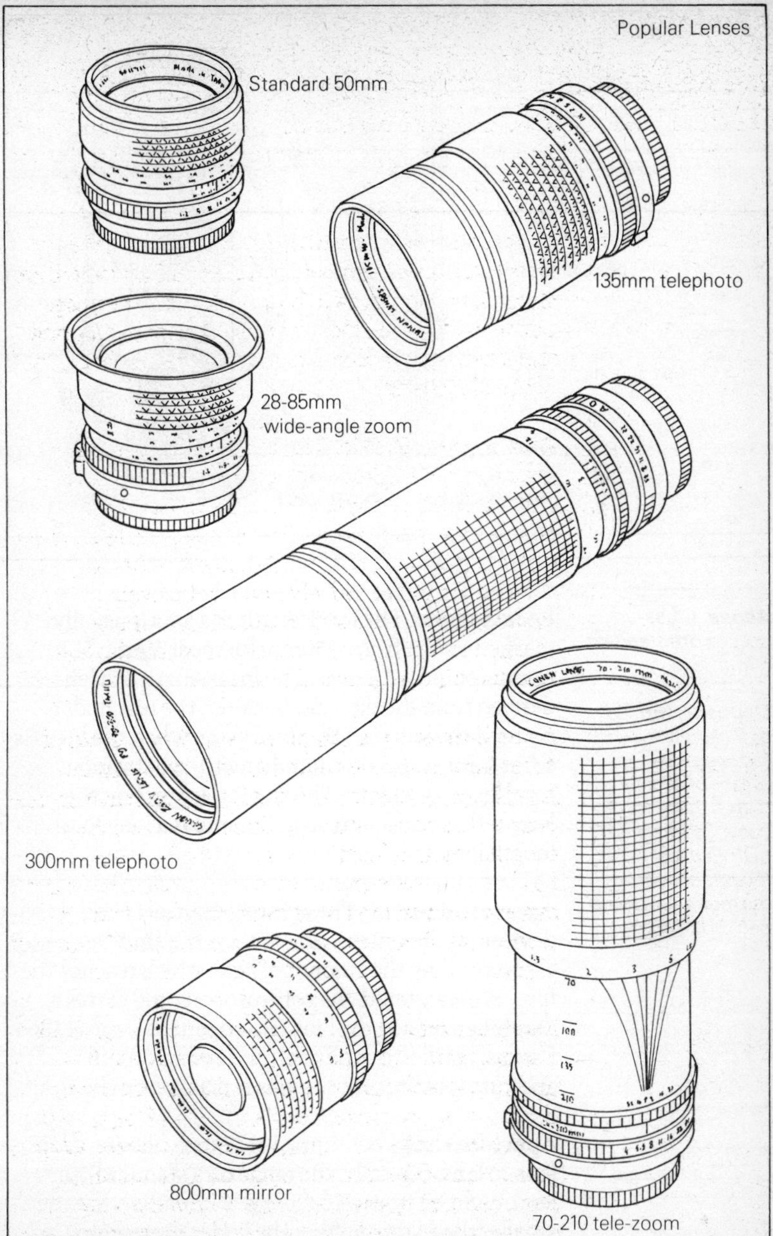

Standard 50mm

135mm telephoto

28-85mm
wide-angle zoom

300mm telephoto

800mm mirror

70-210 tele-zoom

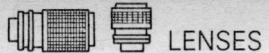 LENSES

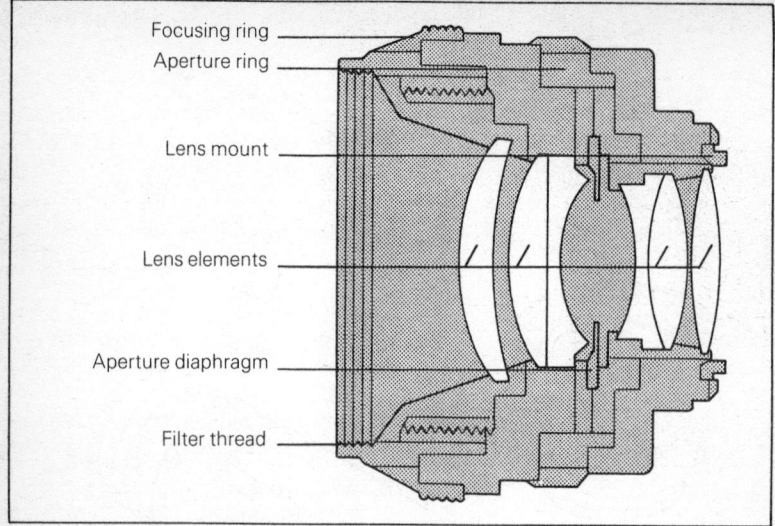

Focusing ring

Aperture ring

Lens mount

Lens elements

Aperture diaphragm

Filter thread

Above Cross-section of a standard 50mm lens.

Opposite, top On SLR cameras focusing is by means of a rotating ring on the lens body. The distance of the subject in focus is shown on the metre/foot scale behind the ring.

Focal length The focal length of a lens is usually marked on the front – 50mm for most 35mm SLR camera standard lenses. The focal length of a lens is derived from the distance between the rear nodal point of the lens and the focal plane when the focus is set at infinity. Become familiar with what various focal lengths refer to. The larger the number, the longer the focal length, e.g., 300mm is a long focal length lens.

Aperture control The aperture control is one of two devices on the camera (the other is the shutter speed) for controlling the amount of light which reaches the film. When rotated, the control opens and closes a diaphragm inside the lens. This opens at stages called f/stops, marked on the control. The maximum aperture (or f/stop) of the lens is marked on the front.

Aperture range The range of f/stops can vary from lens to lens. typically, the range on a standard 50mm lens might be from f/16 to f/2.8. Remember that the smaller the f/stop number the wider the opening, so the maximum aperture of the lens might be f/2.8.

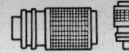

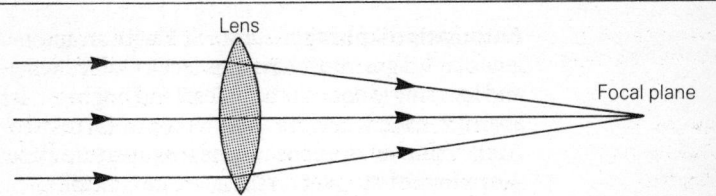

A lens's focal length is the distance between the lens and its focal plane — the point at which light beams converge after passing through the lens.

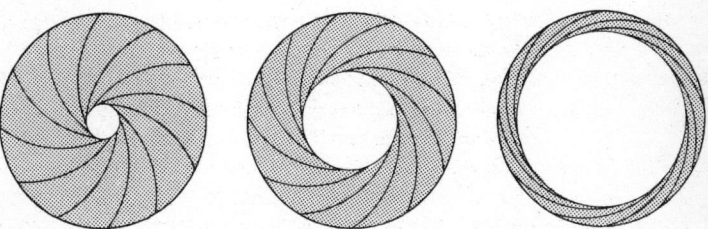

The aperture diaphragm controls the amount of light passing through the lens; it consists of a series of overlapping blades moved by the aperture ring.

Longer focal length lenses usually have a more limited aperture range. A lens with a wide maximum aperture is described as being 'faster' than a lens with smaller maximum aperture, e.g. an f/1.8 lens is 'faster' than an f/2.8. When comparing lenses, choose the fastest lens you can since the wider the maximum aperture, the easier it is to work in low lighting conditions. But remember that the faster the lens, the more expensive it will be.

Depth of field The area of sharpness in front of, and behind, the subject in focus varies when the aperture is changed. This is called depth of field. The smaller the aperture, the greater the depth of field, i.e., the area of sharpness is greater at f/16 than at f/2.8. If you want your subject and the background sharp, use a small aperture (f/16). If you want the background out of focus, use a large aperture (f/2.8). If in doubt, choose an aperture in the middle of the range (say, f/8).

Automatic diaphragm On an SLR with an automatic lens diaphragm (most have this facility) all viewing and focusing is done at the fullest (and brightest) lens aperture, even when the aperture control is rotated. At the moment of exposure, the lens aperture closes-down to the f/stop set on the aperture control.

CHOOSING A LENS

Test reports One way to check the quality of a lens before you buy is to read a magazine test report. If you can not find a report in a current issue, but a test has been done, the magazine can usually supply a copy or reprint. Just write in and ask. A charge may be made, but it can save you from making a costly mistake when choosing a lens.

The standard lens When you buy a camera it either has a fixed standard lens, or a separate standard lens is supplied to fit onto the camera. A standard lens is designed to give a 'normal eye-view' image of the subject. Remember that the focal length of a standard lens varies between some types of camera, relating to the size of the film format. Choose a 50/55mm standard lens for a 35mm SLR and an 80/85mm standard lens for a roll-film SLR. Most fixed lenses in 35mm compacts are slightly wider than standard, at around 38mm, to allow a slightly wider angle of view.

Additional lenses With an SLR you can choose lenses in addition (or even instead of) the standard lens. Select from wide angle, telephoto, zoom and other specialist lenses. But bear in mind that there are more lenses available than you can practically use – so be careful in choosing the lenses that you really need. Money spent on an unused lens would be better spent on a more useful accessory, or on film.

●**Plan your lens system** before buying. Make a list of the lenses that will be most useful to you early on and buy gradually when your budget allows.

System planning Many photographers buy more lenses than they need and it is wrong to think that the more lenses you have, the better your photography will be. Having a choice of lenses in your system is useful, but only if you have chosen them carefully to fit in with *your* requirements. Before buying extra lenses, sit down and think about the photography being tackled and the lenses needed to achieve the best results. A small well-used system is better than a bagful of unused lenses.

Buying a lens When buying a lens, decide first on the type you want (wide angle, telephoto or zoom: see pages 48, 49 and 50) and then decide on the focal length needed (80mm, 135mm, and so on). List the makes available in your camera fitting and check prices carefully. If you decide to visit a photo dealer, take your camera along and try the lens out. Make sure you are happy with the 'feel' of the lens on the camera and check that it has the range you require.

●**Try not to** buy a lens without trying it out first. Make sure it fits your camera properly and check that the controls are easy to operate.

Brand name When buying additional lenses for your camera, you may want to consider lenses of the same brand name, e.g., Canon lenses for a Canon camera. The advantage of this is that the lenses are specifically designed to complete a camera system. Most brand-name lenses offer good quality, but often at a price. Before buying compare cost with other independently made lenses. Don't just buy a brand name for the sake of it, *check that it is compatible with your camera.*

Independent choice There are independently made lenses available for most of the major SLR cameras. Companies such as Tamron, Sigma, Hanimex and others produce lenses in a variety of focal lengths – from wide angle to zoom – to fit the leading makes of SLR. The quality of these independents has improved greatly over the years. Many are as good, and sometimes better, in quality than some brand-name lenses – and they are usually cheaper.

Changeable mounts When you buy a lens it usually has a fixed mount for attaching it to the camera. However, some independent lenses have inter-changeable mounts so that they can be used with a variety of different cameras. For instance, to fit this type of lens to a Pentax camera, choose a Pentax mount. If you change to a different type of camera

●**Never** try to fit a lens with the wrong mount to your camera, or irreparable damage could be caused to both camera and lens.

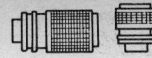

Lens Mounts

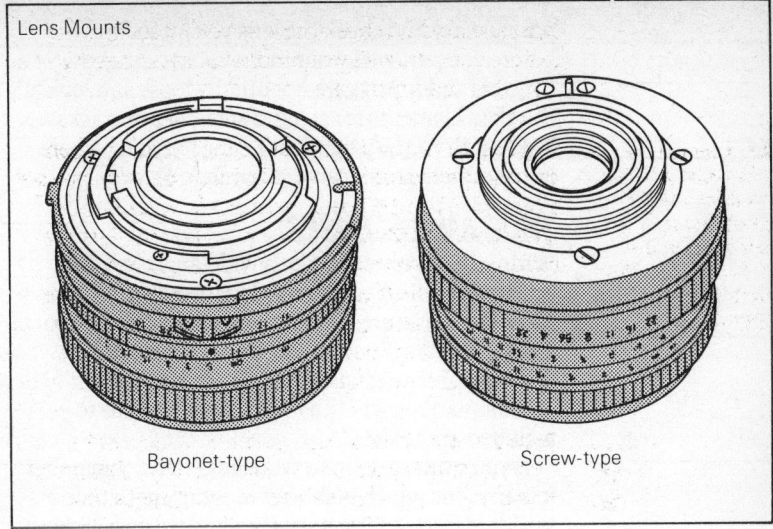

Bayonet-type   Screw-type

later, you don't have to sell your lenses – just buy
another mount with the new camera fitting.

Testing a lens When you buy a lens, put it through
its paces, using a roll of colour slide film (like
Ektachrome 200) for test shots. With the camera on a
tripod or firm support, shoot the same subject (a view
with buildings or other detail is best) at each aperture
on the lens. Then photograph subjects at different
focusing distances, from close-up to far away. When
checking the processed results (an eyeglass helps)
look for clarity of focusing and sharpness at the edges
of the frame, particularly at wider apertures. A
checklist of apertures used and distances will help
your assessment. If you have any doubts about the
quality of the lens, take it (and the pictures) back to
the shop. For a more technical test, special lens-
testing charts are available from most camera stores.

Buying secondhand An inexpensive way to add to
your lens collection is to buy secondhand. Fellow
photographers may wish to sell used lenses to you
direct, or you can check the advertisement pages of
local newspapers or photographic magazines. If

possible, try and check the lens you intend buying before you part with your money. Check that the controls and fittings are not unduly loose and look at the glass elements for signs of scratches or cracks. Make sure you buy the right fitting for your camera. Some camera stores carry secondhand stock.

WIDE-ANGLE LENSES

Wide-angle subjects Use a wide-angle lens for interior shots, when you need to include most of a room in the picture, but only have a limited amount of space available. You can choose a wide angle for photographing groups of people, for landscapes, or in other situations where a large expanse needs to be included in the shot.

If you want to define a wide-angle lens, remember it is any lens which is shorter in focal length than a standard lens. A 50mm lens is standard on a 35mm camera, so a 28mm is wide angle. Bear in mind that focal length varies with the size of the film format. On a 120 roll-film camera, for instance, 80mm may be the focal length of the standard lens, so anything shorter would be wide angle, e.g., 55mm.

Wide choice For most 35mm photographers, the wide angle choice is between either a 24 or 28mm lens. The former obviously gives a slightly wider angle of view and may be handy for certain shots, but the 28mm is perhaps the more useful, and cheaper. The maximum aperture of the wide angle is also a factor – the difference between a 28mm f/2 lens and a 28mm f/2.8 can be as much as £100, but you would seldom use the extra stop provided by the f/2 lens.

Problems By far the biggest problem you are likely to encounter with wide angle lenses is distortion. The purpose of the wide angle lens is to 'bend' detail from the subject into the camera viewing area. In so doing, straight lines in the subject bend in the picture and this is called a distortion. The effect is exaggerated the closer you move in. If you photograph someone too close with a wide angle a contorted face will be the result, so don't do it unless you require this for effect.

TELEPHOTO LENSES

Tele subjects Select the telephoto lens to match your subject. If you shoot portraits, a short telephoto (say, 150mm) is possibly the most useful choice. For shooting sport or other action which takes place some way from your camera position, choose a longer telephoto (200mm upwards).

If you are trying to bring distant subjects closer, try a telephoto lens. The telephoto acts like a short telescope and allows you to photograph far away objects without the need to move in close with the camera. Tele lenses are longer in focal length than the standard lens – if 50mm is standard, then 135mm is typical for a telephoto.

Tele choice There is quite a good range of telephoto lenses for most 35mm cameras. Remember, the longer the focal length of the telephoto, the closer you can photograph your subject. You may need a selection of different telephotos in your system. With a 35mm camera, consider a 135mm or 150mm lens first, then a longer 200 or 250mm lens, and possibly a 300 or 400mm for really distant work.

Problems When you buy a telephoto lens, bear in mind that the focal length is 'fixed', i.e., it cannot be adjusted, as with a zoom lens. You may find yourself photographing too close or too far away for the subject to be in focus, and need to change your camera position since the focal length of the lens cannot be changed. Also, because of the length of some telephotos, the viewing image may seem dimmer because less light reaches the viewfinder. Exposures are also longer, but the TTL metering in most SLRs should cope with this.

ZOOM LENSES

A zoom lens is one which features an adjustable focal length. Typically, a zoom will have a certain focal length range, e.g., 80-200mm. You can select any focal length within the range by moving the zoom control. This is obviously a big advantage over a conventional 'fixed' lens, and some zooms offer the equivalent of

three or four 'fixed' lenses in one lens. One disadvantage is that very long focal length zooms can be heavy and difficult to handle.

Wide zoom For more versatile wide angle-shots, a wide zoom is a good choice. Most wide zooms start at around 24 or 28mm, extending to around 75 or 80mm at the other end of the focal length range. Because of this versatility, many photographers choose a wide zoom *instead of* a standard lens – the zoom can be used at the standard 50mm length, with the added facility of wider and longer zooming.

Medium zoom For most subjects, a medium range zoom is probably most useful. Popular choices in this range are around 70-150mm. The wider end of the zoom range is just beyond standard lens length and is ideal for most close-in photography. At the longer end of the zoom range you can photograph distant subjects, or zoom in more accurately for portraits.

Long zoom If you continually photograph distant subjects (for example wildlife or sport) then a long zoom is a useful choice. Most long zooms start at around 200mm, extending to 600mm in some cases. Because of the long range this type of zoom will only be worthwhile if it suits a subject that you are likely to photograph regularly. It is not worth buying for occasional use.

Zoom control The zoom control varies from lens to lens. For ease of use, go for a 'one-touch' zoom, where one control is operated for both focusing and zooming. Rotating the control focuses the lens, and moving it forwards and backwards along the lens barrel changes the focal length. Some lenses have two separate controls, but the 'one-touch' is quicker and easier to use.

Zoom effects Apart from the advantage of changing the focal length, you can also create interesting effects with a zoom lens. If you use a slow shutter speed (say, ⅛ sec) and move the zoom control *during* the exposure, an interesting effect can be produced (see illustration in the Colour Section, page XIV). When doing this, make sure the camera is supported (preferably on a tripod) otherwise the whole picture will become blurred if the camera itself is moved.

Fixed or zoom? Before you select additional lenses for your camera, think very carefully about whether you should buy 'fixed' focal length lenses, or zooms. Zooms seem to offer the best value since one zoom can often do the job of three or four 'fixed' lenses. They also offer more flexibility when you want to change focal length quickly. If you choose two zooms (say, a 28-70mm and an 80-200mm), most subjects can be covered. Or you can decide to include one 'fixed' lens, like a 28mm wide angle, a zoom in the 80-200mm range, and possibly a longer 'fixed' lens like a 300mm. Plan your system carefully, based on your photographic requirements, and cost.

Zoom lock With some zoom lenses it is possible to move the zoom control accidentally during an exposure, resulting in a slightly blurred picture. Some lensmakers fit their lenses with a 'zoom lock' which is a small button or lever used to tighten the zoom control after it has been set. The only drawback is that you have to remember to unlock it again to adjust the zooming range.

SPECIAL LENSES

What is a special lens? There are some photographic situations which call for specialist equipment, and possibly a special lens. A few different types are detailed in this section, most of which allow you to tackle a particular job more successfully, or in a different way. Consider carefully before you buy a special lens and make sure you can justify the extra expense that may be involved. In some cases, you may be able to borrow, or hire, a special lens and save a lot of money.

Autofocus lenses Many 35mm compacts feature a built-in autofocus lens, which automatically measures

the distance from camera to subject and sets the lens focusing for a sharp result. Recently the same principle has been applied to 35 mm SLR cameras.

Mirror lenses A mirror (or catadioptric or 'cat') lens is basically a compactly designed telephoto lens. Instead of the light entering the lens travelling straight from one end to the other through glass elements (as in a conventional tele lens) a system of mirrors inside the 'cat' lens reflects the light. This enables a long focal length to be achieved within a shorter and more compact lens. Because of the design the mirror lens does not have a diaphragm and, consequently, no aperture control. Light entering the lens is controlled by special filters.

'Macro' zooms To photograph really close-up detail (say, the petals of a flower) you can buy a special macro lens (see next item). However, some zoom lenses offer a 'macro' facility – in most cases this is not true 'macro' since the lens cannot focus as closely as a macro lens can, but it does allow you to move closer than you might with a conventional zoom.

Macro lenses Buy a special macro lens for really close-up photography. A 50 mm macro lens is offered as an alternative standard lens by some 35 mm SLR manufacturers. A macro lens offers good quality, but usually at a hefty price. Macro zoom lenses have an extra close-up focusing facility. Don't buy a lens like this without first considering a zoom lens with a 'macro' facility (good enough for most situations) or using close-up lens accessories (see page 56).

In perspective When shooting buildings or examples of architecture, you will find with some lenses that the verticals in the picture converge, depending on your viewing angle. To put this right, use a perspective-shift lens, whose lens elements can be moved to straighten converging lines. This lens is very expensive and should be considered only by the keenest amateur. For a one-off picture hire one if you really need it.

LENS EFFECTS AND ACCESSORIES

Lens coating When buying a lens, particularly a secondhand – and possibly older – type, try and check that it has coated lens elements. Modern lenses feature this transparent coating which helps reduce 'flare' (see next item) caused by photographing into direct sunlight. Look for words on the lens (or box) like 'multi-coated' or 'super multi-coated' which indicate that the lens has been treated.

Lens 'flare' If you take pictures while facing into the sunlight, or other light source, you may see tiny spots or patterns appearing in the lens. This is known as 'flare' and such patterns will appear on the film and effect your pictures. With most modern lenses flare is reduced by special coating on the surface of the lens elements, but even then it is sometimes impossible to avoid flare with the brightest light sources. Try shooting from a different angle to reduce the flare spots, or use a lens hood over the front of the lens.

Lens support One important fact to remember when using lenses is that the longer the lens is, the more physical support it will need. If you hand-hold a camera fitted with a long lens, it can be difficult to keep both steady, particularly for any period of time. This increases the risk of camera shake spoiling your pictures, especially when using slower shutter speeds. Balance the camera on a firm tripod, or rest the barrel of the lens on a wall, fence or similar support.

Lens care While most cameras can stand a fair amount of rough treatment, lenses are more fragile and require careful handling. The front element is

53

●**Always** use a lens cap when the lens is off-camera. You can buy special tie-on lens caps which hang from the lens when you are shooting, a good idea if you are prone to losing lens caps.

●**Never** take a lens apart – leave that to an expert.

usually the most vulnerable, so fit a lens hood when shooting. Some photographers keep a filter (such as a Skylight) permanently over the front of the lens for protection. Keep the lens caps on the front and back of the lens when it is off-camera. Keep the lens clean and dust-free using a special lens-cleaning cloth, tissue or blower brush (see cleaning hint, page 55).

Lens repair Most photographers can carry out minor adjustments to the lens, such as tightening any loose screws (a set of miniature screwdrivers is a useful addition to your accessory bag for this purpose). Be very careful doing this. You should avoid taking a lens apart, even to clean inside, because this is a job best handled by an expert lens repairer. Your local camera shop should be able to help, or write directly to the lens manufacturer for advice.

Lens hire Some photographers find they have a need for a special lens, but cannot justify the expense of buying it. Hiring is a good alternative and some specialist dealers offer this service, usually in addition to camera hire. Hiring really only pays off when you need one of the more expensive lenses, such as a perspective shift lens or a long telephoto or an extra-wide wide-angle. Shop around for the best deal – but be prepared to pay a hefty (returnable) deposit.

●**Don't** leave lenses lying around – they may become clogged with dust, or even get knocked over and broken. Keep a lens in its original case if possible.

Lens carrying For the photographer on the move, carrying lenses can often be the biggest burden. Although most lenses are fairly compact, having more than two or three can slow you down. Aim to have one mounted onto the camera (carried either around your neck or in the accessory bag) and two more in your bag or in your pockets. Make sure the lenses are well protected, preferably in their own cases.

Lens storage You can keep your lenses quite safely stored in your gadget bag, again preferably in their own cases. Store them in a cool damp-free place and keep the silica gel bag (supplied with most lenses) in the case to absorb any harmful moisture which might affect the lens.

Lens hood Most lens hoods are made of either metal or plastic and fit onto the front of the lens. The hood prevents direct light hitting the front of the lens and causing 'flare', which can spoil your pictures. A hood also helps to protect the front of the lens if something knocks against it. Some lenses have built-in hoods.

Collapsible hood While most lens hoods are 'fixed', you can buy a fold-down, or collapsible, lens hood. This is made of rubber and can simply be folded out when required and folded back when you want to pack the camera into a case.

Space shots If you are trying to take pictures of the sky at night, it is possible to attach your SLR to a telescope for taking pictures of far-off galaxies. A telescope adaptor can link the camera body to the telescope eyepiece, or the eyepiece can be removed in some cases and an adaptor used to fit directly onto the camera.

Binocular fitting You can attach your SLR to a pair of binoculars using a simple adaptor for bird's eye shots. The adaptor fits onto only one of the two binocular eyepieces.

Focusing handle Adjusting the lens focusing on some cameras can be a bit fiddly. If you have difficulty turning the lens focusing control, buy a focusing handle. This is a ring with a handle which fits around the lens and makes it easier to turn, especially while you are looking through the viewfinder and not able to watch your fingers.

Lens-cleaning kits To look after your lenses you can buy special lens-cleaning kits. These might include a lens-cleaning cloth, a blower brush (for removing hidden dust) and some lens-cleaning fluid. Regular cleaning is essential for clear, sharp results, so it is a good idea to keep a kit handy in the gadget bag.

●**Keep a lens cleaning kit** with you so that your lenses can be cleaned on location.

Teleconverters You can take telephoto shots without buying a telephoto lens – by adding a

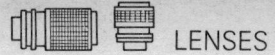

teleconverter to your standard lens. A teleconverter is a simple glass element which fits between the camera body and the main lens, doubling, or even trebling, its focal length. Add a 2X converter to a 50mm standard lens, for instance, and it becomes a 100mm lens. Teleconverters are a cheaper alternative to buying telephoto lenses, but there is a loss of image quality, so bear this in mind when deciding whether the saving is worthwhile.

IN CLOSE

Microscope For extreme close-up photography (or photomicrography) the camera can be fitted to a microscope eyepiece using a special adaptor. In some microscopes a separate optical system is used for the camera, allowing you to view through the microscope in the normal way.

Reversing rings For taking close-up pictures one of the simplest methods is to put your standard lens into the camera the wrong way round for greater image magnification. The lens is attached to the camera via a reversing ring, which screws into the lens filter thread and the camera body. Before you buy a ring the close-up effect can be seen by holding the lens over the camera the wrong way round. With the lens reversed, the coupling for control of the aperture is lost, so set f/stops manually before each exposure.

Close-up lenses You can increase the magnification of your lens for close-up work by fitting a close-up lens. This simply screws onto the front of the camera (choose the size to fit your lens filter thread) and allows close-ups at fixed, or varying, magnification, depending on the type of close-up lens. Use smaller apertures with such a lens to avoid blurred edges on your pictures (f/16 or f/11 should be about right).

Extension tubes The further away the lens is extended from the camera, the closer you can take pictures. You can buy a set of extension tubes (usually three per set) which fit between the camera and lens for close-up work. You can fit one or more tubes

depending on how close you wish to photograph.
Because the tubes are hollow there is no optical
interference with image quality.

Bellows extension The bellows extension works
on the same principle as extension tubes, except that
the bellows are adjustable and thus the
magnifications can be altered – tubes are fixed and
cannot be adjusted. When choosing bellows or tubes
try and choose those with automatic coupling
between camera and lens – this saves setting the
aperture manually each time you take a shot. Bellows
are easy to adjust but require firm support. And make
sure you tighten the adjustment control each time,
otherwise the shot may slip out of focus.

Move closer You don't always have to spend money
to shoot close-ups. The cheapest close-up accessories
can be your legs: in many cases, all you have to do is
move in closer with the camera. The standard lens on
most modern 35mm SLRs focuses as close as 0.5
metre (1½ft) which is close enough to record a large
flower head or an object of similar size. Obviously, if
you need to move in closer, get one of the accessories
mentioned. But try the 'move-in-close' test first.

Cheap close-up Using a good quality magnifying
glass held over the camera lens can sometimes
produce acceptable close-ups. If you have one handy,
give it a try – but use only small apertures (f/16 or f/11)
for best results. Make sure, if you are using this
method, that the glass is held firmly over the lens,
otherwise blurred pictures will result.

Fish-eye effect Ultra wide-angle 'fish-eye' lenses are
expensive to buy, but you can create fish-eye effects
using simple accessories. (Fish-eye lenses are so called
because they show an extremely wide angle of view,
like a fish's vision.) You can buy a fish-eye attachment
which screws onto the camera and costs a fraction of
the price of a fish-eye lens. Or you can make your own
fish-eye attachment by cutting a hole in a spare lens
cap and fitting one of those wide-angle door 'spy'

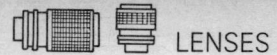

viewers. With the cap over your standard lens you can shoot fish-eye effects easily.

FILTER FACTS

Filter thread You can buy a number of different filters for creating special effects, altering colour or contrast, and other uses. The circular type of filter is screwed into a special thread on the front end of the lens. Check when you buy the lens what the screw thread size is (say, 49mm) and, ideally, buy filters to fit. Don't worry if you have a number of different lenses with varying filter thread sizes. You can buy step-up or step-down rings which allow you to fit the same size filter to different filter threads.

Filter protection A filter is good protection for the front of the lens. Even if it is scratched or damaged, replacement is cheap compared to repairing or replacing a lens. You can ensure the filter does not become damaged by using a lens hood, or fitting a lens cap over the filter when the lens is not in use.

Below A selection of filters and filter components. Detachable filter holders are useful as they enable more than one filter to be used at a time; the better ones (as here) allow attachment of a lens hood.

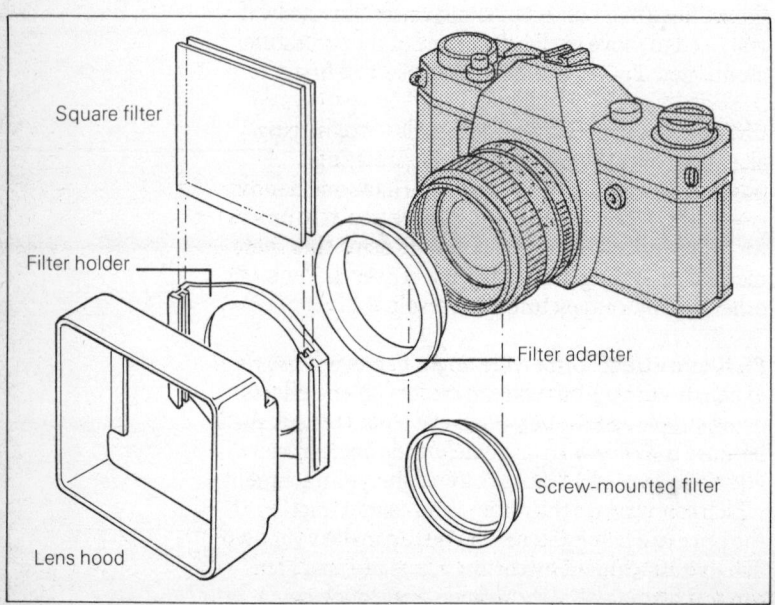

Square filter

Filter holder

Filter adapter

Screw-mounted filter

Lens hood

Circular filters These filters are probably the most widely used, and are available in varying sizes to fit most lenses. Most are made of glass and you should take care when handling them. You can use step-up or step-down rings to fit filters to different lenses, but some larger lenses may require their own filters, which can lead to expensive duplication, so bear this in mind when opting for filters of this type.

Square filter systems If you intend collecting a set of lenses, consider buying a square filter system. This usually consists of a universal filter holder (which can be adapted to fit most lenses via a screw-in ring) and square filters which slot easily into the holder. This type of system is very flexible in that you can change filter quickly without removing the holder and the holder can be matched with most of your lenses. You can start with one filter and build your collection as required.

Filters for black-and-white Don't just choose filters for colour photography – they can be just as important in black-and-white work. Because black-and-white films record colour as tones of grey, it is sometimes desirable to change these tones to achieve the best effect. This might involve bringing out the white clouds in a sky shot, or emphasizing foliage in a landscape, for example. By using a particular coloured filter (red, orange, yellow, blue, etc.) you can make these tonal changes quite easily. The chart here shows which filter colour to choose for specific shots.

Filter choice for black-and-white photography

Subject requirement	Filter colour
Whiten clouds in blue sky	Yellow
Darken sky dramatically	Red
Lighten foliage in scene	Green
Lighten blue sky, losing cloud shapes	Blue

Filter strength The various coloured filters for monochrome work are available in different

strengths (or densities) to match individual picture requirements. A 1X red filter, for instance, would be less powerful (and provide less effect) than a 2X red filter. Use a 1X if in doubt – the density of the image can always be increased later, at the printing stage.

Colour-correction filters Most colour film is balanced for shooting in average daylight conditions. Shoot indoors under artificial lamplight, or outdoors late in the day, and the results may look too orange or 'warm'. To 'cool down' the colour for a more natural colour balance you need a blue colour-correction filter. Similarly if you use a colour film balanced for lamplight (tungsten) in daylight, the over-blue results need to be 'warmed up' by using an orange colour-correction filter. You will also need to filter a daylight film shot under fluorescent light, which can produce a green tinge on the film. The chart below gives the correct filter to use for adjustment to colour.

Colour-correction filters

Film in use	Shooting situation	Filter choice
Daylight balanced	Indoor lamplight	Blue (80A)
Tungsten balanced	Normal daylight	Orange (85B)
Daylight balanced	Under fluorescent lights	FL/D

Special-effects filters While there are many special-effects filters available (see pages 152-3), use one only if the picture really needs it. Filters can improve many pictures, but they can also ruin them. A wrongly used filter can often obstruct the real objective of the photograph.

Other useful filters Two standard filters used by many photographers are the skylight 1A and the polariser. The skylight can be kept over the lens permanently and is useful for absorbing ultra-violet 'haze' in landscape scenes, resulting in clearer images. The Polariser can be used to minimise reflections when photographing glass or water, as well as making a blue sky much deeper in colour shots.

Soft effect It is possible to buy a 'soft focus' effect
filter which will create a misty result around the edges
(for portraits, etc.). However it can be done more
cheaply (and more accurately) by smearing Vaseline
around the edges of a skylight filter. The effect can be
varied and the smear can be wiped off later with a
lens-cleaning cloth. Do not smear the lens itself
otherwise it may be permanently marked.

Lens Comparisons
Equipment described is for SLR cameras prices
typical for 1985

TYPE	TYPICAL FOCAL LENGTH	TYPICAL USES	PRICE RANGE (£)
Standard	50 or 55mm	General Landscapes	Usually comes with camera
Wide-angle	24, 28 or 35mm	Groups Wide scenic views	50-400
Ultra-wide-angle	16 or 21mm	Group close-ups Special effects	60-400
Short telephoto/zoom	35-80mm	Portraits Close action	50-300
Medium tele-photo/zoom	80-210mm	Most sport Distant landscape	50-400
Long telephoto/zoom	200-400mm	Wildlife	60-600
Mirror	500, 600 or 1000mm	Distant action	200-300
Macro	50 or 55mm	Close-ups	150-300
Shift	50 or 55mm	Architecture	150-300
Autofocus	50 or 55mm	General	100-150

Equipment

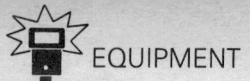

GENERAL TIPS

●**Don't waste money** on accessories you may hardly use. Be selective in your choice.

●**Take your camera** along to the shop when buying any accessories if you are not sure about the type required for your particular camera.

Buying accessories Undoubtedly your photography can benefit from owning a few accessories. But just as with the purchase of cameras and lenses, take care when buying them. Most accessories cost very little in comparison to cameras, so you may be tempted into buying them just for the sake of filling your gadget bag. Make sure you have a real *need* for a particular accessory. You would be better off buying film than a useless gadget.

Accessories *not* to buy Which accessories should you avoid? Well, most photographers work within a tight budget, so avoid any expensive items – at least initially. They can be bought later as your experience grows. Go for cheaper and more useful accessories, such as a small flashgun, or filters, or similar items which will see some regular use.

More than you can carry Many photographers pick up so many accessories that they end up with more than they can practically carry. Even if you enjoy hoarding gadgets, don't be tempted to cram them all into a case each time you go out shooting. Size up the assignment beforehand, make a selective list of the accessories you think are vital, and leave the rest at home.

CHOOSING FLASH

Built-in flash Many simpler cameras and 35mm compacts have built-in flash. This facility means there is one major accessory you don't have to worry about. Of all the accessories available, flash is perhaps the most useful, even vital, in poor light or indoor situations. Consider choosing a camera with this useful facility when shopping around.

Buying a flashgun There is a huge choice of portable flashguns on the market and selecting the right one can be daunting. Just remember that all you are buying is a portable light source and that this must be compatible with you camera. Make sure it can provide the light output you require and is straightforward to operate.

Power output The light output of a flashgun is usually indicated by its Guide Number (GN). The higher the GN, the more powerful the flash. The GN can also be used to calculate exposure required for a correct flash exposure, but most of today's automatic flash units calculate exposure automatically.

Portable power Most flash units are powered by AA-size penlight batteries or by AC mains via a small optional adaptor. Some also accept rechargeable NiCad (Nickel Cadmium) cells which are expensive to buy initially but can work out cheaper than continually replacing conventional batteries, though of course you will need a battery charger. Some larger flash units require a portable power pack which can be recharged before use.

Manual flash This is the simplest form of flashgun. Each time it is fired, the full light output of the unit is discharged. This means you cannot just add a touch of

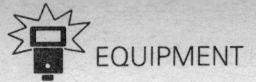

flash light to the subject (as with an automatic unit) and the batteries are drained much more quickly. However most manuals are cheaper than the automatics – it is possible to buy a small manual for under £10.

Automatic computerised flash Most modern flash units now feature computer thyristor circuitry to control light output. An automatic unit can produce exactly the right amount of light for the subject. When fired, light emitted from the subject and a tiny sensor on the unit 'cuts off' the light output to give a correct exposure. An auto unit is the best choice for most types of photography.

Programmed flash Some automatic 35mm SLR cameras offer a 'programmed flash' mode in addition to other automatic exposure functions. When you have this facility, it is possible to set both the flash unit (usually the same make as the camera) and the camera itself for fully automatic flash exposure. Buying such a combination takes much of the guesswork out of flash photography, so consider the option seriously. Occasionally some manufacturers and/or dealers have special offers on SLRs with a matching flashgun in the price, so look out for those.

X-sync and hot shoe When you plan to use an electronic flashgun with any camera, make sure that it is connected for synchronization. Most cameras, particularly 35mm SLRs, feature a hot shoe on the top plate. This provides direct electrical contact, automatically firing the flash when it is attached and avoiding the need for a connecting cable. If there is no hot shoe on your camera, connect the lead from the flash to the X-sync (synchronization) socket on the camera. SLRs have a maximum shutter speed for flash sync; do not exceed it or only part exposures will result. This is usually 1/60 or 1/125 second.

Recycling When taking a succession of flash shots, the speed at which the flashgun recycles itself for the next shot is important. Recycling times vary

Flash Units

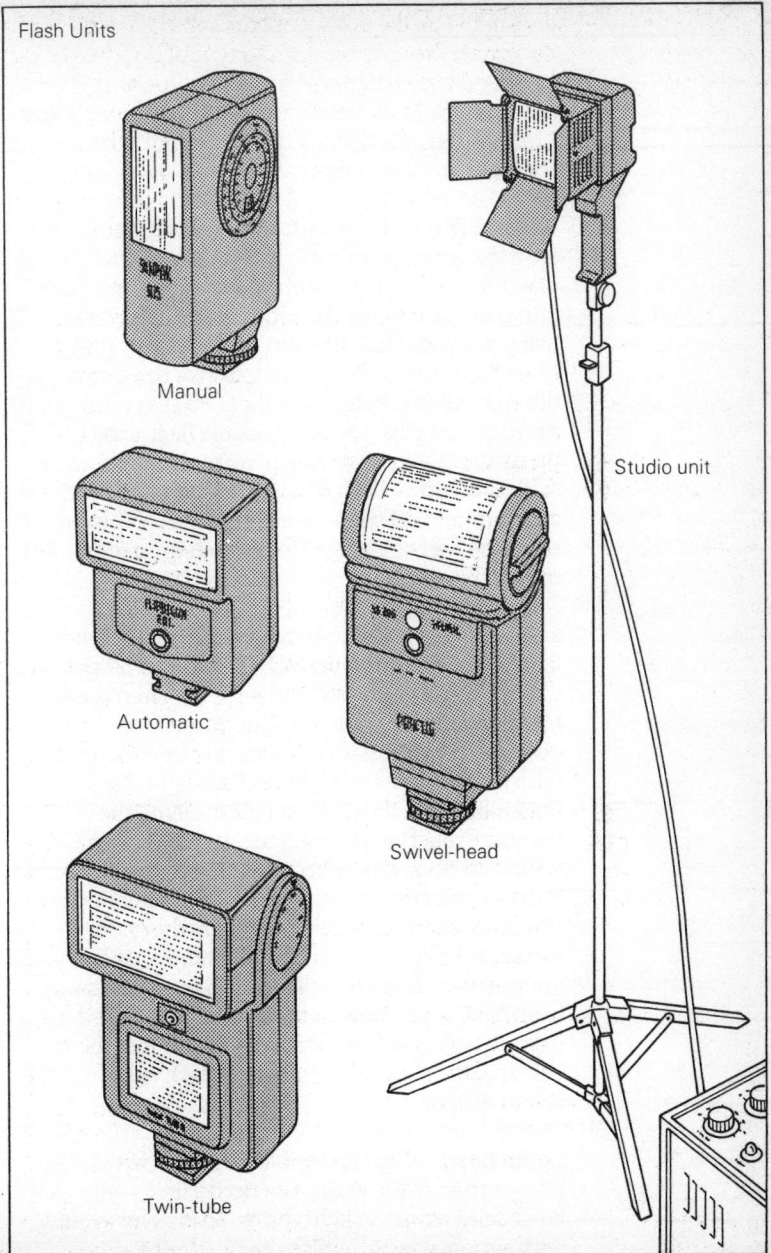

Manual

Automatic

Twin-tube

Swivel-head

Studio unit

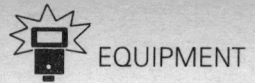

depending on the distance of the subject, the setting chosen on the unit, the age and type of batteries being used, and other factors. Bear this in mind and remember that the manufacturers' claim for recycling time is often optimistic, if only for some of the reasons mentioned above.

Flash settings Even with automatic flashguns there are a few settings to be made, usually on a dial (or dials) on the side of the unit. First, you *must* set the film speed dial to the ISO rating of the film you are using (e.g., with ISO 100 film, set the dial to 100). Most auto units give you the option of three or more different apertures for flash shots, so select the aperture you wish to use. Check the flash subject distance scale against that aperture to make sure the subject is within flash range (if not, go for a wider aperture) and set the sensor at the front of the unit for the same aperture range. Colour coding on most units makes this easier.

Swivel head If you want to vary the angle of the light from your flashgun without taking it off the camera, buy a unit with a swivel head. This type of flash is useful for bouncing light off a wall, ceiling or other reflective surface, allowing a softer effect than with conventional 'straight on' flash light. But remember that, if you do bounce the light, the exposure must be increased because the light has to travel further and may become diffuse. The automatic function on most flash units should compensate for this but make your settings based on the extra distance the light travels from the subject. When you bounce light from the ceiling, calculate the distance from flash to ceiling to subject, not flash to subject as in straight-on shooting. Remember also that the colour of the surface reflecting the flash will affect the colour of light.

Zoom head When taking flash pictures with telephoto or zoom lenses, you need a unit with a longer and narrower light throw. So look for a unit with a zoom control, which can be adjusted from normal flash output to longer throw by simply extending a special magnifying lens on the front. The amount of extension is usually numbered to be compatible with a particular lens focal length.

Twin tube When you take pictures of someone by bouncing flash light off a ceiling, the effect can be rather 'flat' and you can end up with awkward face shadows. To counter this problem, some flash manufacturers offer units with a twin tube. The large main tube can be directed upwards for bounced light, with a second smaller tube facing directly at the subject, adding an extra touch of light to the face and filling-in shadows. A twin tube is worth buying if you are likely to be tackling many flash portraits.

Flash brackets If you have difficulty holding a camera-and-flash combination steady, use a special flash bracket. This type of bracket allows the flashgun to be supported separately off the camera and, incorporating a special hand grip, ensures that both camera and flash can be held more firmly and easily.

Flash accessories It is possible to buy special accessories to fit many flashguns. Coloured filters fitted over the flash tube can create special lighting effects. You can also buy diffusers which 'soften' the light produced by the unit, for a less harsh result in a portrait, for instance. Extension leads can be used to hold the flash away from the camera when trying out different directions for the lighting.

Flash meters With daylight or ordinary lamp light you can measure exposure with your camera's built-in metering, or with a separate hand-held meter. Flashlight is emitted at high speed, so if you take large numbers of flash photographs, consider buying a special flash meter. When the flash is fired, the meter 'freezes' the light reading and the required aperture can be read off a scale on the meter.

Flash slave If you are using more than one flashgun at a time, to provide lighting from a variety of angles,

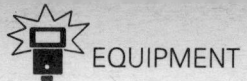

the units don't all have to be connected up to the camera for synchronization. Just connect one unit to the camera and fit a flash 'slave' to each of the other units. This is a tiny photoelectric cell which senses light from the main flashgun and automatically fires the unit it is attached to at the same time. A slave is quite inexpensive and does away with the need for trailing wires everywhere. Many studio flash units have built-in slave units.

STUDIO FLASH

Studio units If you do any serious studio work, you might consider buying special studio flash units. These mains-powered units are generally more powerful than most portable flashguns, they recycle very quickly and can be fitted with a variety of accessories designed to help you obtain high quality results. You can pay a great deal for a professional studio set-up, but there are special budget systems which are adequate for most enthusiasts' requirements. Start with just one flash unit and build your system from there.

Modelling light When using natural light or conventional lights for photography you can see the direction of the light, its strength and where the shadows are *before* you take the picture. This is not possible with flash because the light is emitted so quickly. However, many studio flash units have built-in modelling lights which allow you to set the direction of the light before taking the shot. The modelling light is usually the same strength as the flash, so that you know how well proportioned the light is when using several units simultaneously. The modelling light goes out when the flash is fired and comes back on again for the next shot to be set-up.

Output control Studio flash units are not normally automatic (unlike many on-camera portable units) but many feature output control to allow the right amount of light for the subject. This control is often limited to full power and half power, with lower power settings on more expensive units. This type of

●**Remember** that studio lamps get very hot when they are in continuous use – keep the room well ventilated.

control is most useful for a second fill-in light, with a full-power main light.

Snoots and barn doors Most flash units give a reasonably wide 'spread' of light. To control the light direction you can fit either a snoot or barn doors. The latter are simply four small flaps or 'doors' (as seen on many movie lights) which can be opened or closed to prevent stray light from reaching parts of the scene, or shining on the camera. A snoot is a long tube which allows the light to be directed along a narrow beam.

SPECIAL FLASH

Ring flash For very close-up photography it can be difficult to light the subject with the lens so close to it. If you are likely to do much close-up work, consider buying a ring flash. This is a circular flash tube which fits around the front of the lens and, in effect, takes the flash in as close as the lens.

Infrared flash There are situations – when photographing animals at night, for instance – when you need to take flash shots without the flash being seen. An infrared flashgun emits infrared light which cannot be seen by the naked eye. But, used in conjunction with infrared film, well-lit images can be produced – without the subject knowing anything about it. Infrared flashguns are fairly expensive, but infrared film costs little more than standard film.

Coloured filters When working with studio lights you can change colour and tone by adding filters to your camera (see pages 58-61), or by putting filters over the lighting. You can buy large gelatin filter squares to cover one or more lights. This is particularly useful if you want to make a background a particular colour without affecting the light in the foreground (a lens filter would make the whole scene the same colour).

LIGHTING ACCESSORIES

Umbrellas Direct flash light can be quite harsh, particularly with some of the stronger types of studio

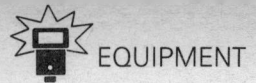

flash. To soften the light, you can attach a reflector umbrella onto the lighting stand. Turn the light source to face into the umbrella (not at the subject) so that the light reflects from the inside of the 'brolly', giving a softer light overall. Umbrellas are commonly used for most types of studio photography, but particularly for portraits. They come in white, silver or gold – white for most uses, silver for a 'harder' effect, gold for a 'warmer' effect, e.g. in colour portraiture.

Diffusers You can soften the light without deflecting it from the subject by using a diffuser. This consists of semi-transparent white gauze material, which fits over the front of the flash and disperses the light in a wider direction for a less intense effect. You can improvise your own diffuser from tracing paper, but be careful because it can quickly become a fire risk!

Reflectors Because lighting is very directional some parts of the subject may be unlit, or in shadow. To fill these areas you can use another light source, but a cheaper alternative is to use a reflector. You can buy reflector squares (white or silver), but any bright reflective surface (even an old white sheet) will do the job. Placed on the opposite side to the flash, and to the side of the subject, extra light will be reflected into the darker areas for a more balanced result.

Tungsten lighting You don't have to use flash in the studio. Ordinary tungsten or photoflood lamps can be used. You can buy special lighting stands with fittings for large photoflood bulbs. This type of lighting is easy to use, but you will have to use film balanced for this lighting when using colour (tungsten or daylight film is available in some types of film) or use colour-correction filters.

Flash lamp A compromise between flash and lamp lighting is provided by a special flash lamp made by AICO. This is a flash tube inside a lamp housing which screws into a conventional lamp fitting. The flash is fired via a built-in slave unit which responds to any other flash fired by the camera.

BAGS AND CASES

Gadget bags You can carry a camera in its case around your neck, in a handbag, or even in a carrier bag, but when you start collecting extra lenses or other accessories, you need a good case to carry them all. Shoulder bags, special fishing bags, or other similar holdalls may be all you need, but some may not offer enough protection from damage. You can buy special gadget bags with compartments for various items. Go for one that is strong, but reasonably lightweight and roomy.

●**Never** use a flimsy bag for your equipment. Make sure it is properly packed and protected.

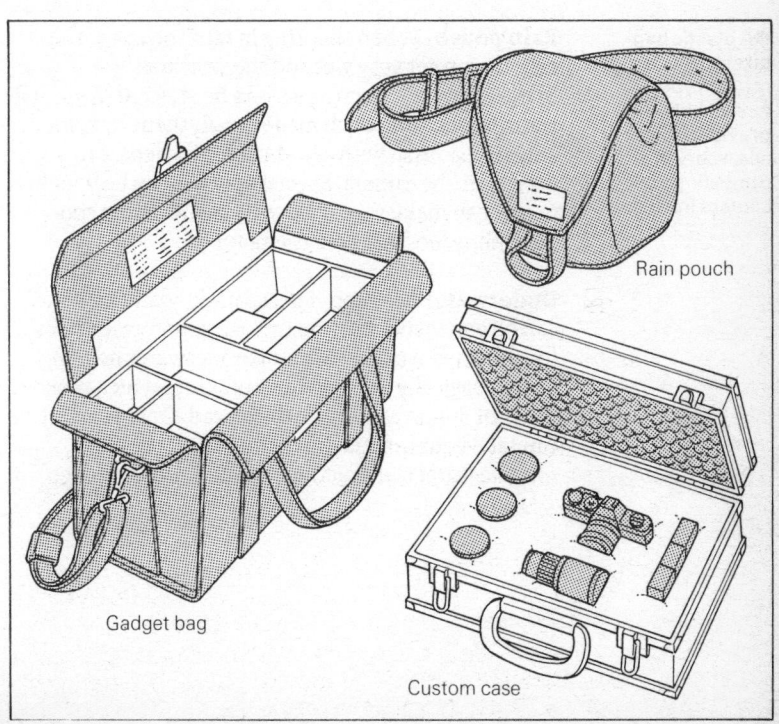

Rain pouch

Gadget bag

Custom case

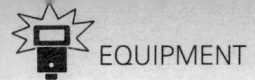

Custom cases Custom-made camera cases offer the best protection for your equipment. Most are made of metal (or metallised material) with a foam-lined interior, which can be cut to fit individual items. These cases are very hard-wearing, but are a bit more difficult to carry than a shoulder bag. However, some come with special shoulder straps.

Ever-ready cases Many 35mm SLR cameras are sold with a carrying case included in the purchase price. However, the case is usually only deep enough to house the camera when fitted with a standard or wide-angle lens. You cannot close the case when you have a longer lens on the camera. If you use a telephoto or zoom lens almost continuously on the camera, it is worth considering buying an ever-ready case, which is larger than the conventional case and can be fully closed.

● **A plastic bag** takes up barely any room in your pocket but could provide a vital accessory in protecting your camera from rain.

Rain pouch When shooting in rain and snow the camera can get very wet and the workings (particularly the electronics) can be affected. A special transparent rain pouch made of polythene or some similar material, with a hole cut for the lens, can be used over the camera. Special pouches can be bought, or you can make your own quite easily on the spot. Polythene food bags are useful for this.

Underwater housing Special underwater cameras can be expensive, but you can use your own camera for sub-aqua work by using an underwater housing. This is basically a transparent unit into which most types of 35mm camera can be placed. Once sealed you can take your camera down into the depths (the manufacturer's instructions will tell you how deep).

CAMERA SUPPORTS

While you can take many pictures simply by hand-holding the camera, there are times when a firm camera support is needed. Supports like tripods are not always necessary – sometimes you can rest the camera on a firm surface to prevent you from shaking the camera during an exposure. Most camera supports are light and compact, however, and it is worth adding one to your list of accessories.

Tripods Of all the different camera supports, the tripod can provide the most flexible range of adjustment. Most tripods are made in light aluminium and are therefore easy to carry, yet firm enough to support your camera. Various sizes are available so, when buying, extend the legs and supporting arm of each type to see which is best for your requirements.

Table-top tripod Consider a table-top tripod for close-up photography or small studio set-ups. This is basically a miniature tripod which can fit into a small area, yet still support your camera reasonably well. It packs quite small and can be carried in your pocket.

Swivel head Some older tripods feature a swivel, or ball-and-joint, head on which the camera is mounted. This can be swivelled in practically any direction so that you can take pictures with the camera at different angles. The swivel head is nowadays giving way to pan-and-tilt head featured on many of today's tripods.

Pan-and-tilt head This type of head has a single arm which you use to tilt the camera up-and-down and from right-to-left. Turning the arm locks the camera angle in position and it can then be loosened when you need to change the shooting angle.

●**Don't** lumber yourself with a tripod that is difficult to use. Before you buy, check that the legs are simple to extend, that they lock into place firmly, and try the camera support head for ease of use.

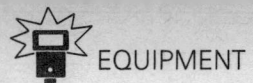 EQUIPMENT

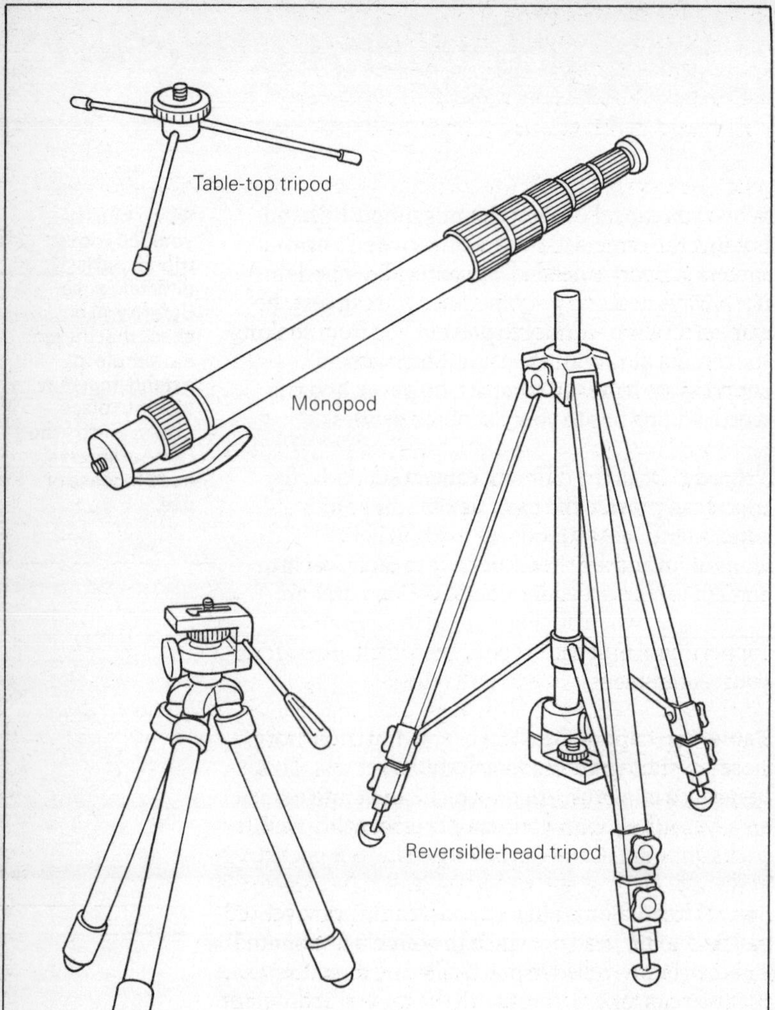

Table-top tripod

Monopod

Reversible-head tripod

Pan-and-tilt tripod

Reversible head On many tripods the legs cannot
be set for very low angle shots. Some types, however,
allow you to remove the centre support holding the

camera and insert it upside down, which can enable you to shoot right down to ground level. You may have to shoot through the gaps between the tripod legs, so bear this in mind when using a wide-angle lens, which might include the legs in the view.

Quick release legs When choosing a tripod, go for one which is quick and easy to set-up (and take down). Some tripods feature screw-on sections, but it can be a lengthy business extending all of the legs. The best type to buy is a tripod with quick-release clamps between each section of the legs. These can be opened and closed quickly and the tripod can be set up within a matter of seconds.

●**Always** tighten the legs of your tripod securely in case it moves during the exposure and spoils your shots.

Monopod If you don't want to carry a tripod around, a monopod can be a lighter alternative. This single pole-like support can be extended telescopically to a reasonable height and will provide a level of firm support, but it may also need to be rested against a wall or tree to prevent lateral movement.

Clamps Probably the easiest and lightest support to use is a clamp. The camera is attached via a special screw and the camera clamp can be fixed to practically any firm surface, such as a post. While easy and quick to use, you will not be able to move around as easily as with a tripod or monopod without continually re-fixing the clamp to different supports.

Rifle grip This is used for shooting pictures, rather than bullets. The extending arm of the support is ideal for camera-and-long-lens combinations and the grip is strapped to one shoulder for extra support. A cable release is fitted to the grip's triggering device for firing the camera shutter. Such a grip is ideal for fast-action photography. (See drawing on next page.)

Pistol grip This type of grip is smaller than the rifle grip and resembles the handle of a pistol. Balance the camera on the grip and you have an easy-to-use combination. A cable release attaches to the grip trigger for firing the camera.

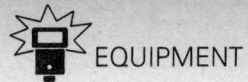

Cheap support It is possible to improvise your own supports for very little cost. One popular idea is to rest any long lens you are using on top of a bean bag, placed on top of a wall or other firm support. The bean bag absorbs any vibration and the beans inside 'mould' themselves around the shape of the lens for rigid support. If you can't buy a bean bag, fill a cloth bag with dried peas.

Below A rifle grip helps to keep camera steady when long-focus lenses are used. A cable release is built into the grip.

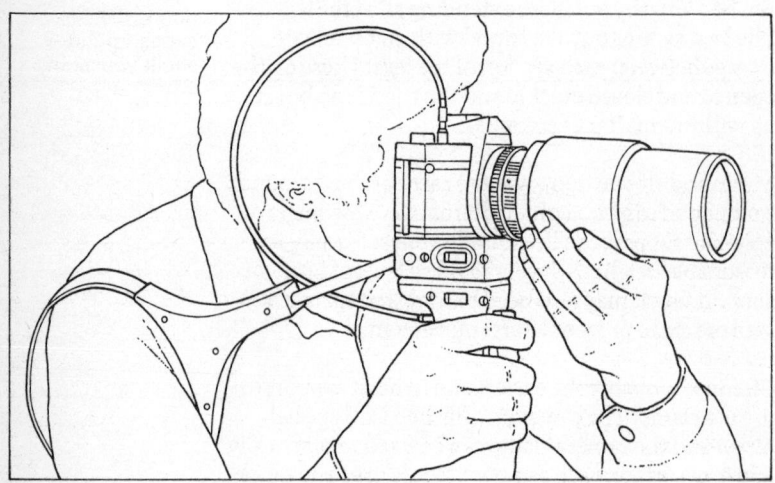

SPECIAL RELEASE AIDS

Cable release One of the hazards of taking pictures is camera shake, when the camera moves slightly during an exposure. The result is often a blurred picture. You can avoid touching the camera at the moment of exposure by attaching a cable release to the shutter release button.

Air release Most cable releases, because they work mechanically, are often no longer than 25cm (12in). If you want to fire the camera from some distance (to include yourself in the shot, for example) you can use an air release. This is basically a long tube with an air bulb at one end. The other end is attached to the camera and, when the bulb is squeezed, air pressure operates the shutter release.

Times You can make the camera operate itself by attaching a small mechanical timer device to the shutter release. Once the shutter has been cocked in the normal way, set the timing device and, after a few seconds, the shutter will be fired automatically. If your camera has a built-in timer, you can use that in exactly the same way for shake-free exposures.

Infrared release If you want to fire the camera from a distance (say, for certain types of wildlife photography where the photographer can hide away from the camera position) try an infrared release. This works on a similar principle to some TV remote control units. An infrared beam is emitted by the hand control to a compatible unit on the camera which fires the shutter. If the camera is also fitted with a motorised film winder, you can shoot a number of pictures continuously (otherwise you would have to keep going back to the camera to wind on the film after each frame had been exposed).

●**Test** any remote-control shutter releases beforehand to ensure they are working properly.

79

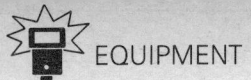
MISCELLANEOUS AIDS

Light meters If your camera does not have built-in TTL (through-the-lens) metering, you can use a separate hand-held meter to measure the light level for a correct exposure. There are many different types, the most common of which is the selenium cell meter. This type of meter is fine for most general use, but you can also buy more expensive and more accurate meters for specialised work.

Spot meter An ordinary hand-held light meter will normally provide a very general reading of the whole scene being photographed. But there are some situations where you may wish to record the light level in only one part of the scene, or the different areas of light and dark in a shot. For this, use a spot meter which has a very narrow measuring angle and can be used to measure any small area of the subject.

Below Hand-held exposure meters: (1) cadmium sulphide (CdS) type; (2) silicon photodiode (SPD) type.

Focusing screens With some cameras (35mm SLRs in particular) it is possible to remove the focusing screen (a rectangular screen, the point at which the

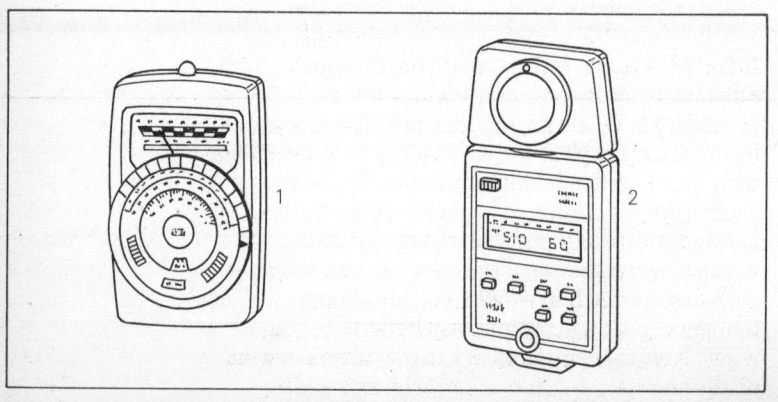

image is focused inside the camera) and insert another type for specialised photography. For architectural work, for example, replace the conventional viewfinder screen with a screen which has parallel lines etched on it. These can be used as a guide for judging the straight lines in the building which is the subject of the photograph. There are also screens for close-up photography and other applications.

Viewfinders In close-up photography you may find that the viewfinder on your camera is not adequate for viewing fine detail. You can change the viewfinder on some cameras for one offering a greater magnification of the viewing image. There are also other types of viewfinder.

Eyecups In bright conditions it is sometimes difficult to see the viewfinder image, particularly if you wear glasses. Fitting a rubber eyecup will keep out unwanted light from the viewfinder and allow you to see the subject image more easily.

Correction for glasses Spectacle-wearers often have difficulty viewing the entire area of the focusing screen. You can dispense with spectacles by fitting the camera viewfinder with an eyesight-correction lens, matched to your optician's prescription. If you buy the lens holder, your optician may be able to have a lens fitted for you. If not, some specialist accessory dealers may be able to help. Mail-order suppliers will also make up lenses to your prescription.

Data backs When shooting many photographs at once, you might want to keep a record of when they were taken, exposure details, or other information. In many cases you can simply write this down when shooting, but an alternative is to use a data back to replace the conventional back on your 35mm camera. The dials on the data back can be preset for any specific numerical information (time, date, frame number, etc.) and this information will automatically be transferred onto the film when you shoot. The

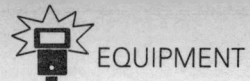

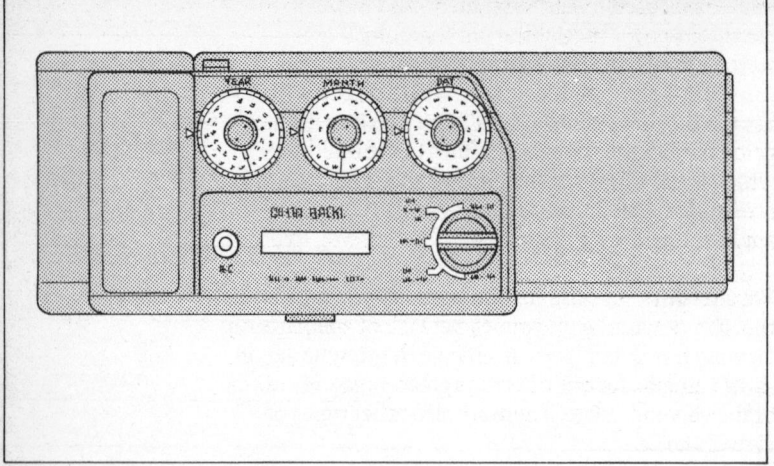

Above *Battery-driven, a data-back replaces the normal back on 35mm SLRs and can be used to inscribe information automatically onto the film's margin as each exposure is made.*

figures will appear at the bottom of the frame. The data back can be switched off if you don't wish to have any information on a particular frame of film.

Bulk film backs. If you use conventional prepacked 35mm film cassettes, the maximum number of exposures you can shoot is 36 with most films. You can increase this considerably by fitting a bulk film back to your SLR. This back accommodates larger rolls of bulk film, which you can buy and load yourself to a required length, which may be up to 30 metres (100ft). A bulk film back is useful for covering events where a large number of pictures need to be taken quickly – a sports event, for example.

Interchangeable backs On many large format SLRs you can change the film back (even in mid-film) to shoot on another type of film. For example, a switch from black and white to colour is possible.

Autowinders For shooting a number of pictures in quick succession, most SLR cameras can be fitted with a motorised autowinder. Some cameras even have this feature built-in. When switched on, it is possible to shoot pictures at around 2 frames per second – fast enough to record most action sequences. The small motor inside the winder is usually powered by four penlight batteries.

Motordrives More expensive SLR cameras can be fitted with a motordrive, which is basically a faster version of an autowinder. Used mainly by professionals, the motordrive allows you to shoot at around 5 frames per second, or faster in some cases. The motordrive is most useful for sports photography, where the photographer needs to record a number of pictures in fast-action sequence.

Other useful accessories Not all the accessories in the photographer's gadget bag need to be photographic. A few household items can also be very handy on location work. Examples which you might find useful include:

A penknife and
A pair of scissors – both useful trimming tools
A ball of string – for tying back unwanted branches in a landscape
A roll of adhesive tape – for taping notes to the camera or fixing backgrounds
A pen and note pad – for notes on exposure, or taking names of subjects
A small penlight – for viewing camera controls at night
A set of small screwdrivers – for minor camera adjustments (experienced photographers only)
A roll of fast film (1000 ASA) – for emergency shots in very bad lighting conditions

Film

FILM BASICS

However you view subjects through the camera, it is how they reproduce on film that will determine the success of your pictures. Choosing a film can be just as important as your equipment selection. Film is cheap compared with almost every kind of photographic hardware, so don't be afraid to try out different types and to experiment.

● **Always** double check that you have bought the right type of film. If buying colour print film, make sure you don't buy colour slide by mistake and vice versa.

Film types All film looks more or less the same. However, the character of pictures produced by different *types* of film can vary considerably. If in doubt, ask for advice at the shop counter. When choosing, consider:
1) whether you require black and white or colour;
2) if the choice is colour, decide whether you want colour prints or slides, and make sure to buy the right film for the purpose.

Film makes Many manufacturers produce film, and choosing between all the film cartons in a store can be difficult. If in doubt, start by going for the big-name brands, like Kodak, Ilford or Fuji. Try different brands over a period of time and see which produces the best results for you.

● **Check** that the ISO speed setting on the camera is the same as that marked on the film.

Film speeds Every film is designed to respond to a range of lighting conditions and this range is denoted in ISO figures on the film or film carton. Generally speaking, the lower the ISO figure, the better the light conditions should be when using it. For example, a film like Kodachrome 25 slide film should really be used only in bright conditions. For very low light, you might need a film rated at around ISO 400. Most popular colour negative/print films are rated at ISO 100, which is a central rating, usually producing acceptable results in reasonable lighting.

Film lengths Make sure you buy a film which is no longer than you need for your current commitments, since it is not a good idea to leave film in the camera over a long period of months. The length of the film denotes how many exposures (or frames) you can shoot and should not be confused with the film size. A 35mm film, for example, might be available in lengths of 12, 24 or 36 exposures. Some films may be available only in one length; e.g., disc film is available only at 15 exposures per film.

Box information Sorting out a film is one thing, but understanding the jargon on the film carton can be quite another. First, look for the film size and length – on a 35mm film this might read '135-36' which means the film size is 135 (35mm) and there are 36 exposures. Next, check that the ISO rating (the ASA rating is the same as ISO) is right for your requirements. The leaflet with the film may carry advice about exposure, but don't worry about that if your camera is automatic. This information acts as a guide for setting manual cameras. Next, check the expiry date – don't use outdated film unless you are prepared to risk poor results. (See the drawing on the next page.)

●**Don't** use out-of-date film – the results may be below standard. The expiry date should be marked on the film carton.

Film storage Most film should be kept in a cool, damp-free place. Storage in a refrigerator is recommended for some colour films. Some films need to be kept in a freezer for long-term storage, but check with the manufacturer's instructions first.

Film markings When a film has been processed, you can see a variety of different markings on the negatives. Each negative should be numbered to enable reprints to be ordered later and this is the only mark which need concern you.

COLOUR NEGATIVE/PRINT FILM

How it works The most popular type of film in use is colour negative/print film. If you want colour prints, you can choose one of these films. When the film is processed you have a set of colour negatives from which your prints are made.

Popular speeds Most colour neg film is available in ISO 100 rating and this is fine for the vast majority of shooting situations. However, if you are likely to be shooting in lower light or bad weather conditions, consider one of the faster films. Kodak, for instance, offer colour neg films rated at ISO 100, 200, 400 and 1000 – a range which should cover most situations.

Right Basic data to look out for on a film carton.

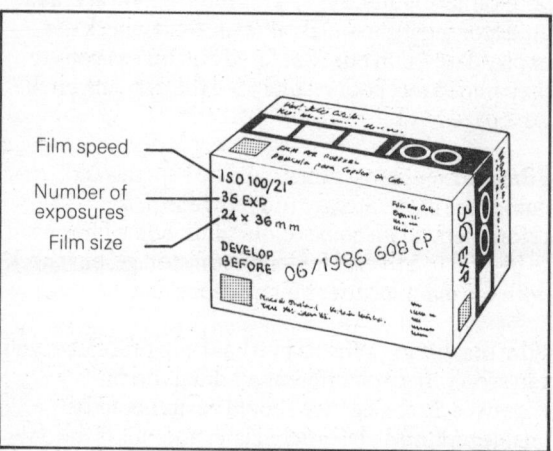

Ultra-fast film Modern colour-film technology has developed in recent years, allowing the production of ultra-fast film, like Kodak VR1000, rated at ISO 1000. While very fast, the special 'T-grain' emulsion used also reduces the amount of grain visible in the result. Many photographers have found this new type of film

better in quality than slower films. It is worth keeping a roll handy for situations where very low light might otherwise make it impossible to take a photograph.

High resolution Recent developments in film technology have produced so-called 'high resolution', or HR, films. Because of the way the HR film emulsion is made, it is possible to achieve much sharper and more colourful results on these films. It probably won't be long before all colour neg films feature the HR emulsion, and they are certainly the best choice for the enthusiastic photographer who is looking for the sharpest possible quality.

Exposing colour neg Accuracy of exposure is important for best results with all types of film. But there is a reasonable amount of tolerance with colour neg film. If you under- or over-expose the film this can usually be corrected at the printing stage. Automatic printing machines at a processing laboratory can usually produce an acceptable result from a wrongly-exposed colour negative. Some photographers deliberately over-expose the film (by one or two f/ stops) for a stronger colour effect. Colours can look 'washed out' if the film is under-exposed.

Orange mask When you have colour neg film processed you will notice the negatives have an overall orange appearance. This orange 'mask' is designed to make printing of the negatives easier and does not spoil your pictures in any way.

Laboratory processing Most photographers send their colour neg films to be processed by a laboratory, either by mail or via a photo shop or store offering this facility. Certainly, this can be the cheapest way of having this film processed and healthy competition in the processing market ensures reasonable quality and prices. Shop around for processing deals and try different outlets to see which is best (see pages 159-61). Compare price, quality, and the time taken – the latter can vary from one hour to several days or even a week. Remember that speed does not always

guarantee good quality. Check prices for extra reprints too. See the Processing chapter, pages 156-63.

Home processing Processing and printing colour neg film is quite easy at home (see Darkroom chapter, pages 164-93), but laboratory processing is so cheap, it isn't a very economical proposition. You do get the satisfaction of producing your own pictures from start to finish, however, and having your own darkroom can start to pay off if you want to do your own enlargements later.

Reprints Always remember that colour quality can vary each time a negative is printed. Even if you use the same processing laboratory, the colours in a second print made from the same negative as the first will usually differ – although you can help by sending the original print with your reprint order so that colours can be matched more closely.

●**Don't** worry too much about brand names when choosing colour neg film – most are made by the main manufacturers anyway.

Colour quality Most film processors monitor the quality of their work very closely and, indeed, large firms like Kodak also monitor the processors to whom they supply materials. If you receive a set of prints that you feel are not of acceptable quality (colour, sharpness, etc.), don't assume automatically that it is your fault. Return the prints *and* negatives, explaining why you are not happy and ask for an explanation. In some cases, a simple reprint may be all that is needed. Many laboratories pride themselves (and indeed sell their services) on quality and will be happy to double-check their work for you.

COLOUR SLIDE FILM

How it works Colour slide film is also known as colour transparency, or reversal, film. The latter name is probably most descriptive because, when you shoot pictures on this type of film, the result is not a negative (from which you would make a positive print image) but a reverse negative, i.e., a *positive* image. So you end up with the colours as seen in the subject.

Film choice Colour slide films are available in various sizes and types. Within all the various makes, there are two basic types of slide film – *substantive* and *non-substantive.* Substantive films contain colour dyes in the emulsion and can be processed by a laboratory of your choice, or at home (see Darkroom chapter, pages 164-93). With non-substantive films, like Kodachrome 64, dyes are introduced at the processing stage and so the films must be returned to the manufacturers for processing.

Process paid With non-substantive films, such as Kodachrome 64, the cost of the film includes processing by the manufacturer. A small return envelope is enclosed with the film – you simply put the exposed film in, fill in your name and address and that of the nearest processing division of the company (a list is supplied), stamp it and the film will be returned after processing, usually within a week or so. Slides are usually returned in plastic mounts ready for viewing. Generally, there is not much price difference between process-paid films and films which you pay to have processed later by a laboratory. Some savings can be made by processing a batch of ordinary films (not process paid) together in a home darkroom.

Popular speeds There is no fixed standard speed for slide film. One of the slowest slide films is

Kodachrome 25, which offers very high quality results, but requires good lighting conditions. Kodak Ektachrome and similar films from manufacturers like Agfa and Ilford are available in medium speed ISO 200, and even faster ISO 400 for low-light work.

Exposure With slide film correct exposure is more critical than with other types of film. This is mainly because there is no printing stage, so a greater degree of accuracy in exposure is needed at the shooting stage. Don't always depend on your camera meter – experiment with under- and over-exposure when using slide film and see how the results can vary.

Film differences Slide films vary in the results they produce. This is often because they are made differently, but even those of similar type have their own characteristics. You can see differences even between Kodachrome and Ektachrome (both made by Kodak) because of their construction and the difference in processes used. Experiment by trying a few different types of film and keep a record of likes and dislikes for future reference. Some films may be more suitable for certain types of picture than others. Kodachrome 25, for example, is more suited to very bright and colourful subjects than a faster Ektachrome, which produces slightly grainier results.

Slide mounts Slide film sent to a laboratory for processing is usually returned in plastic or cardboard mounts ready for viewing. You can buy mounts separately if you wish to mount your own. Some are fitted with glass for extra protection against heat (from a projector lamp) and dust. Sandwiching slides between glass sometimes causes circular coloured rings, known as 'Newton's rings', to appear. Buy anti-Newton glass mounts to avoid this problem.

Prints from slides It is possible to make prints from slides using special reversal slides, like Cibachrome. A laboratory can do this for you (usually at the same price as a print from a negative) or you can print at home using a printing kit (see pages 185-6).

Duplicate slides Like a negative, which must be looked after if extra prints are to be made, an original slide is also precious. To protect yourself against loss or damage, you can have duplicate slides made from your originals on a special duplicator. This can be expensive, although some laboratories offer special deals on a large batch. Buying your own duplicator is an option, but an expensive one. Duplicate at the shooting stage by taking several frames of the subject instead of just one – this is the cheapest option.

Slide storage Once processed, slides should be cared for. Keep them in the slide box in which they were returned from the processors, or store them in a special magazine ready for projection. There are also slide storage wallets in a plastic material for easy storage and quick viewing. These wallets can be kept in a conventional filing cabinet if required. Always store slides in a damp-free place.

Slide 'pushing' As with most other types of film, you can increase the working ISO speed of slide film. For example, you can shoot a 200 ISO film at 400 then increase the development time at the processing stage for accurately exposed results. Most laboratories offer an uprating service for this purpose, but usually make a small extra charge.

Instant slides To produce slides instantly use Polachrome instant-slide film. By means of a special hand-held processor (which can be used in normal light) the exposed film is developed, producing a roll of slides within minutes. This is useful for pictures which are needed very urgently. Results are not usually as good as conventional slide film, but acceptable.

BLACK-AND-WHITE FILM

How it works Conventional black-and-white film captures the colours we see not only in black-and-white, but in all the shades of grey in between. Most of the black and white photography we see is reproduced in newspapers, magazines, books, and so on. Many enthusiastic photographers recognize the individual qualities offered by black-and-white photography, such as its increased emphasis on texture and composition, despite the increase in interest surrounding colour work.

Right Strong, simple shapes like this road bridge lend themselves to contrasty exposures in black and white.

Film choice Most simple cameras are designed for colour only. However, there is a reasonable choice for the 35mm and roll-film camera owner. Black-and-white film isn't cheap, however – it is usually more expensive than colour, mainly because the latter is more popular and is produced in such quantities that prices can be kept lower.

Slow film For high quality results, a slow film (around ISO 50) is the best choice. With minimal grain, the negative produces a very fine image although it can be quite 'contrasty', i.e., with very deep blacks and whites. This contrast can be reduced in processing by reducing the development time. Slow film is ideal for portraits, copying work, or if very fine detail is required.

Medium-speed film The best film-for-all-occasions is a medium speed film of around ISO 125. This is fine enough for good quality results and fast enough for shooting in most conditions. It is a safe choice for portraits or landscapes and the like.

●**Remember** that you can buy black-and-white film in various ISO speeds – experiment so that you can weigh up the pros and cons of different films.

Below Black-and-white film can also go to the opposite extreme, creating subtle graduations of tone as in this shot of cooling towers.

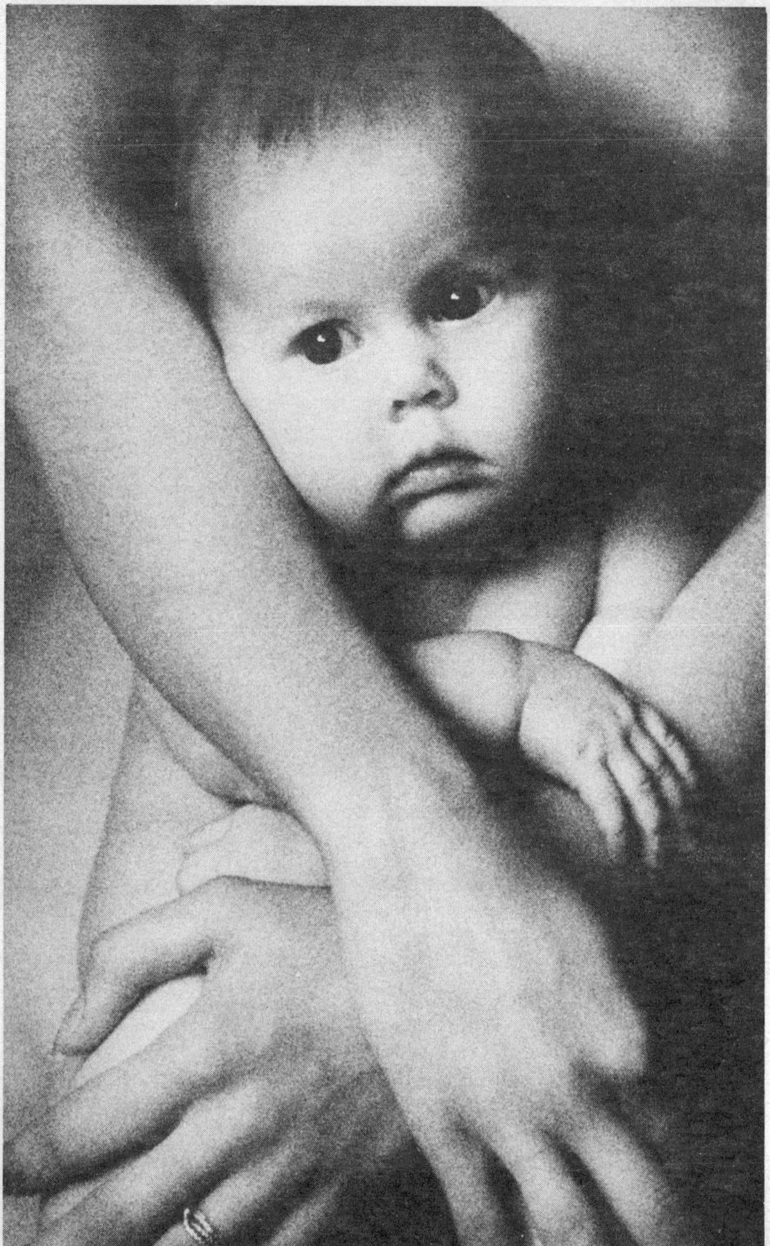

Fast film For low light work (bad weather, indoors, and so on) or situations where you need to use a fast shutter speed (sport, for instance) choose a fast film around the ISO 400 rating. This type of film produces slightly grainier results than slower films, but under difficult conditions, shooting on fast film is better than not getting the picture.

About grain Because black-and-white film is made up of silver halide 'grains' in the emulsion, this graininess can be seen in the processed negative and, consequently, the print. Remember that the faster the ISO speed of the film, the more grain it contains and the more visible this will be on the final image.

Negative points When a film has been processed, check the negatives for correct exposure. There should be even tones of grey, with slight detail in shadow areas. Too black a negative means you have over-exposed and a 'thin' negative with little detail means under-exposure.

Laboratory processing Remember that black-and-white processing and printing by a laboratory is often more expensive than colour. Many laboratories offer a film processing and contacting service, so you can view all the pictures on one sheet of paper, selecting the best for printing later.

Home processing Most serious photographers choose to process their own black-and-white films at home because it is cheaper and more rewarding than laboratory processing. Providing there is space for a darkroom, home processing is within the abilities of most enthusiasts. (See Darkroom chapter, pages 172-9, for advice on setting up a black-and-white photography darkroom.)

Contacting You can buy a special contact printer to hold negatives and paper together, or you can simply lay the negatives flat on the paper and cover with a sheet of clean glass. Expose under an enlarger lamp (or similar light source) and develop the print in the

Opposite The inherent graininess of fast film can often be exploited creatively. Here it lends interest to skin textures that might otherwise appear to lack tonal contrast.

 FILM

normal way (see page 175-6). All the pictures can be assessed on the sheet and selections made for enlargement later.

Assessing prints There is a great deal of trial-and-error involved in printing black-and-white film. Always examine your prints carefully, checking for correct exposure, framing of the negative in the print area (i.e., the composition) and general print quality. Beware of dust and scratch marks which can spoil the print.

Push processing While black-and-white films generally have a fixed ISO speed rating, there may be occasions when you wish to increase the speed (perhaps to cope with bad light). Uprating film will increase the grain and contrast of the image, lowering its quality but often enhancing its atmosphere. If you decide to 'push' the speed of an ISO 400 film to ISO 800, increase the development time at the processing stage if you are doing your own processing or ask the laboratory to uprate the film (otherwise it will be under-exposed). Details for 'push processing' are usually provided with your developer.

SPECIAL FILMS

Infrared Using infrared film you can create special 'bleached out' results for effect. This film can also be used in conjunction with an infrared flash unit (which produces light not visible to the naked eye) for photographing wildlife at night. It is available in both black-and-white and colour versions.

Left *In daylight infrared film produces prints with a mysterious, ghostly pallor.*

Chromogenic films Not all film has a fixed ISO rating. The chromogenic films, such as Ilford XP1 or Agfa Vario XL, are designed for use at practically any ISO speed. You can start taking shots at an event at ISO 200, then switch to 400 *on the same film* if the weather turns cloudy. No change to the processing cycle is needed, and all the shots will be printable. Choose a chromogenic film if you don't want to carry a variety of different films around. You can buy the films with their own special processing chemicals.

Line film For copying documents and other fine detail buy special line film, which is of high contrast and is ideal for this purpose. However, it is available only in sheet form for large format cameras such as 5×4 cameras.

Bulk film You can save money by buying film in bulk lengths. In the dark you can load practically any length of the film into a reloadable cassette using a bulk film loader. While there are cost savings, you have to take care not to scratch the film when loading or unloading from the cassettes.

Instant black-and-white You can shoot instant black-and-white pictures using one of the Polaroid cameras loaded with compatible film. Also some large format cameras can be fitted with a Polaroid back which allows an instant shot to be taken of the subject (to check composition, lighting, etc.) before conventional black-and-white film is used.

Instant colour You can choose from a variety of instant colour picture systems. Polaroid have peel-apart films for their own cameras, and for Polaroid backs on some large format cameras. They also have their own SX70 system for sealed colour prints using their own cameras. Kodak also have a system of instant prints for their own cameras. Look at these systems and see which you prefer. Polaroid also have an instant slide film in 35mm size (see Instant slides page 93).

LOADING/UNLOADING FILM

Simple camera loading One reason for buying a simple camera, like a 110 or disc, is the ease of loading the film. The cartridge or disc can only be loaded into the camera the right way round.

Loading 35mm To load a 35mm film, open the camera and insert the cassette into the left recess (you may need to lift the rewind button first).

Take-up spool In some cameras you have only to lay the end of the film (known as the leader) over the take-up spool before closing the back and winding on. On some, there is a hole or slat into which the leader should be inserted. Make sure both sides of the film perforations are placed over the tiny sprockets to the left of the take up spool, otherwise the film may not wind through.

Tighten rewind With the camera back closed, advance the film frame by frame (pressing the shutter release each time) until the number 1 appears in the film counter window on the top of the camera. Before shooting the first frame, gently turn the rewind lever (usually top left) clockwise until you feel it tighten. After the first shot has been taken, watch the rewind control when you advance the film to the next frame to check that the film is going through the camera. Keep an eye on it as you use the shots – occasionally a film breaks and, if the rewind doesn't move when winding on, this might be the reason.

Autowind Some cameras have automatic film advance. Once the film is in place and the camera back is closed, the built-in motor will advance the film to the first frame ready for shooting. These cameras may also have automatic rewind (see page 18).

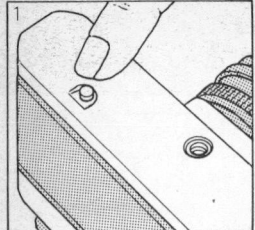 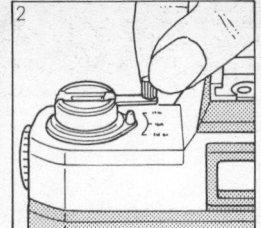 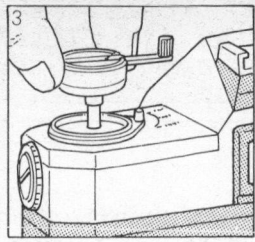

Above *Rewinding film on a 35mm camera: (1) press film-release button on camera baseplate; (2) turn rewind crank clockwise until it swings freely; (3) lift rewind knob to open back of camera.*

Rewinding For manual rewind, press the rewind button (usually in the base of the camera) and turn the rewind control on the top until you feel the film slip off the end of the take up spool. It is then safe to open the back and remove the cassette once the film is fully rewound into it.

Problems Sometimes the film can jam inside the camera. *Never* open the back of the camera in daylight. If you can't inspect the problem and put it right, take it to a dealer who may be able to help.

FILM ECONOMY

Planning shots One of the easiest ways to save money on film is to plan your shooting schedule carefully. List what you intend to photograph, how many shots you will need, and stick to your plan. You won't always be able to, however, so carry an extra roll of film just in case.

Careful shooting Don't take too many pictures of the same subject if you can avoid it. Experience with the camera will tell you when you have a good shot on film. Aim for variety on one film – shoot from different angles, or vary the lighting if possible. Then you will have a better selection than if you had taken pictures in a similar way.

Bulk buying Remember that you can make economies by buying film in bulk lengthways. Only certain films are available in bulk but it is worth looking into costs. You can buy from specialist dealers or by mail order. Remember that you will also need a bulk film loader (not an expensive item) and some reusable cassettes.

Change backs If your camera has interchangeable film backs, you can shoot just a few frames on one film and remove the back, try another type of film, shooting the rest of the first one later if you wish.

Cutting film With 35mm film, you can stop shooting in mid-film, take the camera into the darkroom and unload the exposed section by cutting it and loading it into a tank ready for processing. The end of the remaining film can be cut to feed into the take up spool ready to be finished. This is useful if you want to check the results of your shooting mid-film. You do, of course, lose a few frames because of the reloading.

Using A Camera

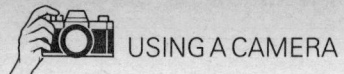

THE BASICS

●**Never** use a
camera until you're
sure how it works.
At best you could
end up with spoilt
pictures – at worst,
you could damage
the camera.

Ready to go Don't use a camera until you know what
you're doing. Just as you wouldn't drive a car until you
had mastered the controls, so you have to be sure of
how the camera functions before 'going on the road'
with it. Cameras usually look more complex than they
actually are. Without the 'frills' each camera is just a
box which transfers an image onto film – all you have
to do is to find out how to handle it before you are
ready to go out taking pictures.

Instructions Always read the instruction booklet
supplied with the camera (if it is new). With the
camera in hand go through each section of the
instructions and familiarise yourself with the various
working functions. If you don't understand
something first time around, move on to the next
section and return to that part later.

Add-on accessories Most 35mm SLRs are
supported by a range of back-up accessories. Find out
what lenses and accessories are available for the
camera so you can develop your use of it as you
become more expert. See also Equipment, pages 63-83.

Check results After shooting and processing a roll
of film, always check the results carefully. Analyse
not just the quality of processing, but your own
shooting style. Can you do better? Is the lighting
right? Can the angles be varied for more interest?
These and many factors can combine to improve your
photography and reduce the wastage caused by bad
shots, and save you money in the long run.

Courses There are many courses on photography
which will help you understand camera equipment
and how to use it. Schools and colleges list courses

locally and you can find short courses advertised in photographic magazines.

HOLDING THE CAMERA

Hand held Remember that the camera is a precision tool and should be handled with care. Hold the camera firmly in both hands, with the right hand controlling the shutter release button and film wind-on lever, and the left controlling the lens aperture control and focusing.

●**Hold** the camera in a comfortable position. If you are happy with the position, there is less likelihood of camera shake.

Horizontal/vertical Most cameras are designed to be held horizontally, for view-shaped pictures. This is fine for such subjects as landscapes or groups of people, but for portraits, tall buildings and so on, hold the camera vertically to include more of the subject and less of any unnecessary background. If in doubt, try both views and see which works better.

Support When you hold the camera, tuck your elbows into the sides of your body to add extra support and to avoid camera shake spoiling your pictures. You can also support the camera on a wall or any similar nearby surface.

Tripod The best way to achieve shake-free pictures is to mount the camera on a tripod. Various types are available – see pages 75-80.

Lying down If you lie on your stomach, you can support the camera with your elbows resting firmly on the ground. This forms a sort of 'human tripod', supporting the camera, but also allowing you a certain amount of movement.

The right film Before shooting make sure you have a film in the camera – even the most expert photographers forget sometimes! Also check that you have the right film before putting it in the camera. Some cameras have a film memo holder on the back – cut off one end of the film carton and place it in the holder. This will remind you which type of film is in the camera.

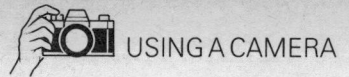
Camera settings Check the camera settings before you start taking photographs. In particular, make sure the correct ISO film speed has been set. See the rest of this section for other important settings.

VIEWING AND FOCUSING

Using the viewfinder In simpler cameras the picture area is outlined in yellow, so keep the subject within these lines. With an SLR, compose the picture within the entire area of the viewfinder screen. The viewfinder in an SLR is also used for focusing. See also pages 24-5.

Heads and feet Avoid cutting off people's heads or feet when framing your pictures. This is easily done if you are shooting with the camera held horizontally, especially if you go too close. Holding the camera vertically will help solve this problem.

Backgrounds When you are shooting a portrait don't forget the background. Look at the detail behind the subject before pressing the shutter release. If there is a tree appearing to 'grow' out of the subject's head, or any unnecessary clutter in the background, ask the sitter to move, or change your shooting position. Check the whole viewfinder area, not just the part occupied by the main subject.

Composing Learning how to compose pictures is one of the most important aspects of photography. You can learn a great deal by simply looking at other photographs (in magazines, newspapers, books and so on). Look at the key elements of each picture, how it was put together, and the general framing of the shot. Quite often, impact relies not on what is in a picture, but what is left out. Avoid clutter – a simple approach usually works best.

Changing viewpoint Don't stay in the same position when you are taking pictures. Move around and try different viewpoints. Don't just shoot a portrait head-on: photograph from the side, or from above or below as well. In a landscape, avoid the

Left Racing cyclists at the Olympics: Eamonn McCabe's shot demonstrates flair in composition, timing, and use of uncluttered background.

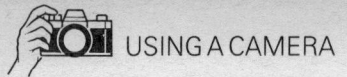

obvious view and try shooting from a high vantage point (like a hill), or walk around until you find a different angle.

Focusing For really sharp results be careful about focusing properly. With simpler cameras, where focusing adjustment isn't possible, most shots should be sharp beyond 1 metre (3ft) – don't go any closer. On 35mm compacts and SLRs where focusing is possible, look at the image carefully in the viewfinder and adjust the lens until the image (or its most important part) is perfectly sharp.

Background focusing When photographing someone in front of a view, don't be tempted to focus on the background. Focus on the main subject – the view should be sufficiently sharp in most cases to show detail. Focus on the distant view if this is the main part of the picture you want to highlight.

Foreground focusing If there is some detail in front of the main subject you want to dominate the picture, focus on this. But remember, the closer the foreground detail, the more out of focus the background is likely to be.

Focus indicators When focusing the lens you can use the focus indicator mark on the side of the lens. This is matched to the distance scale, and depends on how far away the subject of the photograph is. You need only use these markings if you can't focus visually through the viewfinder. Some SLR cameras have focus indicators inside the viewfinder, showing which way to turn the focusing control for a sharp picture. This is particularly useful for photographers with eyesight problems.

No-fuss focusing Choose an autofocus camera if you find manual focusing a nuisance. This automatically measures the subject distance and sets the lens for a sharp picture. Make sure the subject is near the centre of the viewfinder since this is the area used for autofocus measurement.

UNDERSTANDING EXPOSURE

What is exposure? Exposure is the control of light reaching the film for a correct result. Every film has its own ISO speed rating and, consequently, a particular exposure requirement. Once the ISO speed of the film has been set on the camera, the camera metering system can help you work out how much light is needed for an accurate exposure, by using the shutter speed and lens aperture. This can be done manually or automatically, depending on the type of camera.

Using a TTL meter To operate the TTL (through the lens) metering system, first find out how the meter is switched on. This might be via a small switch on top of the camera or, more likely, by flicking out the film wind-on lever slightly from the camera body. Some meters operate by gentle pressure on the shutter release button – don't press too hard otherwise the camera will fire. Watch for indication in the viewfinder that the meter is operating.

Match needle Exposure information is often given in the camera's viewfinder. Some cameras feature a small swinging needle which moves between a '+' sign (indicating over-exposure) and a '−' sign (under-exposure). Centre the needle for a correct exposure by moving the shutter speed or lens aperture control.

LED indicators Modern SLRs have small LED (light emitting diode) indicators to signal exposure. A red light usually means over- or under-exposure, with green signalling a correct exposure.

Manual or automatic? Choose a camera with manual metering if you want to experiment with shutter speed and lens aperture controls. The manual camera can often be more flexible than and automatic camera, which will select the correct settings for an exposure. An automatic camera is the best choice if you want a simpler camera which is easy to use.

●If your camera does not lock onto an automatic setting, make sure you don't knock the control manual when shooting. Use sticky tape to keep the control still.

Meter readings The TTL metering in most SLRs measures a general section of the viewing area. This

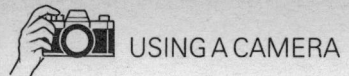

so-called 'centre-weighted' metering measures mainly the middle area of the subject, so bear this in mind when taking readings. For more precise readings, some cameras offer a spot-metering facility, which allows the photographer to take a reading from a small section of the subject.

Manual settings On a manual camera transfer the information given by the camera meter to the camera controls manually. If the meter indicates an over-exposure, either select a faster shutter speed or a smaller aperture (that is, a higher f/number). This will reduce the light reaching the film. Watch for a correct exposure indication in the viewfinder. An under exposure reading calls for a slower shutter speed or wider aperture (see table below).

●**Don't** keep to one exposure setting in changeable weather. If the light varies, for accurate results so should your settings.

Meter reading example

Camera set at 1/125 second (shutter speed) at f/8 (aperture)

Subject indicates	Re-set to
Over-exposure	1/250 second at f/8 or 1/125 second at f/11
Under exposure	1/60 second at f/8 or 1/125 second at f/5.6

You may need to adjust the setting still further until a correct exposure is indicated by the meter.

Shutter priority If you want manual control of the shutter speed on the camera and prefer to allow the camera to select the aperture automatically for a correct exposure (as when shooting sport or action, for instance, and you need to be sure of 'freezing' high-speed motion), choose a camera that offers shutter priority. Select the required shutter speed (say 1/250 second) and set the lens aperture to 'A' (for automatic). When you take the shot the camera will automatically select the correct aperture (say, f/8), which will be indicated in the display area in the viewfinder for your information.

Aperture priority On an aperture-priority camera, you set the lens aperture manually, but the camera automatically selects the correct shutter speed. Set the required aperture (say, f/8) and set the shutter speed dial to 'A' (for automatic). When you shoot, the camera will automatically select the shutter speed needed for a correct exposure (say, 1/250 second).

Program setting If you choose an SLR with a program setting, you won't need to adjust either the lens aperture or shutter speed. The camera will automatically select both for a correct exposure. This type of camera is very quick and easy to operate, and will provide accurate results in most situations. The selected aperture and shutter speed will be indicated in the viewfinder.

Manual override If you want the convenience of an automatic camera, but the possibility of setting the camera yourself, buy a camera with manual override. This is possible on most aperture-priority cameras, which have a full range of apertures for manual settings. Shutter-priority cameras should have a full-range shutter-speed dial for overriding the auto setting. An auto-only camera like the Olympus OM10 has a separate shutter speed control which can be added as an accessory for manual settings.

Backlighting When photographing someone with the camera facing the sun, the camera meter is likely to expose for the bright background rather than the subject's face, which is in shadow. You can increase the exposure manually by using a wider aperture to compensate (say, from f/8 to f/5.6). Some cameras, however, have an exposure compensation, or backlight control (with a range of about ±2 f/stops) for dealing with this kind of difficult light.

Special metering problems While most camera meters are accurate, they should not always be trusted. Test the metering in a variety of lighting conditions to see how it functions. Run a roll of colour slide film through the camera and check the results

for accurate exposure. Pictures that are too light or too dark may indicate problems with the metering. Inaccurate readings from the meter can also be caused by a low battery, so check this first. Don't hesitate to return with the results and the camera to your dealer if you are unhappy.

ABOUT APERTURE

Setting aperture The lens aperture (together with shutter speed) controls the light reaching the film, or the exposure. On some automatic cameras you don't have to set the aperture control manually. On most 35mm SLR standard lenses, the lens aperture ranges from about f/16 (smallest) to f/2.8 (widest). Use a small aperture for very bright weather, and a wide aperture for dull days. If in doubt, use an aperture in the middle of the range – say, f/8 – and match the correct shutter speed advised by the camera's metering system for an accurate exposure.

Depth-of-field scale You can check the area of sharpness at a particular aperture by looking at the depth-of-field scale marked on the lens, near the aperture control. Two aperture scales (minimum to maximum) meet at a middle mark. Focus the camera lens on the subject and you will see the distance opposite this mark. If you have set the camera to, say, f/16, read off the distances opposite the two f/16 marks to find out the depth of field range.

Depth-of-field preview You don't have to guess how much of the picture area will appear sharp if your camera has a depth-of-field preview button. First, compose and focus the shot then, while pressing in the DOF preview button on your camera, select different apertures and watch how the background detail becomes more or less sharp at each aperture. Once you are happy with a particular aperture, release the DOF preview control and take the shot.

ABOUT SHUTTER SPEED

Setting shutter speed The speed at which the camera shutter opens and closes controls the light reaching the film for a correct exposure. Just as important, the shutter speed is used to 'freeze' motion. The shutter speed range on most 35mm SLR cameras is between 1 second and 1/1000 second. The speed is set on a small dial on the top of the camera, or by pressing a button and reading the speed on a small LCD (liquid crystal display) on the camera, or inside the viewfinder. A speed of 1/60 or 1/125 second is safe for most shots, but use a faster speed (1/500 or 1/1000 second) for fast action. Slower speeds may be needed for low light conditions, but beware of camera shake.

Auto shutter speed Some cameras don't have a shutter speed dial. If you can't be bothered with manual shutter speed settings, choose a camera with an 'auto' setting only. Once you set the lens aperture, the camera will automatically select a shutter speed for a correct exposure. Cameras with a program setting, select aperture *and* shutter speed automatically.

Speed effects The shutter speed you select will affect the final result, so take care to choose the right one for the subject. While 1/125 second is about right for most subjects, shooting fast action or movement at that speed could leave you with a blurred picture, because it isn't fast enough to 'freeze' the action. In some cases, however, a small amount of blur can give the *impression* of movement. Experiment with different speeds and see what effects you like.

Shutter speed table

Subject	Shutter speed (second)
Portrait	1/60
Landscape	1/60
Children	1/125
People walking	1/125
Running/cycling	1/250
Medium-pace sport (e.g. football)	1/500
Fast action (e.g. car racing	1/1000

In the case of a moving subject, these suggested speeds should be enough to 'freeze' the action. For subjects moving *towards* the camera (rather than *across* the camera) you may be able to go down by one speed (say, from 1/125 second to 1/60 second). Results can vary depending on the focal length of the lens being used. Generally, the longer the lens, the faster the speed should be to reduce the risk of blur.

Camera shake Most amateur pictures are spoilt by camera shake, i.e., when the photographer shakes the camera slightly at the moment of exposure, causing a blurred result. It is easy to avoid. First, use a sensible shutter speed if hand-holding the camera (no slower than 1/60 second). Second, hold the camera firmly until *after* the shot has been taken. Third, press the shutter release button gently – jabbing at it will shake the camera. Ideally, for completely shake-free exposures, place the camera on a firm support (like a tripod) and use a cable release, attached to the shutter release button, to fire the camera.

Freezing action You can see from the shutter speed table that, the faster the movement of the subject, the faster the shutter speed should be to 'freeze' the action. The speed you choose is often dictated by the amount of light available and it isn't always possible to select the fast speed you want. In low light, use the widest aperture you can (say, f/2.8) and the fastest shutter speed compatible for a correct result.

VIEWING WITH LENSES

Standard view The standard lens on your camera is designed to cover most situations. You can use a standard lens (usually 50mm on a 35mm camera) for portraits, landscapes, groups, and so on. Become familiar with using the standard lens and find out how you can get the best pictures with it before considering adding any other type of lens (like a wide angle or telephoto) to your equipment.

Wide views You may well encounter situations which call for a wider lens. For interiors, where space limits your ability to move back, a wide angle lens will give you a wider perspective. A wide angle will also help you to take in more land detail in a view shot. Don't over-use a wide angle: too many wide shots in your portfolio of pictures can become tedious.

Telephoto view If you want to capture close up detail of a far away subject, use a telephoto lens. On a 35mm camera, a telephoto lens of around 150mm is a convenient length for most shots, although you will need a longer lens of 200mm upwards for very distant subjects. In a portrait you can often get much better facial detail and, in a landscape, foreground and background can appear compressed, creating, as in many paintings, a far more dramatic effect.

Zoom view The zoom lens is the most flexible lens you can buy. Within a zoom range of, say 70-210mm, most subjects you are likely to photograph are within your grasp. A zoom is most useful in sport and action photography, where the subject distance from the camera is always changing. For photographing people, you can alter the subject from head and shoulders to a full length shot by simply zooming out. See also Zoom Lenses, pages 49-51.

Mirror view If you don't want to carry around a long telephoto lens because of its bulk, a mirror lens is a compact alternative. Even a 1000mm mirror lens is no bigger than a short telephoto in length yet you can photograph the most distant subjects. Use a mirror lens for covering sports like cricket, where the action is just beyond the range of most telephotos of usable size, and also for widlife photography.

Straighten perspective Photographing a building or monument can present a problem because the lines of the building can appear to converge, particularly if you shoot from a low position. Changing the angle of the shot can help, but you may have to move much further away from the building to reduce the effect. That isn't always desirable, so a 'shift' lens is needed to eliminate the perspective problem.

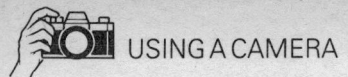

USING LIGHT

Light sources Light is essential to all photography and the camera user has a choice of different types of light sources, both natural and artificial. Daylight can provide the most natural and pleasing results, but you can use lamps or flash as alternatives, depending on your style of photography. Remember, the quality of your photography will depend as much on your skill in using light as on your use of equipment.

Natural light Daylight is the most natural light source for photography – and it can offer the photographer an extremely wide range of effects. The quality and direction changes all the time, depending on the time of day, and year, the weather, and so on.

Bright sunlight Many photographers believe that bright sunlight is best for taking pictures. This can be so – but it also creates problems, such as very harsh shadows. Mid-morning or afternoon is better than midday for this reason. Don't photograph someone with the sun over your shoulder – harsh lighting and a squinting subject don't make a good portrait. Shoot from the side or with the camera facing the sun to avoid awkward shadows on the subject's face. A lens hood will help prevent 'flare' spoiling the shot.

Diffused light Many photographers agree that diffused sunlight, with the sun's rays passing through thin cloud, is ideal for pictures. The light is bright enough for good results, yet the diffused effect reduces the harsh shadows experienced in direct sunlight. On a bright day watch for occasional cloud cover and try shooting when the sun is diffused by it.

Cloudy weather You might not get very bright results in cloudy weather, but you can get some

interesting results on an overcast day. A sky heavy
with clouds can look very dramatic in a landscape
shot, for instance. You might need a fast film when
heavy clouds cause the light level to drop.

Snow and showers Even the most uninteresting
scene can be totally transformed into good picture
material when bad weather strikes. Rain and snow
showers can be particularly dramatic, so don't scurry
for shelter until you have tried to take a few shots.
Shoot under an umbrella or from a nearby covered
position if you are worried about getting your
equipment soaked (see also page 74).

Left Cloud
formations can add
greatly to the drama
of landscape
photographs. The
atmospheric gloom
of this picture was
captured with fast
(ISO 800) film.

TIMING

Time of day Choosing the right time of day to take a picture is important because the quality and direction of the light given out by the sun will effect your results. You can chart this yourself by setting aside a day to photograph a nearby scenic landscape. Start very early (around dawn) and take pictures at hourly intervals until dusk (take a packed meal and something to read in between shots). Shoot on colour film and look at the results carefully after processing. Note how the colour, direction and general effect of the lighting varies throughout the day and use this information for future reference.

Midday sun Try to avoid taking pictures in the midday sun. Because the sun is at its highest point at this time of day, practically any subject you photograph will appear to be very flatly lit, with very few shadows to make the subject more interesting, or perhaps very harsh shadows. Portraits are particularly difficult to shoot in midday light.

Time of year The effect of natural light changes with the seasons. A scene taken in spring, for example, will look very different when photographed in winter snow. Keep a record of these changes by returning to shoot the same scene on different days during each season. Apart from weather effects, note how the quality of the light varies throughout the year.

●**Take** a small torch along for night shots so you can see what settings you are making on the camera controls.

At night You can make an urban scene appear much more dramatic by taking pictures at night. The best time to shoot is around dusk when there is some colour detail in the sky, but the lights from streets and buildings are also visible. Long exposures are usually called for, so take along a tripod. Use a fast film (ISO 400-plus) to keep exposure times as short as possible.

Light sources at night When shooting night shots in colour, remember that most daylight balanced colour films will not be suitable for recording street lighting. The results will have an overall orange cast. Either use a colour correction filter over the lens (80A) or use tungsten balanced film (usually only available for slides).

Moonlight Shooting scenes under moonlight calls for the use of a very fast film (ISO 1000) and long exposures. Results will vary depending on the reflectivity of the scene (from buildings, water, and so on) and the brightness of the moon. Shoot under a full moon only for best results. When photographing the moon itself, remember it is a very bright light source reflecting the sun's rays, so exposures can be short. Expect to shoot at around 1/60 second at f/11 using a medium speed film of around ISO 200.

Night photography exposure guide (using ISO 100 film)

Subject	Suggested exposure
House interior	1/15 second at f/4
Store window	1/15 second at f/4
Brightly lit street	1/15 second at f/2.8
Floodlit buildings	1 second at f/4
Cityscape at dusk	1/15 second at f/8
Moonlit landscape	2 minutes at f/2.8

Note: These figures are an approximate guide. Try shorter and longer exposures. In many cases the camera's metering system should be able to indicate a correct exposure, depending on the light levels though one of the more sensitive hand-held meters might give more accurate indications in poorer light conditions. Exposures will be shorter with faster films.

LIGHT INDOORS
Using available light You don't have to use lamps or flash to shoot pictures indoors. With today's fast films and auto exposure cameras, many indoor pictures can be taken using daylight from a nearby window, door or even skylight. Even if your camera has built-in flash, try a few shots in natural light if the level seems reasonable – you will often obtain a good result which will be much better than a straight-on flash shot.

Window light Daylight coming through a window (or doorway) can provide the most pleasing results, particularly in portraits. Avoid direct sunlight, which throws awkward shadows – bright, but slightly cloudy, days are best. Photograph the subject with the window light on one side of the face.

Reflector One useful and economical accessory for window-light portraits is a reflector. While lighting one side of the subject's face from the window, the other side is cast in shadow. A reflector held on this side will reflect back the light and allow a more even lighting effect. The reflector can be a piece of white card, a sheet, or even a newspaper. You can also buy a special fold-out reflector (called a Lastolite).

Lamp light You can shoot indoors using ordinary household lights. Avoid using overhead lights when photographing people because of the awkward shadows they cast – but they are fine for interior room shots. Table lamps or spotlights can be used for portraits but you may need to use a reflector to fill-in shadow areas. With colour film balanced for daylight, you must use a correction filter (80A) or use tungsten balanced film for accurate colour rendition.

Candlelight To take pictures in candlelight you need a fast film (at least ISO 200, and preferably ISO 1000) and a longish exposure. With daylight-balanced colour film the effect will be warm or orangey, but this enhances the natural effect of candlelight.

Can the film cope? In very low light, where very long exposures are needed, some films (particularly colour) suffer what is called *reciprocity failure*. This simply means that the film emulsion can't produce an accurate rendition of the subject, which may spoil the colour and sharpness of the processed picture. Fast films (ISO 400 upwards) are designed for low light.

Using reflection Always be aware of the effect of reflected light. In a scene, light reflected from glass (in buildings), water (rivers, lakes, fountains, etc.) can add depth to your pictures. Light reflected off strongly coloured surfaces can affect the colours in your main subject. If you photograph someone in a bright green outfit, for instance, green reflections may appear in the person's face, possibly spoiling the shot. Use reflections to your advantage – a dramatic sky or landscape can have twice the impact if it is also reflected in a lake.

Reflected flare Make sure reflections from, or around, the subject being photographed don't cause 'flare' spots to appear in the lens. Flare can be a particular problem when photographing water or glass. A lens hood can reduce flare from outside the picture area, or a polarising filter will help reduce reflection in the subject area.

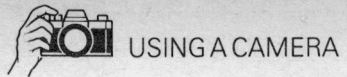

Light direction With any type of light, (from daylight to candlelight), the direction it comes from, and how it hits the subject, dictate the final effect. Try to vary the direction the lighting in your photography and see how the results change. If you can't move the light source (as in daylight photography) move around with the camera or alter the position of the subject.

Right Lichfield's informal portrait of Lord Clark demonstrates effective use of available light to side and rear. Large windows can be used, as here, to produce an interesting inner frame to a composition.

USING STUDIO LAMPS

Photolamps Consider a proper lighting set up for serious studio photography. You can buy special photolamps and stands of various types and sizes depending on your requirements. The lamps need to be quite powerful – and reflectors and other accessories direct the light as needed. Lamps feature a screw thread fitting and have a reasonably long life if used correctly.

Simple set up A typical set up for studio lighting can be one main light with a large reflector, one smaller fill-in light and possibly a spotlight for extra detail or

124

for lighting the background. If economy is a priority, start with a main light only and use white reflector boards to fill-in shadow areas cast by the light. Add other lights when you can afford to (see lighting accessories, pages 70-1).

Direct light For strong lighting the lamps should be directed straight at the subject. Don't go too close – a distance of between 1.5 and 3 metres (5 and 10ft) is about right. The heat and brightness of the light should not bother the subject too much at this distance. Watch out for reflections which can spoil the picture. In a portrait, you may find that you will need to tone down bright areas of the face with a little make-up.

●**Don't** keep photo lamps on when you're not shooting, because the heat will build up in an enclosed studio. A ventilator or fan helps keep things cooler.

Reflected light Most lighting stands have a built-in reflector. This widens the area of light given out by the lamp for a softer, more natural effect. Placing a large white reflector (a painted board will do) opposite the main light, facing in towards the subject, will help to fill-in any shadow areas.

Bounced light As well as using purpose-made reflectors, you can widen the light area, or soften the effect, by 'bouncing' the light off a ceiling or nearby wall. The surface itself however must be light otherwise the light will not be reflected effectively. With the light facing a ceiling or wall, the effect is softer and more diffuse. But bouncing also means a lower light level, so you will need to use a longer exposure to compensate. Take a meter reading with direct and then another with bounced light and see the difference – it is usually a couple of f/stops (say, from f/16 to f/8).

Background Don't think about lighting only the main subject in the studio. It is just as important to think about lighting the background. In some cases the main light may throw sufficient light to provide adequate background detail, but it is usually best to use a separate background light placed behind and to one side of the subject, shining onto the background.

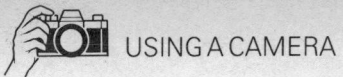

Backlighting In addition to the main light(s) in front of the subject, consider using a backlight as well. Placed behind and to one side of the subject, this light can be used to highlight detail. In a portrait for example, you might be able to place a backlight directly behind a sitter's head (but out of sight of the camera) to give an interesting rim light effect to the hair. Watch out for lens flare, however, when shooting directly into a light source.

Below *Backlighting emphasises form and texture, especially if the subject (here a* Monstera *leaf and stem) is shot against a plain dark background.*

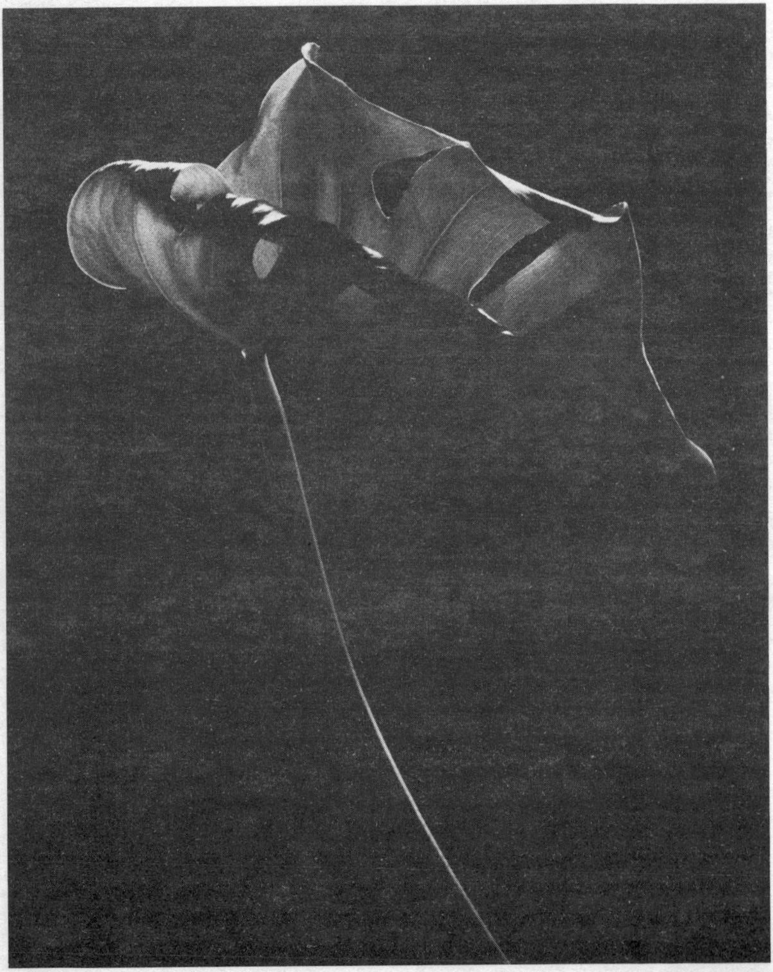

Silhouettes If you use backlighting only, you can produce a silhouette effect. The best way is to place the subject (in profile) in front of a background lit by one or two lights. Don't allow any light to fall onto the front of the subject – the bright background will throw the subject into silhouette.

Multi-lighting Proficient studio photographers can use as many as six lamps in a lighting set up. While most shots can probably be taken with no more than three lamps, some larger subjects may need more light coverage. In a multi-lighting set up, start with one main light and 'build up' the lighting gradually until you are satisfied with the result. Vary the position of each lamp: its distance from the subject as well as angle and height. The type of light (reflector or spotlight) also makes a difference.

●**Always** tape down trailing wires from lamps and flash units to avoid tripping over them.

Light for effect Lighting effects depend a great deal on the angle and height of the lamps in relation to the subject. You can create special effects by lighting from a low angle, casting strong shadows.

Colour effects Change the colour of your lighting by placing coloured filter squares over the lamps. These filter gels can be cut to size to fit your lights – you can use a different colour on each light for effect. You may also use the main lights as usual and put a colour filter over a background light.

USING FLASH

Flash lighting The most portable and easy to use form of lighting is flash. You can use an on-camera flash unit for most pictures and larger studio units are available for home studio work.

Right connection If your camera has a hot shoe connection (which is usually found on top of the camera) you can fit, and fire, practically any portable flash unit. Otherwise connect the flash via a sync lead (supplied with most flash units) to the X-sync socket on the camera (see also page 67). With built-in flash units, just switch on and shoot.

●**Never** be caught out by failing flash batteries. Have at least one spare set handy.

Flash speed Flash light travels much faster than any camera shutter, so the shutter has to begin to open before the flash fires. The timing of this sequence is known as synchronisation. Most SLR cameras have a fixed maximum shutter speed for using flash – usually 1/60 or 1/125 second. This is marked with an X on the shutter speed dial. Don't exceed it, otherwise your flash shots will be spoilt.

Settings for flash Most flash units have a dial for calculating correct exposure. These look more complex than they actually are, so study the instructions carefully before taking any shots.

Manual settings When using a manual flashgun with no automatic settings, set the film speed in use on the calculator dial. Look at the distance scale and, opposite the particular distance your camera is away from the subject, read the required lens aperture on the f/stop scale. Using ISO 100 film, for example, the dial may suggest you use an aperture of f/8 with the subject 3 metres (10ft) away.

Auto settings Unlike manual flash, where the full power of the flash is used each time you shoot, a flash set on automatic emits just the right amount of light for the subject, thus saving power for subsequent shots. Most auto flash units offer a choice of three or four auto settings, depending on which lens aperture you choose to work at. Set the ISO film speed on the dial and check the subject distance against the range of auto apertures on the dial. Set the lens *and* the flash unit to the selected aperture indicated (say, f/11).

Guide numbers The guide number (GN) of a flashgun can be used for manual exposure calculation, and it also indicates the maximum light output of the unit – useful when comparing different flashguns. The GN is the flash-to-subject distance (in metres) multiplied by the aperture needed for a correct exposure using ISO 100 film. For a unit of GN 16, for example, set f/8 on the lens for a subject at 2 metres (6½ft) from the flash.

Flash angles With built-in flash you can direct the light only straight at the subject. Many portable units now have adjustable heads which allow you to point the light in a number of different directions for better lighting effect. Choose one of these units for maximum flash versatility.

Direct flash For the brightest flash effect point the flashgun straight at the subject. Most flashguns are designed to produce their best results within about 1 to 3 metres (3 to 10ft) with direct flash, so try not to go beyond this range.

Bounce effect Most lighting we see in our daily lives is overhead, from the sky outdoors and from ceiling lights indoors. Duplicate this lighting by tilting the flashgun upwards – some models have a swivel head to allow this. Alternatively, take the flash off the camera and, with its lead attached to the X-sync socket, try bouncing the light this way.

No shadows One advantage when photographing someone with direct flash is that it does not cast shadows on the face. However, be careful not to place the subject too close to the background otherwise a shadow of the person's head may be thrown, causing an unsightly black surround.

Diffused flash You can soften the effect of direct flash by using a diffuser over the front of the unit. You can buy special diffuser accessories to fit some flashguns, but a handkerchief, or similar translucent material, held over the flash tube will soften the light output. You can expect to have to increase exposure by up to one f/stop to compensate for the diffusion of the light.

●**Remember** that you can soften direct lighting with a diffuser.

Slave units To provide lighting from several directions at once, in a portrait for instance, use extra flashguns fitted with a slave unit. These tiny light-sensitive cells automatically fire any attached flashguns when the main flash, connected to the camera, goes off (see page 69-70).

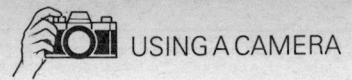

Program flash If your SLR has a program flash setting, you can take fully automatic flash pictures using a compatible flash unit. This is usually produced by the camera manufacturer as an accessory. Camera and flashgun work together to calculate a correct exposure for each flash shot, without the need for any manual settings.

Freezing motion Flash light is emitted at such a fast rate that it can 'freeze' the fastest-moving subject – even if you use a slow shutter speed.

Recycling Once you take a flash shot, remember that the flashgun has to recharge itself. How long this recycling takes depends on the type and condition of the batteries, the amount of light emitted in the last shot, and so on. Wait until the 'ready' light indicates full charge before taking another shot, otherwise under-exposure may occur.

Flash with daylight Don't always save your flash for indoor work. Even in bright sunlight a flash can be used effectively to fill-in harsh shadows. Some of the Polaroid instant picture cameras have automatic sunlight fill-in flash for better results.

Fill-in flash To use fill-in flash outdoors in bright sun first take a normal light reading of the subject and set the required apertures. Then, if you have an automatic flashgun, set the unit to two stops *wider* than this aperture. For example, with the lens set at f/16, the flash should be set to f/8 to produce just a touch of light to fill-in shadows. With too much flash light the subject would be far too bright and the background would darken. With a manual flashgun, set to quarter-power (if it has this facility), or cover the flash tube with a handkerchief to reduce the light output.

Light balance Flash and daylight can be mixed together in the same shot, but it takes some practice to get the right balance between the two. It is worthwhile setting up a flash/daylight shot and trying a number of different exposures and flash outputs. Keep a note of these and refer to them when tackling a similar set up later.

Day to night When photographing someone in daylight you can simulate night by using full power flash at a small aperture about (f/16). The subject will reduce the effect of daylight and darken any natural light in the picture.

Stained glass Never use flash to photograph stained glass in a window or door – it will 'kill' the colour of the panes by ruining the effect of natural daylight filtering through the glass. Take a light reading of the glass in daylight and expose in the normal way.

Large areas You can photograph a large interior with a small flashgun. With the camera on a firm tripod, set the shutter to the open 'B' position and an aperture of around f/11 or f/8. (You need a locking cable release, press in the cable to open the shutter and lock the release tight – when you want to close the shutter, release the lock.) If the camera has a T shutter position, set it and press the shutter once to open it. Then, with a flashgun in your hands, move around the area being photographed, firing the flash off in different directions. This has the effect of 'painting' light over the entire subject area. Afterwards, return to the camera to close the shutter.

Neon signs Don't use flash to photograph neon signs or similar bright light sources. The effect of the flash will cancel out the light emitted from the sign. Just meter and photograph in the normal way.

USING STUDIO FLASH

Studio flash output Most professionals use studio flash lights because they are much more powerful than on-camera flash. Because it is mains powered the studio flash tube is larger and gives a wider spread of light. It can be operated at full power and some offer the option for half and quarter power if fine light control is required.

Light set-up You can take successful studio shots using just one flash unit, in conjunction with a couple of reflectors to widen the coverage of the light. Two studio flashes are ideal – one as a main light, with the other for fill-in or background light. Always try to use brolly reflectors on studio flash for the soft lighting effect produced.

Flash meter The best way to judge exposure for a studio flash shot is to use a flash meter. With the subject set up, hold the meter nearby and fire the flash using the 'test' button on the back of the unit. Transfer the reading given by the meter (say f/8) to the lens aperture for a correct exposure.

Bracket exposure If you don't have a flash meter, most studio units have a scale on the backplate for calculating exposure – depending on film used and the distance from the subject. This is only a guideline and you should try and bracket your exposures. For instance, if the scale indicates an aperture of f/8 take a shot at that aperture, then shoot at one stop less (f/11) and one stop more (f/5.6). Check the processed results and see which is the most accurate.

Polaroid problems If your camera has a Polaroid back facility you can record an instant picture of the set up. However, remember that it can only be a rough guide. The film speed may be different from the film you are using, and trying to transfer exposure detail to a conventional film isn't without its problems. Be aware of this when judging your instant shot before using ordinary film.

Test film For very important flash shots when you have some time to spare, shoot a roll of test shots and process them (leave the camera and lighting set up as they are). Examine the results, particularly the lighting angles and exposures (which should be noted when you shoot), and decide on the best settings. Shoot at these settings for the final roll. If you can't process the test film yourself, use a fast processing lab if you have one nearby.

STUDIO COMPOSITION

Background You can use special background paper, such as Colourama, on large rolls for studio shots. Keep the subject a few feet in front of any backdrop to avoid casting shadows from the lights. Use natural backgrounds (brick walls, etc) only if they complement the subject. If in doubt, keep the backdrop as simple as possible.

Props Add interest to the picture by careful use of props. These can be kept simple in a portrait, for instance, an item of jewellery might enhance the subject. Avoid large props which might stand out too much in the picture.

Left Props can act as visual shorthand in portraits: in Lichfield's picture the cue instantly identifies snooker star Jimmy White.

Poses In studio portraits try and vary the poses as much as possible. As well as poses straight on, shoot the subject from both sides, looking at and away from the camera. Try for full-length and head-and-shoulder poses for variety, as well as standing and seated shots. See also pages 208-15 for more information about photographing people.

Colour &
Black-And-White

WORKING WITH COLOUR

Understanding colour Most photographers shoot colour – but few fully understand how colour works, and how it can be manipulated to produce the very best results. The best way to understand colour photography is to look at some of the best examples, in books, magazines, exhibitions, and so on. See how each photographer has approached a subject and see how the use of colour has affected the final result.

Primary colours Be aware of the three primary colours – red, yellow and blue – which are so important in colour photography. Apart from being strong and effective colours in themselves, these primaries combine to produce other colours, such as green and orange. All three mixed together produce white, an important factor in colour printing.

Colour contrast The impact of a colour picture may depend on the amount of contrast, or 'hardness', in the subject. Bright sunlight usually produces a high contrast effect. Colour contrast also depends on exposure and the type of film used.

Colour in the subject Look for appealing colour in your subjects. Colour which catches the eye easily has the most impact in pictures – for instance, a bright red flower in a landscape. But remember that subtle colour can also produce pleasing effects.

Warm colour Many photographic situations can produce results which are warm or 'orangey' in tone. Examples include a landscape photographed at sun-down, when the light confers a warm ambience. Shooting in lamplight or candlelight also produces a warm effect, especially if you shoot with daylight-balanced colour film.

Cool colour   You can produce a cool 'bluish' tone in your pictures by shooting in wintry daylight. Some films are known for their cool rendering of many subjects, particularly E6 – processed films such as Ektachrome.

Colour and mood   Colour can be a great mood setter, introducing another dimension into your pictures. Apart from warm and cool effects mentioned earlier, some colours dictate a particular mood to the viewer. This is largely subjective, of course, but you can change the impact of a set up by adding a particular colour, restricting the range of colour to emphasize texture and pattern, using props, or lighting, or a filter.

Dominating colour   You can create a strong effect by having just one dominant colour in the picture. A close up of a bright red flower, for instance, can be very effective. Watch for colours that dominate a picture too heavily – the same flower in a general landscape might distract the eye from other parts of the picture.

Mixing colour   Always observe the mix of colours when taking a shot. In some cases it is desirable to combine colours which go together well, with no discordant colour spoiling the impact. The colour mix is not always under your control, in a landscape for instance – but that doesn't matter if you are happy with the result. A filter can sometimes alter subject colour if required.

Colour interest   Quite often the pattern in a colour photograph is as important as the colour itself. Look for natural colour pattern in subjects, or introduce pattern yourself. In a portrait, for example, a bright patterned scarf or material of strong texture can add extra interest to the composition.

Complementary colours   Choose colours which complement each other if you can. A bad mix of colours can ruin the effect you are trying to produce. For example, a yellow rose in autumn will look lost against other roses or trees with yellow leaves, but a low-angled shot that placed it against blue sky would be pleasing.

Colour saturation This is the depth of colour in a photograph. Colour saturation can depend on several factors, including the strength of colour in the subject, the lighting, and even the type of film.

Muted colour Where strong colour is high in impact, muted colour is more subtle – but it can be very expressive. Look for muted colour in most natural landscapes, in grey urban environments, and so on. Remember that colour is muted by the addition of black and grey tones in a picture. This produces an overall bleak effect, with a reduction in colour impact.

Colour variations You can shoot the strongest colours in good sunlight. However, overcast and cloudy weather has the effect of scattering light and thus reducing the impact of the colours in a scene. A foggy or moist atmosphere can produce an overall soft blue cast.

Dawn and dusk You can shoot good colour throughout the day but many photographers find dawn and dusk are the best times. With the sun low in the sky there is a warm directional light which enhances practically any subject, from portrait to landscape. The sky at sunrise or sunset is particularly dramatic in colour, especially if there are interesting cloud formations.

Diffusing colour You can deliberately diffuse colour in a variety of ways. Use a haze or soft focus filter over the lens to soften colours, or smear some Vaseline over a filter for a similar effect (see also page 61). Shoot through a window covered with dust or condensation, or place a slightly patterned piece of glass in front of the lens to scatter the light.

Exposing slide film Shooting on colour-slide film requires a reasonably high degree of accuracy. A correct exposure should produce a clear and colourful image and should reproduce the subject accurately. If you over expose, the image will appear thin and washed out. If you under expose, the slide will appear too dark. Some subjects benefit from deliberate under- or over-exposure; for instance an under-exposed landscape will appear much more dramatic.

Exposing colour negative/print film This type of film is more flexible in exposure than slide film – mistakes can usually be corrected at the printing stage. Under exposure creates a thin, washed out negative, while over exposure produces a dark negative. However, the latter can produce better stronger colours in the print. Some camera meters are deliberately set to over expose for this reason.

Blur A blurred subject can suggest movement, or create an impressionistic effect. If you use a slow shutter speed with a moving subject it will record as a blurr in the picture. The slower the speed, the more pronounced the effect. Blurred colour in the subject can stand out against sharp colour background.

Colour match Try to match your colour film to the subject. A slow film (up to ISO 100) will produce the sharpest and most detailed results. A medium speed film (around ISO 200) is fine for most colour shots, and a softer emulsion (ISO 400 upwards) is needed for low-light colour work. Make sure you use daylight film for daylight work and a tungsten-balanced film for working indoors with lamplight.

Colour imbalance You can deliberately use the wrong type of colour film for effect. Use a daylight-balanced film under lamplight for a warm result in a portrait, for instance. Or use a tungsten-balanced film to make a landscape shot in daylight seem cold and harsh.

Colour correction Sometimes colours may not record on film exactly as you see them because of the limitations of the film, so some correction may be needed. Filters can be used to correct colour at the camera stage (see Filter effects page 60) or, with colour negative film, colour correction can be introduced at the printing stage.

Colour effects Apart from the differing natural effects of colour caused by changeable light, exposure and camera or subject movement, you can introduce colour effects in a number of ways. At the camera stage, special coloured filters can be used to create specific effects. In the darkroom, you can also introduce effects at the printing stage, creating exciting images from quite ordinary negatives or slides (see pages 189-90).

Colour casts Light can produce a single colour cast – in a winter landscape, for instance, there may be an overall blue tinge in the light. However, you should watch out for faulty film casts where a fogged or faulty film can appear to be cast in one colour. The problem may be in the film processing or in the camera. In the first instance check with your processor. If the problem seems to be in the camera, take it and the film back to your camera shop.

BLACK-AND-WHITE

Understand black-and-white Black-and-white photography requires a different approach to colour. The colours in the subject are, of course, converted to monochrome so tone, shape and other factors become more important in the final result.

Black-and-white subjects You can shoot practically any subject in black-and-white – but some areas of photography can lend themselves better to monochrome work than others. Popular subjects include landscapes, particularly when there is a strong linear or textural element, portraits, especially elderly faces, and architectural work, where monochrome emphasizes the lines of buildings.

Left Many photographers prefer to use black-and-white film for portraits: in skilful hands it offers an inexhaustible range of tones and textures with which to delineate character in the human face.

Colour to black-and-white If you are not used to shooting in black-and-white, it may take time to train yourself visually. In a lot of colour work the impact of the subject can rely on the colours. When using black-and-white film look for a good range of tones, interesting shapes, the effect of light, and other factors which will create an interesting effect.

Tonal range Colours reproduce in black-and-white film as a series of tones from black-to-white, with many shades of grey in between. In a landscape, for instance, colours of trees, land and sky appear as layers of tone. The tonal range varies between subjects – in a shot where similar colours dominate the frame they will reproduce as an overall tone of grey. Look for tonal variety where possible.

High key A lot of bright highlights in the subject will produce a high key effect in a black-and-white shot. Shoot in snow, for instance, and most of the shot will be dominated by a white high-key effect. You can make some shots high key in the darkroom by deliberately under-exposing at the printing stage.

Low key A low key picture has plenty of dark tones. A landscape shot in an overcast sky, or someone photographed in a dark room, are examples. You can make a picture low key in the darkroom by over exposing at the printing stage to make the picture darker.

Contrast The contrast (the hardness or softness) of a black-and-white picture depends on several factors. Some subjects are more 'contrasty' than others. Also the strength and the direction of light dictates the level of contrast in your negatives and choose the right paper and developer for increasing or reducing contrast in negatives and prints (see Darkroom chapter, page 178).

Shape and form Without the benefit of colour the shape and form in the subject becomes very important. Outdoors you can find interesting shapes in buildings, monuments and other architecture, as well as in landscape work. In a portrait the shape of someone's face is as important as expression and lighting.

Pattern and texture Be prepared to work hard at bringing out the pattern and texture in the subject to make it seem 'real' to the viewers. Apart from spotting good pattern or finding subjects with interesting texture, experiment with shooting and lighting angles for the best effect.

Weather effects Black-and-white results are as dependant on weather variations as colour. If you shoot the same scene in a variety of weather conditions you can see the changes in light direction, general tone and image contrast. Extreme conditions like snow or heat haze, makes a considerable difference to a scene.

Bright light In bright light you can use a fairly small aperture (say, f/16) with a medium speed black and white film (around ISO 125) for sharpest results. Watch out for high contrast in bright light; a contrast reducing developer may be needed at the film processing stage.

Above The boards of this fence make a background of interesting patterns and textures, but their regularity of colour and shape prevents them from distracting attention from the subject of the picture.

Overcast An overcast sky adds drama to a landscape picture – but it also means you need a longer exposure than would be needed under a clear sky. For a very dark sky where you are not using a fast film you may need a tripod to support the camera while using a slow shutter speed.

Rain and mist If you shoot black-and-white film in heavy rain or mist, remember that there will be a loss of detail, particularly in the distance. Rain has a diffusing effect on light and softens the contrast in a scene. Mist in a landscape can offer an interesting effect but, if you want to reduce the mist for clarity, use a skylight UV filter over the lens.

Avoid grey snow Watch the exposure when photographing snow to avoid the white turning to grey in the final picture. When you take a light reading, deliberately over expose by half or one f/stop to retain the whiteness. Over exposure will also ensure you retain detail in darker shadow areas

Right Snow can be a tricky subject to film. The exposure for this scene is just about right: the photographer has captured some surface detail in the snow while preventing it from taking on a greyish tinge – a common fault of snow-scene photographs.

SIX CONTEMPORARY PHOTOGRAPHERS

This colour section features work by six distinguished photographers – Lichfield, George Wright, Eamonn McCabe, Heather Angel, Adam Woolfitt and Stephen Dalton – and shows their approach to a variety of subjects in colour.

Pictures (L to R, top to bottom) by Stephen Dalton, George Wright, Adam Woolfitt, Eamonn McCabe, Lichfield, Heather Angel.

I

Lichfield

Lichfield is one of this country's best-known photographers. A keen amateur since childhood days, he started photographing professionally about twenty years ago. Renowned for his portraits of famous people, including members of the Royal Family, and of beautiful women, his work is stamped by an engaging informality.

Right *Ballet Girl: Lichfield's daughter, Lady Rose Anson (ISO 200; 1/30 sec. at f/4).*

Left Lord Lichfield's wedding: the bride and groom are at centre in back row; guests in middle row include the Queen and the Queen Mother (150mm lens; 1/60 sec. at f/8, with strobe flash).

Right Model Jerry Hall (150mm lens; 1/60 sec. at f/8 with strobe flash).

Below Designer David Hicks (Ektachrome 64; 80mm lens; 1/30 sec. at f/5.6).

Below, right Decathlete Daley Thompson (Ektachrome 64; 85mm lens; 1/60 sec. at f/11).

III

George Wright

George Wright took up photography while he was studying graphic design in the early 1970s. His first professional assignments were in fashion photography. During the past decade he has built up impressive portfolios of travel and reportage photography in India, the Middle East and the United States. His work appears frequently in *The Observer* and *Sunday Telegraph* magazines.

Right *Girl bathing (Kodachrome 64; 200mm lens, with polarising filter; 1/250 sec. at f/5.6).*

Right *Fishing off a beach at sunset (Kodachrome 64; 300mm lens; 1/125 sec. at f/5.6; tripod).*

Right *Boat trip (Kodachrome 64; 1/125 sec. at f/8).*

Above *Italian seascape (Kodachrome 64; 28mm wide-angle lens, with graduated filter to darken sky; 1/60 sec. at f/11).*

Left *Calais provision store (Kodachrome 64; 28mm wide-angle lens; 1/60 sec. at f/8).*

v

Eamonn McCabe

Eamonn McCabe works for *The Observer* newspaper, covering every kind of sporting event from all-in wrestling to croquet. He has a stylish, often humorous approach to sports work and an unerring ability to capture the essence of a sporting occasion. In 1984, not for the first time, he was voted Sports Photographer of the Year.

Above Big Daddy and Giant Haystacks (ISO 1600; 35mm wide-angle lens; 1/250 sec. at f/2).

Right Three-day eventing (Kodachrome 64; 300mm lens; 1/500 sec. at f/5.6).

Above Olympic bobsleigh racer (Kodachrome 64; 180mm lens; 1/1000 sec. at f/2.8).

Above Olympic swimmers (ISO 100; 600mm lens; 1/1000 sec. at f/8).

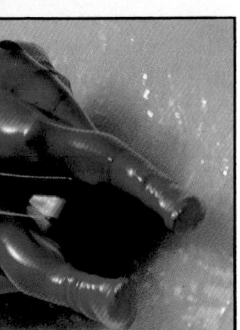

Right Alan Wells in sprint heats, 1984 Olympics (Kodachrome 64; panned shot, 1/60 sec. at f/16).

Heather Angel

Heather Angel is a zoologist and lecturer as well as a distinguished photographer. She has written and illustrated a number of books on nature and wildlife photography, and her work can also be seen in magazines and on television. She has travelled throughout the world in her quest for photographic subjects. She is currently President of the Royal Photographic Society.

Right Council-house garden (Kodachrome 64; 20mm wide-angle lens; tripod).

Below Pond reflections with goldfish (Ektachrome 64; 250mm lens; tripod).

Left *Blue garden at Crathes Castle, near Aberdeen (Ektachrome 64; 150mm lens; tripod).*

Below *Thrift in flower, Land's End (Kodachrome 25; 35mm wide-angle lens; tripod; very early morning).*

Left *Nyssa leaves, backlit in autumn (Ektachrome 64; 150mm lens; tripod).*

IX

Adam Woolfitt

Adam Woolfitt began his professional career in a studio specialising in promotional photography for record sleeves. Today his assignments for major British and American book and magazine publishers take him all over the world. These photographs of buildings demonstrate his mastery of composition and the creative use of light.

Above Cefalù cathedral, Sicily: detail of ceiling (Kodachrome 64; 85mm lens; 2 sec. at f/5.6, with fill-in flash).

Above Château Chambord, Loire, at dusk (Kodachrome 64; 35mm wide-angle lens; 1/60 sec. at f/5.6).

Right Aalto library, Feinäjoki, Finland (Kodachrome 25; 28mm shift lens; 1/60 sec. at f/8).

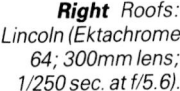

Right Roofs: Lincoln (Ektachrome 64; 300mm lens; 1/250 sec. at f/5.6).

X

Left Interior; available light (Ektachrome 64; 35mm wide-angle lens; 1/30 sec. at f/5.6).

Stephen Dalton

Stephen Dalton, one of the leading British exponents of insect and bird photography, has spent many years perfecting his skills and developing special equipment for filming fast-moving subjects. He has won numerous awards for his work, which has appeared in many magazines and books, notably his own *Miracle of Flight*.

Far left Fox cub
(Kodachrome X;
200mm lens).

Near left Bumble
bee (Kodachrome
25; 1/2500 sec. at
f/16; electronic
flash).

Below Harvest
mouse
(Kodachrome 25;
1/2500 sec. at f/11;
electronic flash).

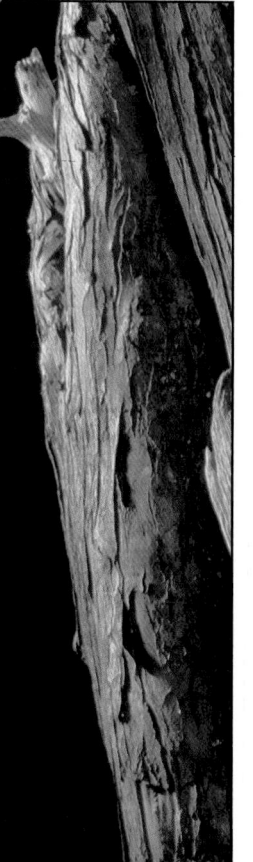

Right Bushbuck
(Ektachrome 100;
600mm lens;
1/250 sec. at f/5.6)

Left Owl in flight
(Ektachrome 64;
1/2500 sec. at f/11;
high-speed flash).

SPECIAL EFFECTS

Many of the most spectacular special effects in photography can be created in the darkroom. On these two pages and overleaf, however, are some examples of the ways in which lenses of different focal lengths and various types of filters can achieve useful effects in terms of composition, selection of detail, colour emphasis and colour correction.

Above *Use of a perspective-shift lens to provide 7mm vertical shift (28mm shift lens; Fujichrome 50; 1/60 sec. at f/11)*

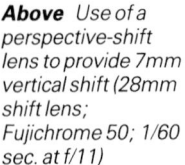

Right *Moving zoom lens during exposure (28-50mm zoom lens; ¼ sec. at f/8; tripod).*

Above *Colour enrichment by filtration: amber filter enhances golden radiance of sunset in the Western Isles (Kodachrome 64; 50mm lens).*

Right *Use of soft-focus filter and backlighting in portraiture (ISO 64; 1/60 sec. at f/8).*

Above *Using a polarising filter to intensify the blue of a pale sky and emphasise cloud forms (Fujichrome 50; 24mm wide-angle lens).*

Above Twilight effects: long exposure converts car tail-lights into red streamers (ISO 64; 2 sec. at f/11; tripod).

Right Slide sandwich: figure was shot on black-and-white film, underexposed to produce silhouette; sunset was shot on Ektachrome 64.

Snow colour and texture Try to shoot snow when the sun is low – the reddish sun will warm up the cool snow colour and the texture of the snow will be more visible because of the sun's low angle.

Wrong film If you don't have the right film for an assignment, don't worry. You will nearly always be able to shoot an acceptable result even if you have the wrong speed film. If a picture situation calls for a slow film for maximum detail, but you only have a fast film, *down rate* the film speed by altering the ISO speed on the camera from the film manufacturer's recommendation (from ISO 400 to 200, for instance) and process the film in a fine grain developer at slightly reduced development time, or ask the laboratory to do this. If you have only a slow film for a fast film subject, *uprate* the film (from ISO 50 to 200, for instance) and increase development time at the processing stage.

Film rating When processing downrated or uprated film you must make adjustment to development time at the film processing stage. This varies depending on the type of film and developer. Most manufacturers detail the times needed to develop a particular speed of film in the developer instructions. Read these carefully before proceeding.

Black-and-white filters You can change the tones in black-and-white picture by using coloured filters over the camera lens. For example, to bring out cloud detail in a blue sky, use a yellow or orange filter. (See Filters, pages 58-61).

Over-exposure When you over expose black-and-white film the negative appears to be dark, particularly in lighter areas of the picture, (white reproduces as black in the negative). Slight over exposure helps retain detail in snow and other situations where lighter tones dominate. If you over expose by mistake you might be able to compensate for this at the film development stage for a more evenly exposed result.

Under exposure When you under expose a black-and-white film the negative appears to be 'washed out' with little detail, particularly in shadow areas. You can create a low key, or dark effect, by deliberately under exposing the film (by one f/stop or more). If the under exposure is accidental, you can correct it by increasing the development time when the film is processed.

Correct film For the best black-and-white results choose the right film for the subject. For most situations choose a medium speed film (ISO 125) but, for more detailed work (close-ups, copying, etc.) a slow film (ISO 50) is best. For fast action and low light photography use a fast film (ISO 400 or faster).

Printing effects You can change the impact of a black-and-white picture in the darkroom. Apart from increasing and reducing the size of the image in the enlarger, you can make the shot seem darker (by over exposing). Using various simple printing tricks you can radically alter how a mono picture looks. (See Darkroom chapter, page 177-9).

Composition If you have sufficient detail in the negative, but you are not happy with how the shot has been framed, for a more pleasing result, you can select any area of the negative to print, leaving out any detail not required.

Print trimming and presentation There are several ways of presenting a black-and-white print. First, decide if you want a white border around the edge of the print. Most enlarging masking frames leave a thin border – you can trim this off later if necessary, or print without the frame. Some photographers print on larger sheets of photographic paper, about 38 × 30 or 51 × 41cm (15 × 12 or 20 × 16in), but print only on a small section, leaving an area of white surrounding the picutre, creating more impact than a picture which covers the whole paper area.

FINDING FAULTS

If you look at your processed pictures and there is something wrong with them, the first thing to do is identify the fault so that you can work out how to avoid it happening again. Most faults occur because of one or more of the following factors:
- Wrong camera setting (exposure, focusing etc.)
- Equipment fault
- Faulty film or film loading
- Faulty processing.

Wrong camera settings If your results appear too light or dark, you may have set the exposure controls incorrectly. For blurred pictures you may have selected too slow a shutter speed, focused incorrectly, or the cause may be camera shake.

Equipment fault If you consistently get poor results there may be a problem with your camera. Take the camera *and* the pictures back to the shop and ask for a check to be made.

Faulty film and film loading If you end up with a completely blank film it may have been loaded incorrectly and not passed through the camera. Faulty film is rare but you may come across a roll which is poor in colour or detail, or one which is marked. You can try complaining to the manufacturer but liability will probably be limited to replacing the film.

Faulty film processing Faulty processing (by a laboratory or in the home darkroom) can be a common problem in picture faults. For colour and black-and-white films check the prints *and* the negatives if there is a fault. If you have streaky or blurred prints but the negatives are clear and sharp have another set of prints made.

147

Special Effects

CAMERA EFFECTS

Frame up Create a slightly distorted effect by moving in as close as possible with the camera. This close framing works particularly well with a wide-angle lens (say, 28mm) and can be most effective in exaggerating the shape of someone's face.

Using blur Set the camera to a slow shutter speed (slower than 1/30 second) for a blurred effect. Move the camera around in a circular direction for an impressionistic effect – this works best in colour because the different hues run into each other. Follow a moving object in a panning motion, using a slow shutter speed to create a blurred background. If you want the subject to be blurred as well, do not follow the movement through.

Aperture effect How the aperture is set will affect the depth of field, or area of sharpness in the picture. You can effectively dissolve the background detail by using the widest aperture on the lens, 8.

Double exposure Superimpose two pictures by using a double exposure technique. Some camera have a superimpose button – take one shot, press in the button and advance the film wind-on lever to cock the shutter (the film stays where it is for the second exposure). Take a second shot of the subject for a superimposed image. If your camera does not have a superimpose button, press in the rewind button in the base of the camera and hold it in as you wind on (35mm cameras only). For a correct exposure, divide the exposure indicated by the meter by two.

Masking To make someone appear in the same scene twice, use a mask. Black out half of a circular filter and opaque card and, with the camera on a tripod, expose the left side of the picture with the person in view. Reset the shutter (using the superimpose or rewind button), rotate the mask 180 degrees and, with the subject in the right side of the frame, take the second exposure. The result will show the person appearing on both sides of the same shot.

Slide sandwich You can create unusual effects by sandwiching two different slides in the same mount. Look through your slide collection and combine subjects which differ in size and perspective for best effect. Each slide should be as light as possible otherwise the final sandwich will be too dark. Project the slides or make them into prints.

Panoramic viewing To record a very wide angle of view – when shooting a large expanse of landscape, or a large group of people – consider a special panoramic camera. A Widelux camera shoots through 180 degrees horizontally, while the Globuscope shoots a complete 360 degree circle. You can produce strange effects with a panoramic camera by moving or tilting it during an exposure, or by pointing it upwards or downwards for distorted perspective.

3D effect To shoot 3D images with your camera, fit a special stereo attachment which records a pair of images on each frame. Use slide film and view the results in a stereo viewer. Alternatively, tape two SLR cameras baseplate to baseplate, make identical exposures of the same subject and view using a stereo slide viewer. Or project the slides using two projectors, fitted with a red and green filter respectively, and provide red and green 3D spectacles for the viewers. The Nimslo 3D camera is a 35mm compact which uses conventional film to produce individual 3D colour prints via a special laboratory process.

LENS EFFECTS

Zooming Create streaky lines coming out of the subject by zooming in or out with a zoom lens. With the camera firmly supported (preferably on a tripod) select a reasonably slow shutter speed (1/15 or slower) and move the zoom control during the exposure.

Distortion effect Any subject can be completely transformed by fitting an ultra wide-angle lens. An 8mm *fisheye* lens will distort detail giving a 180-degree viewing angle. An *anamorphic* lens attachment can be used to 'squeeze' the image horizontally or vertically for effect.

Mirror image Create an unusual effect by photographing someone's reflection in a mirror, or the subject and the reflection. Some mirrors have natural flaws which can produce slight distortion, or you can use trick mirrors as seen in many fairgrounds. Reflections in other surfaces, like some metallic objects, can also produce odd effects.

FILTER EFFECTS

Deeper colour effect For better colour saturation like a deeper shade of blue in a sky shot for instance – fit a polarising filter. Rotate the filter and watch how the sky appears to deepen in colour, revealing any white cloud detail.

Graduated colour A graduated colour filter is half clear, graduating to a deep colour (as in some sunglasses). This can be particularly effective in a landscape, where the land is seen in its normal colour, but the sky takes on the colour of the filter (red, blue, brown, etc.).

Colour spot A colour spot filter is a one-colour filter with a clear hole in the middle. Keeping the subject in the centre of the viewing area, it will retain its true colour, but be surrounded by the diffused colour of the filter. Try using this filter for portraits, shots of flowers, and so on – but be careful to match the colour of the filter to the subject as carefully as possible.

Colour layers You can produce the effect of layers of colour in a picture by fitting a two or three colour filter. This type of filter has two or three different colours, one on top of the other, so that you can produce a sort of colour sandwich. This effect doesn't work well with all subjects and is perhaps most suitable for landscape work. Use it sparingly.

Diffraction There are many filters available which can diffract light for special effect. A 'starburst' filter turns a single bright light source into a star shape – effective in a sunny landscape or with street lamps. Other diffraction filters create a 'rainbow' effect where there are lights in the picture.

Multi-image Use a prism filter to make the subject appear several times at once in one shot. When photographing someone with a prism filter, keep the face in the centre of the picture – several faces will then appear around the frame for a multi-image effect. The number of images depends on the number of 'faces' in the prism – you can choose between three or five, sometimes more. Preferably use a three-face prism to avoid a cluttered picture. Always use a simple background to avoid spoiling the effect.

Soft focus Introduce a softer effect (in a portrait for instance), by fitting a soft focus filter. You can simulate the effect by smearing Vaseline on a Skylight filter, or shooting through misty glass – keep it close to the lens to avoid reflection.

Below Moonlight seascape? In fact, the picture was shot by day, the photographer achieving this effect by underexposure and use of an orange filter.

OTHER EFFECTS

Unusual angle One of the easiest effects to produce is to shoot a familiar subject from an unusual angle. After trying the obvious straight- or side-on approach, try shooting from a high or low angle for effect – you might end up with a better picture as a result.

Coloured light There are plenty of ways you can change the colour of light for special effect. In daylight use coloured filters on the camera. When using flash or lamps cover them with coloured gel filters, adding different colours to the main subject or to the background. Experiment with different colours and see which ones work in particular situations. See also Filter effects, pages 152-3.

Strobe effect If you have the use of a studio and want to capture several repeated images on one frame, use a strobe light. This gives out regular pulses of light and 'freezes any motion into several overlapping images. For instance, you can capture a tennis player at different stages of a serve, all in one picture. To use strobe, place the subject in front of a black background, open the camera shutter (on the 'B' setting) and start the strobe during the action. Alternatively, fire a flashgun at regular intervals for the same effect.

Back projection You can make your subject appear in practically any location in the world – by projecting a background using a back projection unit. With the subject a few feet away from the projection screen (to avoid casting shadow), you can back project a scene at 45 degrees from the screen. Use tungsten lamps to light the subject so that you can keep a good balance between the lighting and screen brightness, · otherwise the illusion won't work.

Front projection A front projection unit can produce special backgrounds behind the subject even more effectively than back projection – using mirrors. A projector is fitted to the front of the camera via an angled mirror. In the viewfinder you can see the subject straight ahead with the projected background appearing behind.

Beyond the camera Apart from effects created with the camera and accessories, there are plenty of effects which can be created after the pictures have been taken – in the darkroom. There are many printing techniques for both black-and-white and colour which can transform your pictures. See the Darkroom chapter (pages 177-9, 189-90) for some tips, and look out for advice on darkroom effects in other books and magazines.

Below A starburst filter enlivens night (or day) scenes by adding star-like flourishes to bright sources of light.

Processing

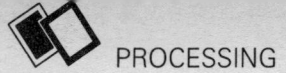

HOME OR AWAY?

Choosing a laboratory Most people choose a processor by convenience; often a nearby shop, chemist or department store. Prices vary and are not always a good guide to the quality and service available. In the photographic magazines, however, dozens of mail-order processors spell out their charges and details of the services they offer. A close study of these advertisements could save you several pounds every time you have a film to develop.

High Street costs The following costs are the average in 1985 of six different processors, and have been rounded off. Sometimes you pay more for speedy service. Column (A) represents shops, chemists and others acting as agents for processing houses which may be local or national; (B) represents a large department store with its own national processing department; and (C) represents processing chains with their own shops.

	(A)	(B)	(C)
Develop and enprint 36-exposure colour negative film	£3.99	£4.79	£4.99
Develop and enprint 20-exposure colour negative film	£2.99	£3.79	£3.00
Delivery time	6-24 hr	48 hr	48 hr
Surface choice (silk or glossy)	both	both	both
Credit for blank frames	yes	yes	yes
20 × 25cm (8 × 10in) enlargement	£2.52	£3.30	£2.95
Cheap, own-brand film, 36-exposure (cost of top brand about £2.30)	no	£1.99	£1.99

Mail-order costs These have hardly changed over the last two or three years, and the figures below are the average of six processors who advertise a service for amateurs in photographic magazines. Categories are as above.

Develop and enprint 36-exposure colour negative film	£2.90
Develop and enprint 20-exposure colour negative film	£2.20
Delivery time	5-10 days
Surface choice (silk or glossy)	some
Credit for blank frames	yes
20 × 25cm (8 × 10in) enlargement	£1.50
Cheap, own brand film, 36-exposure	some, £1.90

Free films From time to time a mail-order firm, directly or through a promotion organised with a national company, will offer a free 'own-brand' film with your current or next print order. At one time, such 'own-brand' films came from many sources. It was possible to buy two or even three different makes under a single brand name, and the quality varied. Nowadays, practically all own-brand films come from a major film maker and are of top quality. When you compare the cost of your order with what you can obtain from other mail-order firms, you will see that the 'free' film is well paid for.

SERVICES OFFERED

Negs and enprints This is the basic order, enabling you to see all the pictures taken, and from which you can later order re-prints and enlargements. Standard enprints are about 9 × 12.5cm (3½ × 5in) from 35mm negatives, though from other negative shapes they will differ slightly. They are ideal for carrying around, or for the album. Handle the negatives by the edges only, as fingerprints and scratches will show up on subsequent prints. Some firms now offer 30 per cent bigger enprints at no extra cost.

Enlargement sizes Postcard (9 × 14cm, 3½ × 5½in) is no longer considered an enlargement, as enprints are about this size. Processing houses for amateurs offer the following as the most popular enlargement sizes: 12.5 × 17.5cm (5 × 7in), 17.5 × 25cm (7 × 10in), 20 × 30cm (8 × 12 in). The last two conform to the rather long 2.5 × 4cm (1 × 1½in) shape of a 35mm negative; 12.5 × 17.5cm looks good in a strutted frame on a side table; 17.5 × 25cm would take pride of place on a mantelpiece; 20 × 30cm is good for framing and hanging. Only sharp, well-exposed negatives yield good enlargements.

Enlargement costs Mail-order costs may be as much as 40-50 per cent cheaper than shop prices. Here is an average from mail order houses: 12.5 × 17.5cm (approx) from any-size negative, 60p; 17.5 × 25cm from 35mm or 20 × 25cm from other negatives, £1.00; 20 × 30cm from 35mm, or 25 × 30cm from other negatives, £1.60.

Paper surfaces Most prints are made on paper with a textured surface, commonly called silk, lustre or lustrelux, which some people consider more artistic. Glossy paper, however, is capable of showing finer detail in the print, especially in smaller sizes. Examine both glossy and textured prints before making your own choice. Before ordering, make sure that the firm can print on the type of surface you specify.

SLIDE FILMS

Processing costs Nearly all slide films these days are compatible with the Kodak E6 chemistry formula, regardless of make, so processing by independent laboratories is universal. The few remaining films requiring different chemistry sometimes take longer to process as they have to be sent away, but they cost no more. Average costs for mounted slides at the beginning of 1985 were:

	High Street	Mail Order
12 exposures	£2.80	£2.50
20 exposures	£3.20	£2.50
24 exposures	£3.20	£2.65
36 exposures	£3.60	£3.25

Slides: mounted or strips? Most photographers
want their transparencies returned ready in standard
5×5 cm (2×2 in) mounts made of plastic or stout
card. These mounts are unglazed – that is, they do not
have cover glasses. Photographers who like to mount
their work at home in glazed mounts, which afford
better protection, order 'process only', their film being
returned in strips in see-through sleeves. This is
cheaper, about £2 as against £3.25 for 36-exposure
films; but of course the glazed mounts have to be
bought separately.

PERSONAL SERVICE

Complaints The bigger processing laboratories
differ in their attitude towards complaints. Some will
instantly put things right, while others appear to
leave such matters to the lowliest, and sometimes
most muddled, member of staff. It is fair to say that
photographers often lay the blame for their own
faults at the door of the processor; but it is equally true
that no processor is invariably blameless. Courtesy
and service usually go hand in hand with good results;
if you get the former, expect the latter.

Custom processing Professionals use processors
who cater specially for them. Usually such customers
establish a personal relationship (at least by
telephone) with the printer, telling him exactly what
he or she wants – which may include individual
details such as lightening shadows or darkening a
sky. Naturally, this service costs more. Such
laboratories will sometimes accept amateur work;
their names can be found in professional magazines
such as *The British Journal of Photography* weekly.

Borders Enprints are normally made without
borders, thus giving maximum print area. If an
enlargement is to be mounted, a border may be
unnecessary, but if it is to be framed a border is
advisable, otherwise the frame will mask part of the
image. To get a frame that fits your enlargement
perfectly, you may have to go to a framer, rather than
buy a frame ready made.

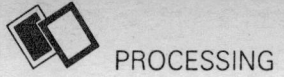

D-I-Y PROCESSING

Processing costs at home It surprises most beginners that the cost of D-I-Y processing is seldom less than commercial charges. This is because the big laboratories buy paper and chemicals in huge quantities and have little wastage. It has been estimated that the amateur who buys paper and chemicals in small packs, wasting 2 sheets of paper in every 10, and with an 80 per cent economy rate on chemicals, can produce one 20 × 25cm (8 × 10in) enlargement, or four 10 × 12.5cm prints on one 20 × 25cm sheet, for about 40p. For the first few printing sessions, however, while you are getting the hang of it, wastage is usually much higher.

Expertise After printing his first two or three films the amateur should be able to get full value from the colour paper and chemicals that he buys, and this would include a small amount of wastage. No true comparison can be made of commercial and D-I-Y costs, as no such measurements can take any account of the pleasure derived from home processing. Printing economy depends partly on equipment (see the next tip).

Equipment costs Many amateurs arrive by experience at a 'standard' filtration for the enlarger, and make any necessary variations by guesswork, whether good or bad (see the Darkroom chapter, pages 167-193). A proper colour analyser (see page 187) will cut down on wastage by eliminating such guesswork, and it is faster in use than making colour-test strips. It can cost between £50 and about £300, but will pay for itself in the long run. The more sophisticated models incorporate an exposure-compensating device. Other equipment is a convenience rather than a necessity.

SLIDE MOUNTING

Glazed or unglazed Mounts which incorporate cover glasses hold the film flat, so that it cannot 'pop' out of focus when warmed in the projector. They also protect the film surface. They are invariably chosen by experienced photographers for regular projection. Unglazed mounts, as supplied by processors, are much cheaper, permit the surface of the film to be dusted, but offer the film no protection. An outfit for mounting glazed mounts includes a cutter and a jig. The transparency is located in half the mount, the other half placed on top, and the jig clicks them together.

Mounting at home Tiny spots of dust or hairs look enormous when projected, so everything must be spotless when mounting transparencies. Put the cut transparencies and mounts on clean white paper. Polish the inside surface of each glass with a fluff-free cloth, and clean the transparency with a camelhair brush. After the two halves of the mount have been joined, polish the external glass surfaces.

A sorting desk This consists of a box with a frosted glass top, illuminated from below on which slides can be sorted in various ways. First come the 'keep' and 'throw away' categories, followed by division of slides according to use. This would include sorting into subjects or sequences for home shows, and so on. Sorting desks are sold by, or can be ordered from, photographic dealers. The best are lit by cold fluorescent tubes; the cheaper ones use tungsten tubes and get uncomfortably hot.

The Darkroom

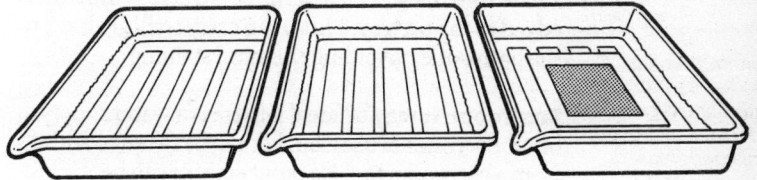

DARKROOM LAYOUT

FINDING SPACE

Bathroom This makes a good temporary darkroom, provided you arrange sessions to give least inconvenience to the rest of the family. At night, a blind over the window can give adequate blackout. A good, firm board across the bath can be used for dishes, tanks and beakers, but the enlarger and other electricals, such as the safelight, must be kept well away from the wet area. If the board across the bath is edged to form a tray, a hose can carry spillage direct to the bath outlet, avoiding chemical staining.

Below A simple darkroom set-up in a bathroom. Wet (developing) and dry (enlarger) areas should be kept separate.

Box-room It may be ideal if there is a water supply, but for occasional use a bucket can be taken to and from a bathroom tap. Blackout screens can be constructed of ply, the edges backed with felt, and

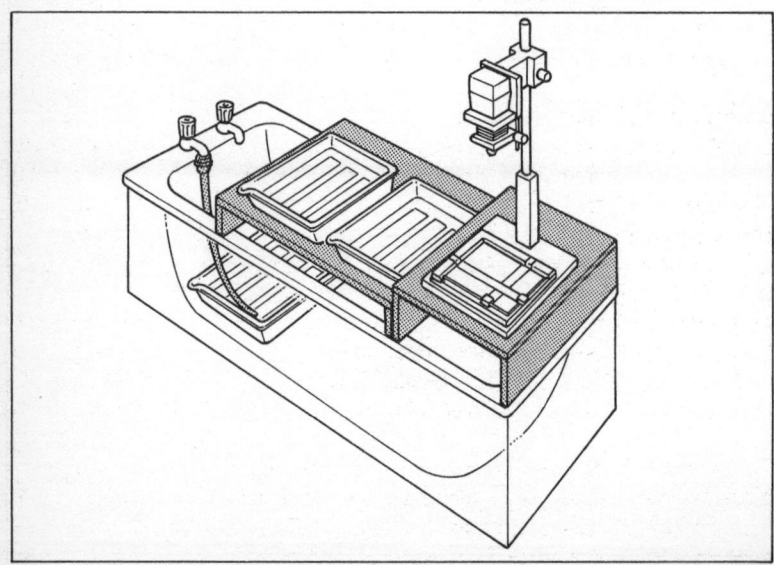

fitted tight with turnscrews to the window frame. A
bench is more useful than a table, as an undershelf is
handy for storage. Measure the bench space needed to
take enlarger, dishes and so on, and plan the work
surfaces accordingly.

A screen Do you remember those bedroom screens,
used for modest dressing by the Victorians? Many of
the less ornate ones are still available, or four large
sheets of framed hardboard can be hinged to form a
similar screen. This can be used to darken a corner of a
bedroom or bedsitter, if heavy curtains or blinds are
drawn over the window. While not exactly a purpose-
built darkroom, it should be adequate for the
occasional printing session.

Changing bag This is sometimes called the smallest
darkroom. Obtainable through dealers, a changing
bag is usually a double-skinned square bag of black
opaque material. There is a lightproof zipped entry for
a developing tank, film, scissors, and elasticated
sleeves which pull up over the wrists. Inside, you can
easily draw a film from its cassette and load it into the
tank, ready for processing (see page 173). It is
adequate for film processing, as all further stages can
be carried out in normal light.

PLANNING A DARKROOM
For black-and-white The loaded tank and beakers
of developer, stopbath and fixer can be contained in a
large dish to confine spillage. This can occupy part of
the area normally used for three dishes when
processing prints. Three 20 × 25cm (8 × 10in) dishes
need about 90cm (3ft) of bench space. The average
enlarger will occupy about 45 × 55 cm (18 × 22in),
but workspace alongside is needed for boxes of
printing paper. Allow sufficient height above the
bench for the enlarger head to be fully raised.

For colour printing Enlarger space is the same as for
black-and-white, but colour printing is now done in a
cylindrical drum, which occupies less space than is
needed for dishes. An area 30 × 60cm (12 × 24in) is

Opposite A small
darkroom containing
basic equipment
necessary for
developing and
printing. A layout of
this size would fit
into a large under-
stairs cupboard or
the corner of a
basement room —
both locations easy
to black out.

adequate. Total darkness is required for colour printing, and even a small chink of light can cause unwanted colour casts. Older houses may still have a cupboard under the stairs, which makes a good small darkroom, but beware vibration from people using the stairs while an exposure is being made.

For slides Although developing slide films calls for careful attention to detail, very little room is required. Darkness is needed only while loading the film into the tank, which can be carried out in a changing bag. After that, subsequent processes are carried out in normal lighting. Unless processing is to be carried out in an auto-processor (see page 181), a plentiful supply of hot water will be necessary.

Electricity If you have a room specially for the purpose, make sure you start out with sufficient plug points. For serious work, you may eventually need points for enlarger, timer, safelight, colour processor, film dryer, print dryer and heater.

USING SPACE

Wet and dry Depending on the space available you should try to keep wet and dry areas separated, as in professional darkrooms. In a small area, this may be achieved simply by erecting a dividing board between the dry and wet ends of a single bench or table. There is usually the odd drop of spillage when transferring prints from dish to dish, and a divider prevents a splash reaching unprocessed, and expensive, paper.

Left to right Everyone has a way of working that comes easiest to them. Ideally, arrange the layout so that you work from enlarger to wet processes and then direct to the sink. Having the wet processes closest to the sink makes for easier mopping up. Whether your prints are air-dried in a rack or passed through a dryer, keep them well away from the sink after washing.

Storage This is often an afterthought in the amateur darkroom, but a little pre-planning leads to much

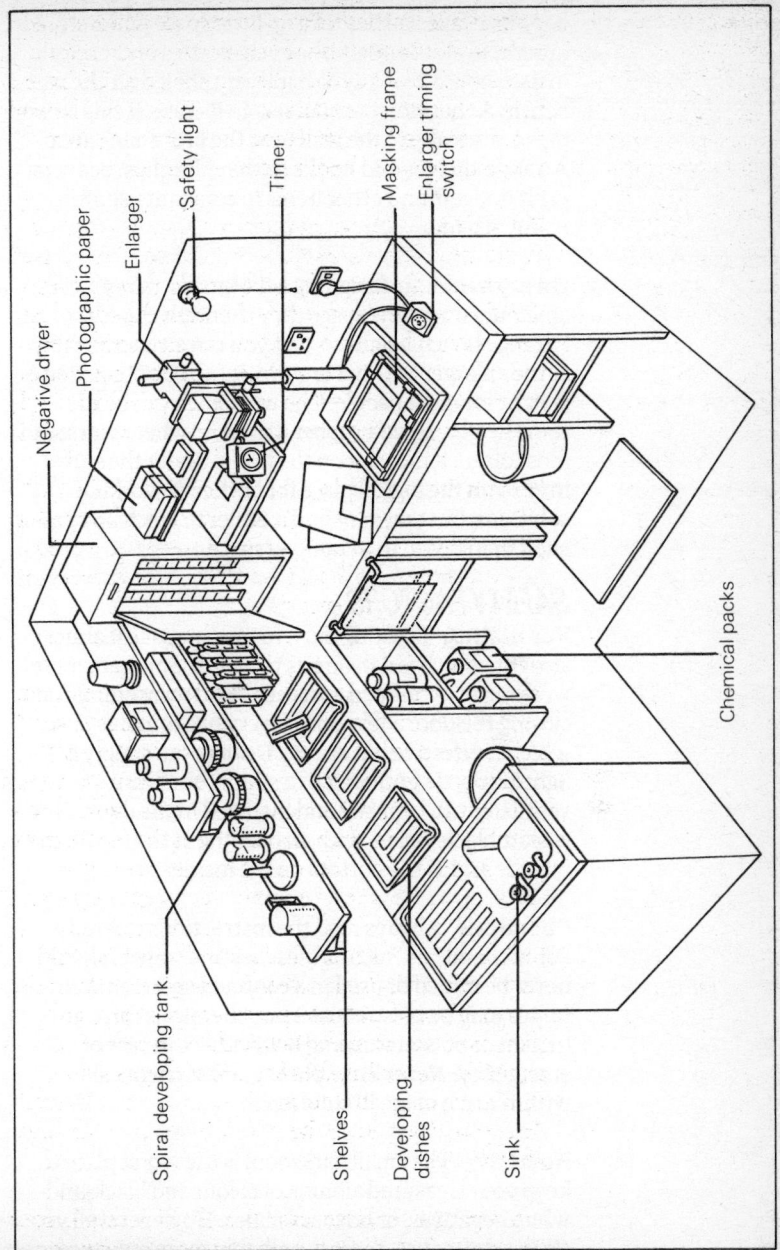

Negative dryer

Photographic paper

Enlarger

Safety light

Timer

Masking frame

Enlarger timing switch

Chemical packs

Spiral developing tank

Shelves

Developing dishes

Sink

happier usage. Dishes take up little space when stored upright in slots under the bench. Bottles of chemicals in use should be ready to hand on a shelf over the wet bench. A thermometer can rest in its case, if this is taped vertically to the wall near the processing area. Arrange shelves and hooks so that film clips, beakers, print dodgers and other items in constant use are ready to hand.

On my back! In designing a darkroom, many amateurs forget the space they themselves occupy. Arrange bench height so that you can sit comfortably at the enlarger without crouching. About 71cm (28in) is right for most people. The wet bench can be the same height. Have a rubber mat here, where you stand most often: it is easier on the heels. Under the sink may seem the logical place for bottles of working solutions, but you may find it easier to reach up to a shelf than down to a cramped space.

SAFETY FACTORS

Ventilation Blacking out a room can make it almost airtight, which is dangerous to health. Some amateurs working in a confined space make do by opening and closing the door a few times every five minutes or so, which is effective but erratic. Dealers can supply a light-trapped ventilator, or a simple boxform ventilator can be made and installed in the door. This is matt black inside, with an opening at the top on the outside and at the bottom on the inside.

Chemicals Always read the instructions carefully. Some chemicals, such as bleaches and toners, should never be mixed or used in a confined space, as their fumes may be poisonous. Some chemicals carry an irritant or poison warning, with advice in case of emergency. *Never* leave photographic chemicals within reach of small children.

Humidity The small darkroom is the worst place to keep your treasured albums of colour and black-and-white negatives, or boxes of slides. However well you clean up after use, there is probably more moisture in

the air here than elsewhere in the house, and this can lead to mould on the emulsion. Take negatives into the darkroom only for a printing session; then remove them to a dry room.

A safety routine Don't just develop prints – develop a safety routine as well. After you have taken a sheet of paper from its packet or box, close the container immediately. There is nothing more irritating to a photographer than discovering, when he or she switches on the light to examine a print, that an expensive stock of unexposed paper has been ruined. If you are exposing several sheets of paper before processing, keep them in a closed box.

A lethal mixture Water and electricity don't mix. One plug per socket should be the rule. We know of an amateur who had a two-way bayonet adaptor hanging on a nail which came out of the wall, allowing the adaptor to fall into the dish of developer he had his hands in – until just one second before the lethal flash! A properly wired darkroom is worth its weight in longevity.

BLACK-AND-WHITE FILM

Equipment For black-and-white processing of film, you need only a tank and a thermometer. Extras are a set of beakers and a film wiper. The same beakers can be used for making up chemicals for processing black and white papers. For the latter, you will need a set of three dishes to hold developer, stopbath and fixer. Opaque or coloured bottles with good stoppers are useful for storing used solutions.

Chemicals When a picture is taken, the image on the film cannot be seen until it is 'revealed' or developed. This is the job of the developer. What it does, in fact, is to blacken the tiny grains of sensitive silver in the emulsion which have been affected by the image projected on the film by the lens. When sufficient developer action has taken place, the developer is poured out of the film tank and replaced with a stopbath, an acid solution which arrests the development process. Finally, the film is immersed in a fixer, so-called because it washes away the unexposed silver grains and 'fixes' the negative image. The film is then washed and dried.

Paper The light-sensitive emulsion of black-and-white printing paper is similar to that of the film, but slower acting. It is composed mainly of light-sensitive crystals (or grains) of silver halides. When the negative image is projected by the enlarger lens on to the paper, the sensitive silver is affected. On development, those areas which received most light blacken most, those which received least light stay lightest. As the negative was a reversal of the original scene, we now have a negative of a negative, or a positive print. If the negative lacks tonal contrast, it needs a vigorous grade of paper to compensate and give a bright print, full of contrasting tones.

Conversely, if the negative has too much contrast, a less vigorous paper will reduce that contrast to normal. Thus, printing papers come in various grades of contrast, usually from 0 to 5. Grade 2 or 3 is considered 'Normal', 0 is softest and least vigorous, and 5 is hard and extremely contrasty.

Special paper is available called 'variable contrast'. By using combinations of yellow and magenta filters in the enlarger, the contrast grade of the paper can be adjusted over a wide range. See Multigrade II, p. 179.

Economy It is important to read the instructions that come with all chemicals and materials. If the solution is only partly used, and has not been in the dish too long, it can be stored in a full bottle for future use. Stopbath is often supplied with an indicator colour, which changes as the solution becomes exhausted. Fixer, especially, should never be kept beyond the throughput recommended in the instructions, or your prints may fade or discolour.

FILM PROCESSING

Loading the tank Before processing, the film has to be wound into a spiral. This device ensures that no part of the film touches any other part, and the developer, stopbath and fixer have free access to all parts. Most spirals load from the outside towards the centre, though a few load from the core outwards.

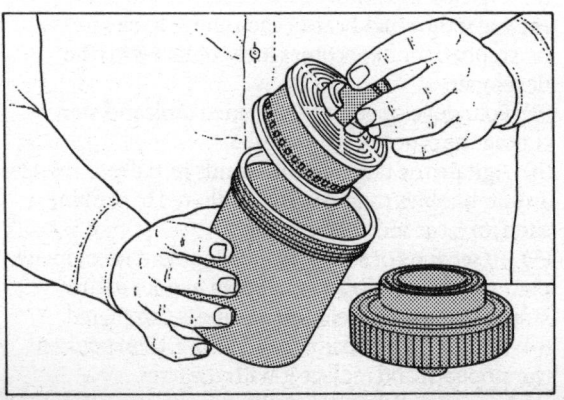

Left A roll of 35mm film, wound onto a spiral, is loaded into a developing tank with a light-tight lid.

173

(1) In the dark, the shaped leader edge of the film is cut off, and the film gently pushed into the spiral. The instructions packed with each tank show how this is done.

(2) The spiral is then placed inside the tank and the light-tight lid clipped on.

(3) The light can then be switched on and processing carried out in comfort. Loading is greatly simplified if practised first in room lighting, with a strip of waste film.

Time and temperature To ensure that the negatives will be of the right density and contrast to provide good prints, it is necessary to develop by what is known as time and temperature. Both density and contrast increase as development progresses, and the rate of increase is also affected by (a) the temperature of the developer, and (b) the amount of agitation given to the solution. The warmer the developer, the quicker it acts. Similarly, constant agitation, by inverting the tank, speeds development. Most manufacturers recommend 10 seconds initial agitation when the developer is poured in, followed by 5 seconds every minute. This is equivalent to inverting the tank and righting it once.

If the instructions recommend, say, 9 minutes development at 20°C (68°F), proceed as follows:

(1) Have developer, stopbath and fixer ready in three beakers.

(2) Check temperatures with the thermometer, rinsing it thoroughly after each check to ensure that no stopbath or fixer comes into contact with the developer.

(3) Pour developer into the loaded tank and start timing the process.

(4) Agitate the tank for 10 seconds initially to release any air bubbles that may have adhered to the film, then for 5 seconds per minute.

(5) 10 seconds or so before development is complete, pour out the developer, and begin to pour in the stopbath just as development time is completed.

(6) Agitate occasionally for 1 minute, then pour out the stopbath and replace it with the fixer.

(7) Agitate occasionally until fixation is complete; the exact time varies according to the make of fixer.

(8) Wash for 10 minutes with the open tank under running water, then hang the film to dry in a dust-free atmosphere. A pair of film-wiper tongs will remove excess moisture from the film, speed drying, and help ensure a clean film.

PRINTING AND CONTACTING

Printing from a negative Because our camera produced a negative – that is, an image of the original scene with the tones reversed – we now have to produce a reversal of the negative. That is, a print with the tones the right way round, with sky a light tone, shadows dark, and so on. A negative may be pressed into contact with a sheet of printing paper, exposed to light and developed, but the image is too small for general viewing and display. So we enlarge it.

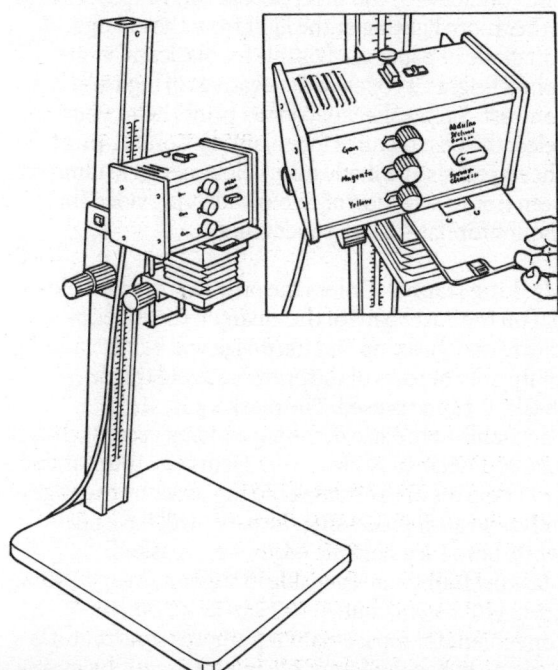

Left A modern enlarger. Both head and lens can be adjusted for height and focusing. Inset: head includes dials for cyan, magenta and yellow filters. Negative is inserted into head in a special film holder.

The modern enlarger is rather like your camera. The negative is inserted in a carrier beneath an illuminated lamp-house. The enlarger head is then raised to give the desired amount of enlargement, and the lens is focused until the image projected on the baseboard is clear and sharp.

When the negative image is viewed on the enlarger baseboard or the paper-masking frame, the desired grade of paper is selected (see Paper, page 172), and the enlarger lamp is switched off. The paper is then loaded into the masking frame, the enlarger is switched on for the required duration of exposure, and then the paper is developed.

Making contact sheets If a 36-exposure 35mm film is cut into six strips of six negatives each, the whole film can be printed on a single sheet of 20 × 25cm (8 × 10in) paper. Normally, the negatives are pressed into contact with the sheet of paper and exposed to either room lighting or the light from the enlarger. A soft grade of paper is advisable for black and white contacting, as it copes with negatives of high and low contrast. Such a sheet of contact prints helps you select the best pictures for enlarging. Contact-print sheets can also be made from colour negative films, or even from a selection of colour slides, provided that the appropriate colour paper is used.

Masking frames Unless the printing paper is held flat on the baseboard of the enlarger, the edges or centre may curve up and the image will be clear and sharp only in parts of the print. To avoid this, a masking frame is used. The masking frame is adjustable to the size of the paper being used, such as 12.5 × 17.5cm (5 × 7in), 20 × 25cm (8 × 10in), and so on. The arms of the frame hold the paper by the edges only, and after processing the paper will have neat white borders where the edges were masked. Masking frames are available in larger sizes up to 40 × 50cm (16 × 20in), but 20 × 25cm (8 × 10in) is convenient for most amateur purposes. One type has a magnetic base and movable metal corners, by means of which a borderless print can be made.

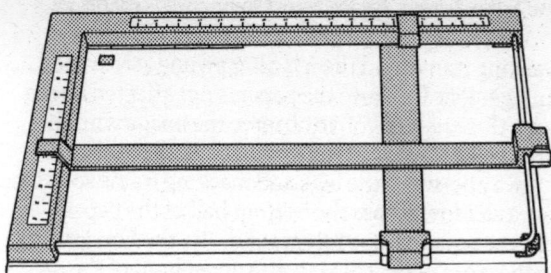

Left *Masking frame is placed on enlarger baseboard. Its movable arms can be adjusted to required size and shape of print.*

Dish development It is best to have three dishes for black and white paper development, one for developer, one for stopbath and one for fixer. Always work from left to right or from right to left. The paper is slid under the surface of the developer with one smooth motion and the dish is then gently rocked, back and forth and from side to side. The key word here is 'gently'. This ensures that the image develops evenly, without streaking. Just before the end of development the print is lifted by one corner, drained, and transferred to the stopbath for a few seconds, then lifted and drained again, and transferred to the fixer. After fixation the print is transferred to the wash water.

SPECIAL TECHNIQUES

Adding a sky Sometimes a pleasant landscape picture is spoiled by the absence of a good cloud formation or, at worst, there is a black sky. In such a case, it is possible to 'print in' the sky from another negative. Indeed, some photographers collect negatives of good sky effects just for this purpose. You start by composing the landscape picture the way you want it, using a sheet of plain writing or typing paper in the masking frame. On this you pencil the horizon line. A small strip of printing paper is then exposed and developed, to determine the correct exposure for the foreground. The negative carrier is then removed from the enlarger, and the negative replaced with one containing a suitable sky. Its image is enlarged and adjusted until it looks natural above the horizon line

177

you have drawn. Again, a test exposure is made.

A sheet of printing paper is now inserted in the masking frame, and the red filter swung across the enlarger lens (because the paper is not affected by red light, this enables you to observe the image without an exposure being made). Now hold a sheet of card midway between the lens and masking frame so as to cast a shadow across the bottom half of the paper – that is, the landscape foreground. Use the horizon line on the plain paper to locate the upper limit of the shadow. Then swing the red filter to one side and make the correct exposure for the sky, moving the card gently, just an inch either way, to prevent the formation of a hard, tell-tale edge to the landscape exposure. Now replace the sky negative with that of the landscape and, using the same technique, expose for the foreground. If the sky on the landscape is blank it will be dark on the negative, so for this part of the operation it will not be necessary to shade the sky area with the card.

High-contrast printing The appearance of a black and white print can often be vastly improved by using a high-contrast printing paper – say, grade 5. If, for example, the picture contained a great deal of foliage taken under dull lighting conditions, the many twigs and leaves would merge into a mass of similar shades of grey. By using a high-contrast printing paper, the effect of a line etching is achieved, with all the minute detail standing out in good contrast. This technique is excellent for old stonework and similar textures.

Toning It is quite easy to apply sepia toning to modern black-and-white prints. Simple kits are available from photographic dealers complete with instructions. Blue and green toners are also available.

Converging verticals When the camera is tilted upwards, the verticals of buildings tend to converge. This phenomenon is acceptable to many viewers, but is considered unpleasant or unnatural by others. Converging verticals can be corrected as follows: one side of the enlarging paper mask is tilted upwards until the verticals appear parallel again. The image is then re-focused at the centre, and the enlarging lens stopped well down so the whole image is sharp.

ECONOMY

(1) Developers keep longer in dark-glass bottles. They will, however, deteriorate if the bottles are only partly filled. To get around this problem, buy a number of bottles of different sizes, especially 500ml (1 pint) and 1000ml (2 pints) for storing part-used developers, filling each to the brim. Another way around this problem is to buy aerosols of inert gas. A squirt of this will find the air space in a part-filled bottle and prevent oxidation, so that the developer stays active for much longer.

(2) Fixers for films are usually more concentrated than those used for papers, so it is false economy to use a film-strength fixer for papers. Moreover, paper fixer is generally used in an open dish, where it can attract dust, hairs and so on. If the same solution is then used for fixing a film, these bodies may adhere to the drying emulsion, resulting in spots and hair-lines on the prints.

(3) The biggest economy tip: always read the instructions carefully. This can result in great savings on film, paper, chemicals – and aggravation!

Variable-contrast paper The advantage of this type of paper is that different grades of contrast are obtainable simply by using yellow and magenta filters, singly or in combination, on the enlarger, making it unnecessary to buy packets of paper of different grades. The only variable-contrast paper at present available in Britain is Ilford's Multigrade II, though Kodak Polycontrast is available in the United States and elsewhere. Ilford can supply a set of Multigrade II printing filters which can be used in a holder under the enlarger lens; but this is unnecessary with most modern enlargers, which incorporate a colour head with which the required yellow and magenta filtration is simply dialled in. Multigrade II paper is similar in price to conventional enlarging papers.

COLOUR TRANSPARENCIES

EQUIPMENT AND CHEMICALS

The tank Almost all tanks used by amateurs today are made of plastic and are impervious to the chemicals used in photography. The same tank will serve for both black and white and colour films, provided scrupulous cleanliness is maintained. Stainless steel tanks are also available, but these are best used for black-and-white processing, as most become badly discoloured when in contact with colour chemicals. The discoloration may contain residues that could cause unwanted colour casts in subsequent colour-films. The popular plastic tanks will also fit the auto-rotating processors (see below), which is not possible with stainless steel tanks.

Chemicals Practically all modern slide films can be processed in Kodak's E-6 chemistry. Thus, they are termed 'E-6 compatible'. Basically, the succession of chemical stages are: (1) first developer, (2) reversal bath (to change the image from negative to positive), (3) colour developer, (4) bleach-fix. Other firms produce packs of similar chemicals. Two of these, Photo Technology Chrome Six and Paterson 3E6, incorporate the reversal bath in the colour developer, reducing the process to three chemical stages.

Similarly, packs of chemicals for colour-negative films are available following the basic Kodak C-41 process, which has the following chemical stages: (1) developer, (2) bleach, (3) fixer, (4) stabilizer. Most photo shops also stock a simplified version of C-41 chemistry, in which the bleach and fixer are combined and the stabilizer eliminated, leaving (1) developer, (2) bleach-fix. With an additive, the same chemicals can be used to process printing papers compatible with the Kodak Ektaprint 2 process. Photo Technology Photocolor II includes a bottle of this

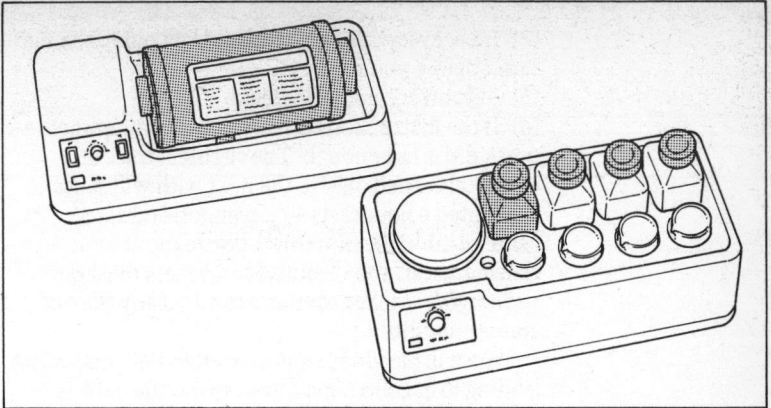

additive, while in Paterson 2NA (which means 2 bath no additive) the extra ingredient is incorporated in the two solutions.

For making prints directly from slides you can use Ilford Cibachrome paper and associated chemicals, or Kodak Ektachrome 14 paper processed in Ektaprint R14 chemical. Again most photo shops stock non-proprietary versions of these processes.

Ancillary equipment A really good thermometer will serve for both colour and black-and-white processing. Choose a thermometer specifically marked for colour. Firms such as Jobo and Paterson now supply auto-rotating processors. In these a water jacket and the various chemicals contained in bottles are maintained at a precise temperature. The tank containing the film, or a similar drum containing colour paper, is held in the processor and rotated at a precise speed in the water jacket, ensuring exact temperature control at each chemical stage.

Cleanliness As successful colour processing depends on meticulous adherence to routine coupled to scrupulous cleanliness, follow these rules:
(1) Equip yourself with a reliable time-keeper. A proper darkroom clock has a sweep second hand and is easier to read than a wristwatch. Any large clock is suitable, provided the minutes and seconds can be accurately read.

Above Auto-processors. Upper drawing: developing tank or colour paper can be loaded into this rotating, thermostatically heated water-jacket. Lower drawing: a thermostatically heated bath keeps bottled chemicals at required temperature for processing.

181

(2) Have everything to hand and laid out in the right order before you start.

(3) Rely on accuracy, not luck!

(4) If the instructions call for a one-minute wash, a quick dip is not enough. The slightest trace of chemical carried over to the next bath will cause unwanted colour casts – or even total disaster.

(5) The tank, the film spiral, bottle caps, thermometer, and chemical containers must be *thoroughly* washed after use to avoid any trace of contamination.

This will pay dividends in trouble-free processing, leading to excellent negatives, prints and slides.

DRUM PROCESSING

Drums and tanks Just as a film is loaded into a tank for processing, so a sheet of colour paper is loaded into a drum. In fact, the paper drum, which is cylindrical and made of plastic, looks just like a tank designed to hold several films. Unlike the film, however, the paper does not have to be fed into a spiral, but presses against the inner wall of the drum. Today colour paper can be processed at room temperature, whereas a few years ago a temperature as high as 38°C (100°F) was required. It is no longer necessary to have thermostatic control of solution temperatures outside and inside the drum. Instead, the drum is rolled back and forth on the bench during the successive stages: (1) water for pre-heating the drum, (2) developer, (3) stopbath, (3) bleach-fix, (4) wash.

With the drum rolled on its side, as little as 50 ml (2 fl oz) of each solution is needed for a single sheet of 20 × 25 cm (8 × 10 in) paper.

Preparation of chemicals: Until recently as many as six liquids and powders were needed to make up a set of colour-processing solutions. Nowadays the job is simpler and ready-to-dilute liquid concentrates are the order of the day. The following are the chemical stages needed for the various colour processes:

(1) Colour negative: (a) developer, (b) bleach fix.

(2) Colour print from negative: (a) developer, (b) bleach-fix.

(3) Colour-slide film: (a) first developer, (b) colour developer (containing reversal agent), (c) bleach fix.

(4) Colour print from colour slide, using Cibachome process: (a) developer, (b) bleach, (c) fixer.

(5) Colour print from colour slide, using Ektaprint R14 process: (a) first developer, (b) stopbath, (c) colour developer, (d) bleach fix, (e) stabiliser. Equivalent processes with only three chemical stages are available from independent manufacturers and are stocked by most photo shops. Always follow carefully the instructions for mixing as well as use. Instructions differ, but all emphasize the need for scrupulous cleanliness and for avoiding the slightest contamination of one solution by another.

TEMPERATURE CONTROL

Accurate temperature: This comes first in all processing, especially of colour-slide film. Here are some tips for getting and maintaining the right temperature:

(1) Ask your dealer for a colour thermometer, which is more accurate than ordinary types.

(2) Even with black-and-white film, do *not* pour warm developer into a cold tank. Warm the tank first, on the outside, by standing it in a bowl of warm water.

(3) A tank containing colour film, or a drum containing colour paper, needs to be pre-warmed. If it is not, the temperature of the solution will drop as it is poured in. To overcome this, the instructions for the process usually include a nomograph. This tells you the required temperature of the pre-heating water that should be poured in for the first minute; it varies according to the ambient temperature of the darkroom.

(4) Some colour processes are now panthermic – that is, they can be carried out at lower temperatures than formerly; in some cases little more than room temperature is required and this is easily maintained. The processing time will be longer at the lower temperature, but this allows a far greater margin for error. For instance, a timing error of half a minute represents 20 per cent of a processing time of 2½

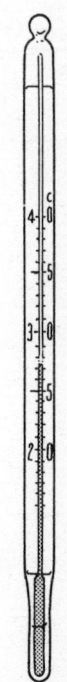

Above *A photographic thermometer calibrated for colour processing.*

183

minutes but only 5 per cent of 10 minutes. In the former case it could result in severe under- or over-development, but in the latter its effect would be insignificant.

Thermo-units Apart from the automatic print processors with thermostatic control already mentioned, there are other ways of maintaining even temperature during processing. A separate thermostat and water heater can be purchased and used in a convenient receptacle. In such a set-up it is necessary to move the water around occasionally so that temperature remains even in all parts of the vessel. Even the heater and thermostat used for fish tanks may be suitable for colour processing at lower temperatures.

Wash water With most colour processes the temperature of the water used for rinses between the chemical stages should be fairly close to that of the chemical solutions. This may entail having a large bucket of warm water standing in the sink or nearby. The temperature can be maintained with an occasional splash from the hot tap or a kettle. Special 9-litre (2 gal) buckets with extra space for mixing are available.

If you process black and white film in cold weather, lower the temperature of the final wash water two or three degrees at a time, for periods of half a minute, until tap temperature is reached. This can be done by pouring from a jug into the tank, then topping up the jug with tap water.

INSTANT SLIDES
Polaroid This has already been described in the Film chapter (see page 93). Briefly, there are three types – for ordinary colour slides, for black-and-white slides of normal tone, and for high-contrast black-and-white slides. Processing is carried out in room lighting in a small machine.

COLOUR NEGATIVES

Simple processing A black-and-white film requires only developer, stopbath and fixer. A colour negative film is just as easy to process, the three stages being developer, stopbath and bleach-fix. Bleach-fix serves a double purpose: fixing the image, and removing the unwanted dye present in the filter layers of the film. Typical chemical stages for colour films and papers are given under Preparation of chemicals, page 182.

Ancillary equipment Three things are required to ensure perfect film processing. First is a reliable thermometer. Make sure the dealer offers you one suitable for colour processing. Second, you need a pair of film-wiper tongs. This will remove all surplus water from the emulsion after processing, leaving spotless negatives. Third, choose the most dust-free room in the house for drying the film. This is usually the bathroom. If dust or hairs adhere to the emulsion while drying, these will appear as white spots or lines on the print.

FILM PROCESSING

Home or away There is no financial advantage to be gained by processing colour-negative films at home. Even without wastage, the price of an amateur chemistry kit is such that each film developed will cost almost as much, and sometimes more, than is charged by a commercial processing house. Nevertheless, by processing your film at home you get something extra – excitement, a sense of achievement, and the chance to see your negative shortly after the pictures are taken.

Step by step Having prepared the three solutions (developer, stopbath, and bleach-fix) for processing your colour-negative film, the process is as follows:

(1) Stand the film tank, with the film inside, in a dish to collect any drops that may be spilled.

(2) Check the temperature of the developer. When it is correct, pour it into the tank and start the clock. Snap on the tank-port cap and apply the initial agitation given in the instructions.

(3) As the development time draws to a close, pour out the developer. Pour in the stopbath just as the clock indicates that development is complete. Agitate occasionally for the required period, usually a minute.

(4) At the end of the period, pour out the stopbath and pour in the bleach-fix; fixation takes about six to eight minutes.

(5) When the time is up, pour out the bleach-fix, wash the film, and hang it up to dry.

Dry and file A wet film usually has an inward curl but flattens as it dries. Even when it appears fairly hot to the touch, it may still hold a slight amount of moisture and a further half hour's drying will do no harm. In a proper film dryer, a bone dry film can be obtained after only seven to ten minutes. The film should then be cut into strips and filed.

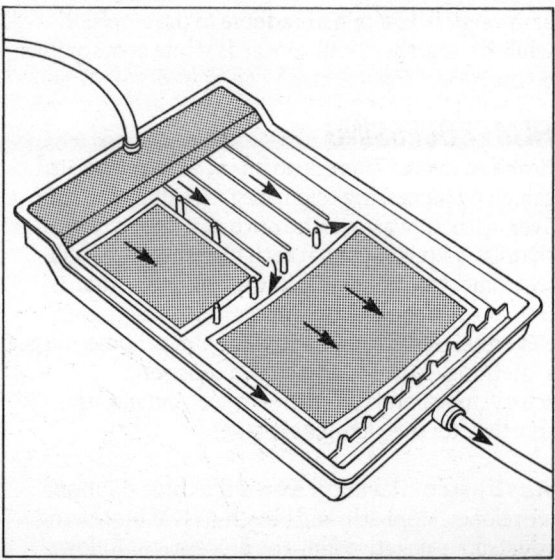

Right This high-speed print washer provides a constant flow of water through tray. Pins keep prints of different sizes in place.

PRINTING

Contact sheet This consists of six 35mm strips, each of six negatives (i.e. 36-exposures), printed together on a single sheet of 20 × 25cm (8 × 10in) paper. This can be filed alongside the negative sheet in an album, either colour contacts, or some photographers are satisfied with contacting on ordinary black and white enlarging paper. At all events, a contact sheet enables you quickly to locate and select your best pictures.

Filtration and analysers Colour negatives have an all-over orange tinge which makes it difficult to observe the colours on the film, which are the reverse of those in the original subject. (A red object, for example, is green on the negative.) The orange tinge is, in fact, a mask. Its job is to cut down on the amount of filtration necessary in the enlarger. In simple terms, the head of the colour enlarger has dials for yellow, magenta and cyan filters which can be introduced into the light path in controllable amounts. For printing from colour negatives only yellow and magenta are needed (cyan is used only when printing from slides), but the right combination must be chosen if the colours in the finished print are to look natural.

The correct balance of filters is achieved by means of an analyser, though you will find that, with experience, you can make a fairly accurate guess. To use the analyser, a diffuser is put in front of the

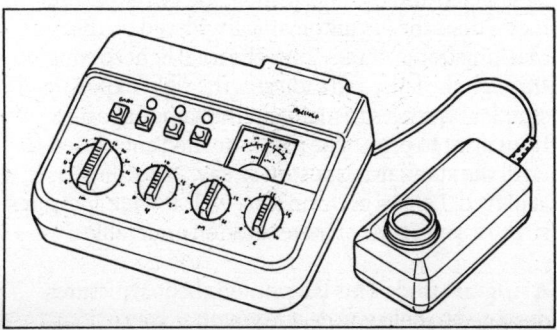

Left Colour analyser. Light-sensitive head (right) is placed on masking frame and analyses colours projected from negative in enlarger. By adjusting filter dials on panel (left), correct filtration and exposure time can be determined.

enlarger lens to 'scramble' the image. The dials of the analyser are then turned until a diode indicates that the depth (value) of each filter is right for that particular negative. A simple analyser may cost about £50; an analyser/meter, which will also indicate the correct exposure for each print, may cost at least four times as much.

Exposure and meters The correct enlarging exposure depends on four things: the sensitivity or 'speed' of the paper; the illumination in the enlarger; the lens aperture chosen (it is easier to judge other variables if the lens is always stopped down the same amount – for instance, two or three values down from maximum aperture); and the total density of the filter pack. 'Filter pack' is a term describing the combined filtration you have dialled in, such as 50Y 20M (50 yellow and 20 magenta values). The term originated in the days when it was common practice to combine small sheets of filters into a pack for insertion in a drawer in the enlarger head, between lamp and negative. Only the cheapest enlargers still work on this system.

Naturally, the denser the filter pack, the less light will reach the paper and the longer will be the exposure required. This can be determined by means of a test strip. A small sheet of paper is uncovered, in sections of an inch at a time, for about five seconds per section; in other words, each section will have been exposed for five seconds longer than the section that follows it. After development, the best exposure can be selected and the final print made. An exposure meter does the job automatically. Placed on the masking frame, it measures the total light coming through the lens, and indicates the right exposure. A simpler type tries to maintain the same exposure from print to print. The lens is opened and closed until the standard exposure of, say, 20 seconds, is achieved. Lenses perform least well at wide apertures, so the former type of meter is often preferable.

A ring-around This is a printed sheet of pictures designed to help you decide whether your colour

prints have natural colour or contain what is known as a cast. When a colour print is made, it should ideally have a pleasing similarity to the colours of the original subject. In many cases, though, there will be a cast towards yellow, magenta, cyan, red, blue or green which needs to be corrected in the next print from the same negative.

At the centre of the ring-around is a small picture of good colour. This is called neutral. There will then be series of pictures radiating from the centre, like a six-pointed star. Each 'ray' will have perhaps four pictures with a particular colour cast, progressively more pronounced the farther they are from the centre. The yellow pictures, for example, will be marked with values such as 05Y 10Y, 20Y, 40Y. Other casts will be similarly marked. When you have decided on the cast value of your print, you can read off the amount of corrective filtration required, and this is dialled in to the enlarger's filtration controls. These are continuous, usually covering about 0-130 values of yellow, magenta and cyan.

SPECIAL TECHNIQUES

Shading and burning-in Part of a print can be darkened or lightened by giving more or less exposure to a given area. For example, a sky can be darkened by giving it extra exposure while shading the foreground with a card. An area that appears too dark can be shaded during part of the exposure by means of a dodger, a small piece of card fixed to a thin wire handle.

Colour control We have already seen how a ring-around, used in conjunction with the filters in the enlarger head, helps to correct colour casts and produce a print of pleasing colour. There is, in fact, no need to aim always for a true colour rendering. If, for example, the original scene looks rather cold and sunless, extra yellow can be added. This is done by *reducing* the yellow value in the filter pack when negative materials are used, or by *adding* yellow in the case of reversal papers. Similarly, extra blue may be added to produce a moody effect.

Using effect filters on the enlarger There are now many effect-filter systems available for cameras, producing graduated colour effects, star-bursts, multiple images, and many others. Few photographers think of using the same filters on the enlarger lens, and yet this can produce highly creative, weird and sometimes humorous effects. Because of the smaller size of most enlarger lenses, some effect accessories have minimal effect, and you would need to experiment with these. With graduated and centre-spot filters, for example, the best effects will be obtained with the lens at full aperture, and this may lead to very short exposures. For the keen darkroom worker, the variety of results is well worth the effort.

Multi-mask Makers such as Paterson and Jobo provide a multi-mask which acts as a normal masking frame, giving a white 20 × 25cm (8 × 10in) border to paper, but also serving an equally important purpose. Various sections of the mask can be uncovered independently, so that four 10 × 15cm (4 × 5in) test or finished prints may be made on a single sheet of 20 × 25cm paper. This is also useful for making a series of test exposures in steps from the same image. One type has five separate 'fingers' which can be lifted one at a time to give successively increasing exposures.

PRINTS FROM SLIDES

Internegs and reversal prints There are two ways to obtain a colour print from a colour slide. The one more often used is to photograph the slide on colour negative film, and from this negative to print on colour paper in the normal way. Because such a negative represents an intermediate stage between slide and print, it is called an interneg. The second way is to put the colour slide in the enlarger and make a print directly. This calls for the use of reversal-type colour paper.

Internegs Commercial or by copier? An interneg can be made by a commercial house so cheaply that it is hardly worth the amateur's while to produce one. The enthusiast, however, will want to have a go, using his or her normal colour-negative film. The easiest method is to use a slide-copying device containing its own lens, the body of an automatic single-lens reflex camera being fitted at one end and the slide to be copied at the other. Some of these copiers, such as the Panagor and the Ohnar, have an adjustment permitting just a part of the slide to be enlarged to the full 35mm frame. With daylight-type film, the copier is simply held up to the sky, preferably when some sunshine and clouds are present, the exposure being left to the automatic metering of the camera.

Reversal papers Ektachrome paper will give a print directly from a slide, and has the advantage of not increasing the contrast of the original. In recent years Cibachrome paper has become popular, owing to its clean whites and to the fact that the colours fade far less than on most other papers. With Cibachrome, though, there is a slight tendency towards an increase in contrast, so that best results are obtained with slides of modest contrast.

Lighting and colour balance A colour film is balanced to give good results with *either* daylight *or* tungsten light, and this is marked on the carton. If daylight film is exposed in tungsten light without a compensating filter, the result will be reddish; if an artificial-light film is exposed to daylight without a compensating filter, the result will be very blue. With the recent introduction of ultra-fast films, the situation has changed slightly. Pictures taken with these fast films in mixed lighting, as in a room artificially lit but with daylight coming through a window at the side, give more pleasing results than are obtainable with slower films.

FINISHING

Drying the film The sensitive emulsion of the film is protected by a layer of super-coating, which helps prevent damage caused by accidental touching of the film, particularly in its wet stages. Even so, touching with the fingers, especially fingernails, or against the workbench, may still cause scratching unless great care is taken. The rule is to handle the film only by its edges, never gripped between the fingers. The film will also pick up hairs and dust if left to dry for too long in a damp atmosphere, or if people are constantly moving to and fro.

Drying prints Most amateurs nowadays use RC (resin-coated) papers. In these, the very thin sensitive sheet is protected on both sides by a thin plastic coating. This allows quicker access by the chemicals and much faster washing times than when fibre-based papers are used. Washing time may be only 4 minutes for RC papers but 30 minutes for fibre-based ones, in running water. If wiped free from surface moisture and stood in a record rack, RC prints will dry flat. Double-weight fibre-based papers may be wiped and laid face-up on absorbent paper or other material, but single-weight glossy fibre-based papers are glazed in contact with a chromium sheet in a drying press.

A TRIMMER IMAGE
Borders and blades Most paper masks used to hold the printing paper while enlarging cover the edges of the paper, leaving a white border. Such borders are acceptable if the print is to be hand-held and unmounted, but need to be trimmed away if the print is to be mounted. The cleanest way to do this without special equipment is to put the print face-up on a piece of stout cardboard, such as artboard, and trim the edges off using a steel ruler and a craft knife. Chemists

as well as hobby shops sell scalpels with detachable blades in packets of six. Buy the blades with a long point, as these can also be used for gently scratching away any black spots on prints.

Trimmers Quicker than a ruler and scalpel is a trimmer specially made for the job. These come in two types. In the desk type, the edge of the print is pushed under a clear acetate guard and the sloping top board is gently pressed down against a spring to lower the blade. More popular are wheel trimmers. In these the print is held square to the trimming edge, a circular steel blade attached to a hand grip. This is simply slid along to trim off the white border.

MOUNTS AND MOUNTING

The modern mount The very ornate mounts of yester-year are still made, but are seldom purchased these days. Print presentation in most camera clubs and exhibitions is now almost entirely limited to plain white or cream mounts. The print itself is mounted flush with the edge of the mount, or with several inches of mount forming a border, wider at the bottom than at the sides and top. If the edges of the print happen to be rather light, it is common practice to 'separate' the print from the mount by drawing a black line round it with a felt-tip pen.

Stick it flat! Most pastes and mountants used in offices are water-based and, if applied to the back of a photographic print, tend to make it swell so that it will not lie quite flat on the mount. Special photographic mountants are available, including one which is simply sprayed on to the back of the print and the mount. Properly applied, with the print then rolled down on to the mount with the aid of a ruler, these work very well. Even better, but more expensive, is a dry-mounting press. A sheet of dry-mounting tissue is tacked with a small iron to the back of the print, which is then positioned on the mount and placed in the press for a few seconds. Secondhand presses, quite adequate for amateur use, are sometimes advertised by professional dealers.

Storage
& Display

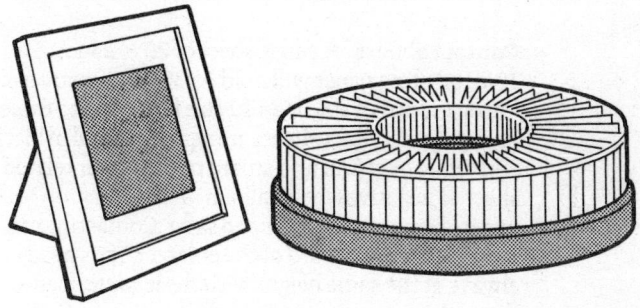

STORING YOUR PICTURES

NEGATIVES

Albums with sleeves If you send your films away for processing, they will come back in some kind of envelope or sleeve; provided you mark these and file them consecutively in a drawer, it will never take very long to find the ones you want. There is no doubt, though, that the filing albums you can buy in photo shops afford better protection and give readier access to the negatives you want. The negatives are held in strips in transparent sheets. If each of these has its own sheet of contact prints, choosing negatives and marking off the areas to be printed is easily carried out without handling the negatives themselves.

Contact sheets A single sheet of 20 × 25cm (8 × 10in) printing paper will hold 36 35mm negatives, cut into six strips of six, or a 120-size film cut into three or four strips. Contact sheets are equally useful in black and white or colour and stored next to their related sheet of negatives in the album, make selection of a particular negative easier and safer. Contacting can be done on the baseboard of the enlarger. If its head is always at the same height with the lens stopped down the same amount every time, the required exposure will seldom vary.

SLIDES

Magazine storage As most amateur slides end up in magazines ready for projection, it seems logical to store them the same way. This is certainly the case if you are in the habit of going through your slides carefully and presenting them, perhaps 36 or 50 at a time, as part of a properly programmed show. Apart from those selected for regular viewing there will always be a greater number of 'overs' which need to be stored for later selection. See next section.

Slide boxes Every dealer who sells slide projectors also sells special boxes in which 100, 200 or more slides can be filed close together in numbered slots. These are not only economical of space, but are probably the best way of storing slides which are not wanted for immediate projection. These boxes become a self-contained filing system if used in relation to a card file, in which different subject headings are used, such as landscapes, cloudscapes, children at play, and so on. Reference can then be given to the box and slot number of relevant slides.

Albums Twenty transparencies in thin card or plastic mounts are not very heavy, and can be easily filed in albums consisting of special leaves in heavy-quality clear acetate with twenty pockets, one for each mounted slide. Ring-binding at the side is adequate for this type of slide, but if the more sophisticated type of glazed mount is used, it is best to choose a special colour album in which the ring fitting is at the top. Because the leaves are clear, the complete sheet can be taken from the album and laid on a viewing box or held to the light.

Hanging files If you intend to amass a great many slides, it is worth thinking about a proper filing cabinet as used in most offices. Specialist firms, recommended by your photographic dealer, can provide tough but transparent filing sheets which are suspended from the usual type of metal bar. A single drawer in a filing cabinet will hold as many as 150 of these suspended files, equivalent to far more than 150 films, taking into account a certain amount of wastage on each film. And here is an extra tip: government surplus filing cabinets can still be bought at very low cost from dealers in secondhand office equipment.

PRINTS

Your enprints Replacing the old family albums in which prints are laboriously stuck with photo-corners, are new albums with self-stick pages. These are now offered for sale in High Street stores. Each album page is faced with a dry stick-down sheet. This is simply peeled back, the enprints arranged on the page, and the cover sheet pressed down over them. It is quick and easy, and if you don't like the arrangement, or want to change it at a later date, all you have to do is peel back the sheet, change the page layout, and press down the sheet again.

Filing and finding If you are going to be a really productive photographer, it will be best to start a filing system at the beginning of your career rather than a year or two later, when the task can be quite daunting. A simple but very highly effective system is to keep a job book in which each film is entered under brief descriptive headings with a consecutive number and in chronological order. This is used in association with an index file.

Writing on prints Any type of ink or pencil can be used on fibre-based black-and-white papers, but RC (resin-coated) prints will neither absorb free-flowing or ball-point inks, nor accept pencil. If a ballpoint pen is used, the ink will smudge, even days later. Fine-writing, fibre-tipped pens are available, containing a spirit ink which will adhere and dry almost instantly on RC surfaces, as well as glass and most plastics. These look like ordinary small ballpoints, so do not confuse them with the broader felt-tipped pens used for parcel writing. If there is a print of which you are particularly proud, leave a wide white border at the bottom where you can put your signature with one of these pens.

Keep them dry If negatives are properly fixed and washed, and filed in a dry atmosphere, they should last a lifetime. The dyes used in colour slide films are less stable. Professionals who project their slides regularly to audiences through powerful projectors, claim that the colours lose their brilliance after a couple of years or even less, and tests would seem to verify this. Sunlight is the worst offender, but this will have no effect on your slides unless you are living in a sunny climate and showing your slides to people two or three times a week.

DISPLAY

Framing it Taking good pictures is one thing, presenting them is another, and pride of place these days is split between the album and the conventional frame. Frames are available in great variety in most chain stores; the prices vary enormously, so shop around. If you wish to frame a favourite print, take it with you while shopping for a frame to ensure that the sizes match and the frame colour is suitable.

The corkboard A must these days in every teenage bedroom is a gadget every adult photographer can learn from! This is a cork or felt board on which your pictures can be pinned on a temporary or permanent basis. Small and large prints can be pinned up singly or overlapping as montages, and there is added interest in being able to see the cream of your output of the last few months all together at one time.

From key-rings to murals In all hobby magazines you will see advertisements for the incorporation of your own photographs in items ranging from key-rings to giant murals. A well-defined subject, such as a pet or a car, will look fine on a key-ring and could make a useful present, but beware of those murals. Some of them have an attractively bargain price, but are printed on cheap-looking paper.

Making a collage To make a montage you cut out prints, overlap them, putting them together in an interesting design. You do the same with a collage, except that you can introduce other materials as well as three-dimensional objects. You could, for instance, stick a child's toy trumpet over the mouth of a friend.

Laminates and canvas bonding The British firm Ademco has recently introduced a series of laminate tissues. When one of these is pressed down on to a photograph with a smooth surface, it is given an textured surface. Initially supplied for professional use, packs of these Ademco laminates should soon be available through amateur photographic shops, or to special order.

VIEWING YOUR SLIDES

Table viewers Having produced a set of 24 or 36 exciting slides, you will want to view them without delay, and it is not always convenient to set up a slide projector on its stand and black out a room. Even for the keen-eyed, a 35mm slide is too small for direct viewing and a table viewer is the handiest and best means of examining the slides or showing them to friends. The very simplest type of viewer depends on daylight or room lighting, which is often adequate but on occasions can be irritatingly dim. For a few pounds more you can obtain one of the battery or battery-and-mains operated viewers, which have a magnifying lens at the front, something like a mini TV set.

Projectors According to cost, a modern slide projector for amateur use will have some or all of the following facilities. A remote control handset by means of which slides can be changed forward and backwards, plus remote focusing. Re-focusing is necessary with unglazed mounts, as the film buckles out of the plane of focus as it warms up. More sophisticated units have an autofocus mechanism which, by means of a servomotor, re-focuses each time a slide pops out of register. The projector will take either straight magazines holding 36 to 50 slides each, or rotary magazines which hold about 80 slides. Among makers of amateur equipment, straight magazine types seem to be preferred. An 85mm lens is considered standard for home projection as it will, for example, give a screen image 1.8m (6ft) wide at a convenient room distance of 2.5m (8½ft).

Daylight-viewing attachment This is a device used in conjunction with a slide projector, but not requiring the room to be darkened. Its big advantage is that the

image, usually about 20-25cm (8 × 10in), is easier to view by the whole family at one time. There are two types. One is a bookform stand which incorporates a mirror held at 45° to the projector lens, and a ground-glass back-projection screen; it is set up at right-angles to the projector lens and about 30cm (1ft) away from it. The other device attaches to the front of the projector but requires the standard lens to be exchanged for one of shorter focal length.

Light box and sorting desk This is a useful device, and some would insist that it is indispensable, especially to the photographer who takes his slide projection seriously. Basically it is an opal translucent surface lit from behind, on which a number of slides can be examined and sorted, ready for correct placing in a magazine. Warning: there is one cheap type whose small tungsten lamps inside create a great deal of heat, which will buckle slides if they remain in position for more than a few minutes. The best kinds have fluorescent tubes which remain cool.

SLIDE SHOWS
A word for beginners A good slide show is characterized by three things. First, it holds the audience's interest right to the end. Second, it entertains or informs the audience. Third, it should be seen under comfortable conditions.

One projector Because of the vast amount of audio-visual equipment on the market, many novices are led to believe that a good slide show can only be presented with a thousand pounds' worth of equipment. This is not the case. With careful selection and preparation, a brilliant slide show can be given with just one projector. The modern projector blacks out momentarily between slides and continuity is maintained with a careful combination of spoken commentary and music. The following sections will explain how success is easily achieved.

Commentary Keep a brief note on your travels of names and places, as well as interesting information about the subjects you take. Later, when arranging your slides for a programme, rehearse what you are going to say with your notes, so that on the night you will be word perfect.

Music by hand The addition of suitable music will greatly enhance your slide programme, but does not call for expensive equipment. You can have a tape recorder with a suitable piece of music of the right length standing beside the projector position. You can 'play in' with the music, then turn down the volume when you start to speak. If there is a short sequence of particularly beautiful slides which call for no spoken commentary, you can turn up the volume as you stop speaking, and turn it down again when the commentary begins again.

Silence is golden Even a trained voice of flawless accent will become boring if it continues too long. It is an old saying among experienced projectionists, that the best parts of the commentary are the pauses between speech. Not only do the ears of the audience get a rest, but the eyes are able to take in a particularly lovely sequence without audible distraction.

Using two projectors This is the simplest form of audio-visual, or A/v as it is known. By means of a dissolve mechanism the picture from one projector fades down on the screen while the image from the other projector is fading up to full power. Audio-visual is not merely a pleasant means of changing slides without a blackout between images, but it can be an exciting and creative medium. The projectors have to be placed side by side or one above the other so that the two lenses are close. This facilitates accurate matching of the margins of the two images on the screen. This is known as obtaining register.

A manual-dissolve unit In its simplest form a dissolve unit consists of two shutters, one being placed in front of each of the two projector lenses. By moving a control lever, the projectionist can close one shutter while the other is opening, and vice versa. In

this way one image fades down while the other fades up. At the end of each lever movement a button works the slide-change mechanism of one projector. Other dissolve units work on a rheostat principle, dimming one projector bulb while bringing the other to full power.

A programmer A programmer is connected to both projectors and to a tape or cassette recorder; there are several models by major equipment companies. The programmer receives inaudible signals from the tape as it is running and transmits these alternately to each projector. Each lamp is dimmed and brightened at a variable rate determined by the projectionist, and slide changing is automatic. Most dissolve units have a handset with which the programme is laid down on the tape and the same programmer can be used to dissolve manually.

Pulsing a tape Although there are variations, it is common for programming to be done on a 4-track tape. The first and second tracks are used for left and right stereo sound, voice and music, the fourth track receives the pulses which are the signals conveyed to the two projectors by the programmer, while the third track separates the stereo tracks from the signal track and prevents feedback, or sound interference.

Projection accessories Don't buy a good projector and use the dining room table as a stand. It will be too low, making it necessary to point the projector upwards, which gives an elongated 'keystoning' effect on the screen. Do the job properly. As a once-and-for-all outlay, buy a good quality pack-away projection stand, which will also hold the magazines of slides to be projected. A pressurized air bottle can be used to 'sweep' the slides in the magazine just before projection, ensuring a clean presentation. If you are going into full audio-visual, you will also need a programmer, cassette recorder, pre-amplifier and speakers with extension leads. Have as many electronic items as possible from the same maker, thus ensuring compatibility.

Harmony Except when your programme includes an intentionally startling sequence, the combination of slides and music and the way slides dissolve into each other on the screen should follow a few rules of harmony. Greens dissolve beautifully into other quiet colours, such as greens, blues and greys; reds dissolve nicely into pinks, oranges and browns. Dissolve slowly from one calm, pastoral scene to another, but where traffic and busy movement is involved, a faster slide-change and dissolve time are suitable.

How many slides? Just because every slide taken on a trip is correctly exposed doesn't mean that it should find a place in your slide show. Be quite ruthless in your editing. Assuming an average screen time per slide of 6 seconds, which is quite a long time on the screen, plus an average of 3 seconds dissolve time, you have a showing time of 7½ minutes per 50-slot magazine. Two or three magazines, together with short breaks, are adequate for a half-hour show, which is quite long enough for most audiences.

How many minutes? When arranging your slides and deciding on commentary and music, there is no need to start with an estimated programme length to which you must adhere at all costs. Start the work visually, sorting the slides into a harmonious arrangement. This is best done on a light box or by clipping series of 20 slides in transparent filing sheets against a window. While doing this, your mind should be busy with suitable commentary and music which will fit well at different parts of the programme. The harmony of the finished programme, after cutting and rearranging, will decide the number of minutes the programme should run.

Audience comfort According to the room size available, an audience for a slide show should never exceed the number that can be seated comfortably at a good viewing angle, and distance, from the screen. White and pearl screens give the brightest image from the front, but beaded screens give a brighter image when a section of the audience is forced to sit at an acute angle to the screen. More than ten or so people tend to create a sense of claustrophobia in a smallish living room, especially if some of them are smokers. Tip: keep the smokers well to the side, otherwise their fumes in front of the lens will show on the screen. Put the lights out, together with a little 'playing-in' music, fifteen seconds before the first slide is shown, which allows the eyes to become accustomed to the darkness, and ensures that the screen images will be seen to best effect.

Screen types and viewing angles What size screen should you buy? Here is a table that will help you decide, depending on the size of the room you have available.

Lens focal length	Screen distance	Screen image
85mm	2.59m (8½ft)	1.02m (40in)
85mm	3.10m (10½ft)	1.27m (50in)
85mm	3.96m (13ft)	1.52m (60in)
85mm	4.57m (15ft)	1.83m (72in)

A lens of 150mm will give the same size screen images at 4.6m (15ft), 5.8m (19ft), 6.7m (22½ft) and 8.2m (27ft) respectively. If your room is sufficiently long to sit everyone fairly well to the front, you could choose any type of screen surface. However, in a short room, where it is necessary for some people to sit well to the side, remember that glassbeaded screens give relatively better illumination at acute angles.

The projectionist Putting over a well-prepared slide show and knowing that the audience enjoyed it can be a very satisfying experience. The same applies to a well-prepared slide lecture, basically for information rather than entertainment, but even here an appropriate touch of humour can maintain audience interest at a good level. It has often been said that the good projectionist is the one who has done his homework so that the audience are treated to the results of his labours, rather than the labours themselves.

Special Skills

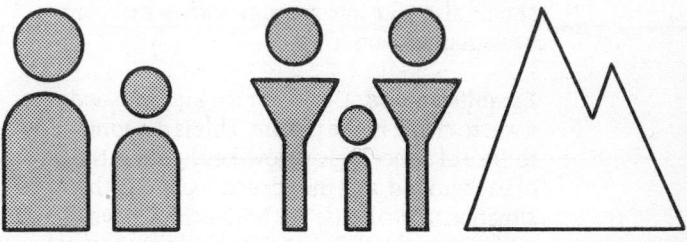

PHOTOGRAPHING PEOPLE

SUPER TIPS BY LICHFIELD

Use your imagination Before photographing someone, determine how you want the picture to look. I would try to see the whole thing as a finished shot in my mind – you can even do a rough sketch of what the shot should look like. Decide if the picture is for an album, or a photo frame, and whether it will be portrait-shaped or horizontal. Your initial concept should also take into account clothes, make-up, backgrounds, and so on.

Establish mood Decide on the kind of mood you want to create in the picture. This is determined by the use of either high- or low-key lighting, the choice of background, and the general 'feeling' of the situation. Also decide on the direction in which you are going to shoot. Try to go to the location first to have a look round if you are unsure about any aspect of it.

Making the formal informal You can reduce the formality in a portrait by carefully avoiding staid poses and expressions. When you have put someone into a pose, 'rough up' their clothing or hair a bit – they won't look quite so staged. The real secret is to get people to *react* to you. That doesn't mean make them scream with laughter – it's hard to live with a photograph of someone absolutely beaming, but a half-smile will do. You must make them feel they are not just an object you're going to click at. After all, they are the *raison d'être* of the photograph.

Overcoming shyness Choose the time of day when the subject might be most relaxed, with not too many distractions. Don't photograph girls before 11am as their faces take longer to 'wake-up'. Establish a confident rapport – a good chat between the two of you may help. Ask how the person would like to be photographed and perhaps look through a few pictures first. Try to be relaxed yourself. If the photographer is preoccupied with his or her own nerves, there will be little chance of noticing that the person being photographed is probably more nervous.

Where to shoot If you have to decide between shooting someone in the front room or the nearby park, I'm all for going to the park. People react better in a 'natural' situation than in a studio set-up, providing there is some privacy. The front room might be crowded and may have walls which will affect the result if you are using colour. Outdoors, try to use backlighting: never shoot with the sun behind you, otherwise you get screwed up eyes and shadows on the face.

Timing When shooting anything scenic, always get ready before dawn. With colour film, the low sun will make everything very 'warm', shadows will be blue, and it is generally a good time to shoot. For people who don't want to get up that early, the twilight time in the evening is excellent, too.

At weddings (1) For church weddings get everyone outside in a group, preferably somewhere where there are few onlookers. (2) When the bride and groom come out of the church, be ready to photograph there and then. Be careful not to have people in the background when photographing the couple coming out of the church. (3) Talk to the couple beforehand to find out who they want in the groups.

Catch their attention It is important to get everyone looking at the camera at the same time. You can use a whistle for this. One golden rule is to position everyone so they can see the camera – which means the camera can see them. Make some alarming noise to get them all to look at you – the first shot will be one of 'shock-horror', but the second one can record their amusement at their reaction, so be ready for that. If possible, stand on a wall or pair of step ladders and a plank to give you a better vantage point, and also to get their attention.

Look for candids Keep a second camera, loaded with fast film, for taking candid shots at the church or reception. Often the best pictures are those that are unrehearsed and unplanned. Compact cameras with autofocus and flash are a good choice for this. Try to photograph everyone you can, but be as unobtrusive as possible. Use flash only as a last resort.

People in b & w Many photographers believe that black-and-white is the better medium for portraits. B & w requires a slightly different approach to colour. In particular, the infinite variations of tone that make up a portrait in black and white depend greatly for

Right *Lichfield's wedding picture of Lady Sarah Aspinall, focused on the bridal veil rather than on the face behind it, has achieved an effect similar to that of a soft-focus filter.*

their effect on how the subject is lit. You can create subtle or harsh b & w portraits, depending on your lighting (and printing) techniques.

THE RIGHT APPROACH

Setting up a portrait Try to establish a rapport with your sitter and keep chatting during the session. If your subject appears nervous take a few pictures with out any film in the camera – then load up and start shooting when he or she is relaxed.

Expression Try for a range of different expressions – laughing, smiling, frowning, and so on. If the sitter cannot naturally produce a range of expressions, you may have to do some cajoling.

Poses How you pose your subject can be crucial to the success of a portrait. The person may be more relaxed when sitting directly in front of the camera. Ask if he or she has a 'better' side; and photograph this first to give the person confidence. Try varying the pose so that the subject is looking at the camera from different directions.

Character Some people's faces are full of natural character and can be easy to photograph. Character can be captured in facial expression, movement, and so on. It is often easier to capture someone's character by shooting informally, possibly from a discreet distance using a telephoto or zoom lens.

Surroundings You can express a great deal about a person by including their immediate surroundings in the picture. Try this if the subject has a particularly interesting occupation or interest – an artist surrounded by paints and easels, for example. Take the opportunity of involving the sitter in his work or hobby, using the surroundings as a backdrop.

Variety Advanced planning of a portrait session is useful, but don't go in with too many fixed ideas. Allow for some flexibility in your approach to lighting, camera angles, and how you want the subject to look. Vary the backgrounds if possible, and ask the subject to try different clothes, or try changing props.

WORKING WITH PEOPLE

Individual portrait One-to-one portraiture, with photographer and subject facing each other, is the most challenging – and sometimes the most difficult – to tackle. If time isn't a problem take the session at a moderate pace and allow time for yourself and the person being photographed to 'break in'. Good communication will help the results, especially when you want to vary location, lighting or other factors. Take a break if your subject becomes tired or bored – if you need more pictures, start again later.

Couples Two people photographed together can be easier than portraying them individually. Allow the couple to chat between and even during shots to establish a relaxed atmosphere. As well as looking at the camera, they can look at each other for variety. Watch for differences in height, particularly in close-ups; the smaller person can always stand on a box for extra height to 'level out' the portrait – unless, of course, the height difference is part and parcel of the 'flavour' of the portrait.

Small groups Photographing a small group requires some 'people management' on the photographer's part – and a bit of space. Avoid a 'firing line' approach with everyone facing the camera – a slightly side-on profile, with the people less close together, looks more relaxed and maximises space. For unusual shots place individuals in different parts of the picture, and possibly at varying distances from the camera.

Larger groups Don't line up a large group in a straight line – you will either not get them all in or, if you do, their faces will be too small to recognise in the picture. Form them in a semi-circle in front of the camera, in rows if necessary. For formal occasions, like weddings, important people should be at the front, not stuck behind others. Use chairs or raised platforms if needed so that all can be seen.

People in action If you photograph someone engaged in a particular activity you should still concentrate on facial expression – you are aiming for a portrait, not merely an action shot.

People at work When you photograph someone at work, follow the person through a range of activity.

Below *The most natural and often the best shots of children can be taken when they are at play and unaware of the camera.*

213

This might involve a sequence depicting something being made. Lighting in offices, factories and shops can, however, be quite harsh. If there is a lot of fluorescent lighting, you may need to use a colour correction filter (FL-D) for daylight film, or use flash.

Babies Most babies are easy to photograph because they are blissfully unaware of the camera. Try to use daylight for indoor shots because flash is likely to frighten a baby. Give your subject a toy to play with: young babies have far livelier facial expressions when their attention is concentrated on something.

Children Some children are 'naturals' in front of the camera; others are painfully shy. To avoid curious fingers covering your camera, shoot from a discreet distance – a telephoto or zoom lens can be useful for this. Children can produce a wonderful range of expressions, so always be ready to fire quickly. Shy subjects are best photographed at play. The more shy they are, the longer you should allow them to become absorbed by their activity before you start shooting. Again, shoot from a distance with telephoto.

ADDED INGREDIENTS

Sequences Make the most of a portrait session by shooting a sequence of pictures. This sequence can take a particular direction, depending on your requirements. For instance, you can follow a sequence of activity, or ask the subject to try a range of different expressions (happy to sad), or you can simply change the surroundings for each picture. Not all the pictures may work but, with a good choice, you can select the best from the sequence.

Humour Always be on the lookout for naturally funny situations. It helps if you always carry your camera, so that you can snap amusing situations as they happen. You can find humour at organised events, on the street, or even around the home. Many pictures are funny because they juxtapose two separate elements, not amusing in themselves, in a humorous way.

PHOTOGRAPHING BEAUTY

Taking a beauty shot The first essential ingredient for a successful beauty shot is the right model. An experienced model will be familiar with expressions and poses and may well be able to provide her own make-up and clothes, as well as props such as jewellery. With an inexperienced model you may need to spend some time beforehand to plan the shot. Try and use diffused or bounced lighting (daylight or flash) and enhance the effect with a soft-focus filter.

Nude photography It helps if you have worked with a model clothed before asking that person to pose nude. Decide on your approach beforehand and discuss your ideas with the model before you start. Try lighting from different angles to emphasise shape and skin texture. When working in a studio keep it warm for the model's comfort.

Model release You can acquire full legal rights to the use of your photographs (in publication, for example) by asking your sitter to sign a model release form before you take the pictures.

PORTRAIT PRESENTATION

Choosing the best shot After processing, look carefully through all your pictures and decide on the best ones from the session. With b & w, for which you do your own processing, contact all the strips of film onto a single sheet of photographic paper and select the best for enlargement later. Colour enprints can be examined and the best selected for reprinting at a required size. Examine slides closely, using a magnifying glass or by projecting them.

Adding effects Make your pictures more interesting by adding effects at the darkroom stage. When making a print you can use techniques to alter the impact of the shot (see pages 177-9).

Keeping an album Store pictures of family and friends in an album. Don't crowd the pages with too many pictures, and vary the sizes of prints.

HOLIDAYS & TRAVEL

SUPER TIPS BY GEORGE WRIGHT

Preparation Make sure that all your equipment is fully serviceable and comprehensively insured. Too obvious to state perhaps, but mishaps have an uncanny habit of catching all photographers unawares from time to time. A service for well-used camera bodies, a critical eye over scratched filters, sufficient spare batteries for those parts that always run out at the most inconvenient moments, and – if you can afford it – a few more rolls of film than you reckon on shooting: all these are wise precautions.

Research Find out as much as you can about where you are going *before* you get there. Check with travel agents and tourist boards for the times and dates of any special events. Plan a photographic itinerary of possibilities. Read about and look at pictures of the place, and, most importantly, buy maps and study them. If it is going to be hot, remember that you are going to have to keep your film cool at all times (never leave it in the boot of a car left in the sun). Sand in the form of desert or beach requires extra thought in the camera-cleaning department.

Travelling However you are travelling, give extra thought to how you pack your camera bag. Know where each item is and always keep a loaded camera ready for recording your journey. If you are going abroad ensure that you know the requirements for customs clearance. Carry a typed list, in duplicate (leave one copy at home), of your numbered equipment. Customs are not usually a problem for most people on holiday, but restrictions vary from country to country and it is always best to check them out first. If you are flying, carry your gear in a case or bag that conforms with hand-luggage requirements.

Arriving Resist the temptation to rush out on the first day and shoot too much film. Always carry your camera, but try and decide what it is about the place that draws you while being ready to get the picture that you never saw again the whole time you were there. It is always worth looking at local postcards; they can be extremely informative, if only in showing you what to avoid. Keep a notebook so that you can caption your pictures with the relevant details.

People They make the place what it is, and you are probably going to want to photograph them. Observe local customs (in some parts of the world being photographed is considered a grave infringement on personal privacy) and, when appropriate, ask permission. This may well get you invited into a part of life that most tourists miss. A Polaroid camera for giveaway pictures is often a rewarding thing to carry, as the unwilling can often be softened with the promise of an instant print.

Shops and markets These are good places to photograph everyday local life. Spend some time looking around a market and you will come up with

Below The humour of George Wright's Calais pavement scene derives from the way the symmetry of the composition is opposed by the strongly contrasting figures on the bench.

that universal image of commerce with its own particular local flavour. An overcast day is usually an advantage, as harsh sunlight and hard shadows will cause problems of excessive contrast. Look for details, signs and shop fronts as well as the general activity. Piles of produce make good still life subjects, but always ask permission to photograph inside a shop. And always be ready to shoot inside the bar!

In the city A map of the city centre and a good pair of shoes are indispensable. It may be worthwhile to go on a sightseeing bus tour; at least it will give you a convenient if predictable view of the obvious sights. Take your family or friends on the conducted tour so that you can feel justified in returning at a later date on your own. Find a tall building with public access to photograph the city from a high viewpoint: the tourist-information office will usually be able to help you here. Night shots – especially after rain, when the pavements reflect the neon lights – are worth considering, so you will need to carry a tripod for long exposures. Some museums allow visitors to take photographs as long as no flash or tripods are used, so you may want to carry some fast film for such occasions; but never take pictures in such places without prior permission.

Tourist sites Do not discount the obvious: it does not matter how many times a famous place has been photographed, there is always a different way of looking at it. After all, it would be a singular photographer who visited Agra and declined to take pictures of the Taj Mahal simply because it is the most photographed object in Asia. Go there at less-popular times of day; at dawn for instance, when the other tourists are still in bed. Look for new angles, odd juxtapositions or reflections. With imagination, a national monument that has become a holiday-snap cliché may well be seen in an original way.

Events and carnivals These always provide strong, colourful pictures. The participants in a carnival will not object to being photographed; they expect it and invariably play up to the camera. The problems encountered when photographing such events will more likely be to do with finding the best place in the crowd, so arrive before the action starts. This will give you the chance to select the best viewpoints before everyone else gets there, and also provide the opportunity to record the preparations and behind-the-scenes activity.

PREPARATION

Where to go Choose somewhere that will inspire you to take good photographs. Countries with interesting scenery, architecture and local costumes offer great scope for photography. The mountains and lakes of Scotland or the Alps may appeal, or the ornate buildings of Amsterdam, or the bridges of Venice. Also consider the likely seasonal weather.

What to take Take only what you plan to use. A simple automatic compact camera is sufficient for holiday snaps, but for greater flexibility take a 25mm SLR camera with three lenses – a 28mm wide-angle, 50mm standard and 100mm or 135mm telephoto. A ×2 teleconverter will extend your lens range still further. Protect your lenses with skylight filter. Two camera bodies enable you to take black-and-white and colour at the same time. Take more film than you think you will need – it may be difficult to obtain, or more expensive abroad. Include a flashgun with spare batteries. Use a lens hood to reduce flare and to protect your lenses and filters.

Instant pictures Producing a picture 'On the spot' can be a great advantage. You can give an instant snapshot of a subject to someone who has helped you to set up the picture, while you can take other shots with your SLR camera. An instant camera can also be used when quality is not a top priority. With this type of camera you are more likely to take pictures on occasions when you might not have bothered with your SLR.

Underwater cameras Most cameras dislike water. Water damages camera electrics and salt corrodes the metal body. With an underwater camera you can take pictures without damage. Small 110 underwater cameras have built in flash, and some have automatic wind-on. The 35mm Nikonos IV has interchangeable lenses and a built-in light meter, but it requires a separate underwater flash. It can be used to a depth of 50 metres (165ft). You can get an underwater housing for your conventional camera; or you can use a plastic inflatable bag with a clear 'porthole' in shallow water.

Carrying your gear Take a soft camera bag as hand luggage on a plane and stow it under the seat. Most bags have padded partitions to separate lenses and cameras. A robust aluminium case with foam padding inside offers greater protection. The case can also be used as a seat or to stand on in order to see over a crowd of people. Aluminium reflects the sun and keeps film and cameras cooler. But a hard case is not as easy as a soft shoulder bag to dip into when you want to change film or lenses. It is also a more conspicuous target for thieves.

Additional pouches Put each lens into an individual pouch in the camera bag to give it more protection. If you are planning to be very active, do away with a large camera bag and use a purpose-made bag or pouch which threads onto a belt, harness, or straps; some of these pouches are waterproof. This will leave your hands free.

DEPARTURE

Insurance Consider insuring all of your photographic equipment. Don't assume that it is included in a policy which covers personal effects: read the small print, and note the exclusions. Some policies may cover your gear worldwide, *but not in transit.* Others do not pay out if you lose or damage a camera while taking part in a 'risk' sport, such as scuba diving or rock climbing.

Avoiding theft Keep your gear tucked under your jacket or in a camera bag. Don't flaunt expensive equipment – in some countries that's asking for trouble. Even if you are insured, loss of camera gear can be very inconvenient.

Before you go Clean and check all your gear before your trip. Put at least one test roll of film through a new camera and have it developed before you go. Include some flash shots. This gives you time to iron out any problems – under- or over-exposure, faulty connections, etc. Camera repairs abroad are at best inconvenient, at worst impossible. There may be no repair shop for 100 miles, or the work may not be completed before you have to move on.

X-ray machines The faster the ISO rating of a film, the more vulnerable it is to the effects of airport X-ray machines. In some countries machines which claim to be safe for film are not. In most British airports the machines have been tested and proclaimed safe for films up to ISO 1000. If your films are going to pass through several airport X-ray machines, this could have a cumulative effect on the emulsion and fog the film. Insist on a hand search of your camera bag. Make this easier by having all your film in one separate polythene bag. An alternative is to pack most of your film in your suitcase, which is checked in. This luggage is seldom subject to X-rays – but it can go astray.

Expect the unexpected Always be ready to take a picture. Know where your camera is, have a place for each item of equipment and return it there after use. Make sure the camera is always loaded and there are several frames left on the roll. Learn to operate the controls quickly. Pre-set the aperture and shutter speed for an average exposure – perhaps 1/125sec at f/8 with medium-speed film.

Photographs from the air Try to get a window seat on a plane, in front of the wing. Clean off any bits of dirt on the inside of the window. Don't worry too much about odd scratches since they will be out of focus and hardly discernible in the photograph. Set the focus at infinity and hold the camera close to the window. Avoid taking pictures looking obliquely through the perspex window, as this usually gives a blurred image. An ideal time for taking pictures is when the aircraft is banking in a turn, so that you have a clear view of the ground beneath.

YOU AND YOUR SUBJECT

Choice Choose what interests you. Monuments, landscape, moody shots, local people, members of your own travel group or whatever – but don't restrict yourself to obvious subjects. Look for detail in local craftwork, or focus on just one aspect of a building, or a close-up of someone. These details often say more about a community than an overall view.

Tell a story Build up an overall picture of your trip through sequences of photographs. Depict where you are staying, what the scenery is like, how the locals dress, and so on. Include pictures of daily activity, whether that is simply people lying on the beach or doing something more imaginative. Record people at work – mending nets, working in the fields, or selling vegetables. A coherent view of your trip will be more interesting and rewarding than a set of unrelated pictures.

Which lens? Use medium telephoto lens (100mm or 135mm) to photograph people without getting under their feet. This lens is also ideal for portraits. The small depth of field makes the subject stand out because the background is thrown out of focus. This length of lens also flattens, rather than exaggerates, facial features. A wide-angle lens (28mm or 35mm) can add drama to a picture: any thing close to the lens will be exaggerated.

Keep on clicking Film is much cheaper than the cost of your trip, so don't be miserly with it. When you see an interesting subject don't just take one picture – keep on clicking. People can often be very self-conscious at first. Once you have taken a photo they relax – that's when you should take more shots. Use a motordrive or autowinder to shoot fast sequences.

Friendly help When travelling with a friend, he or she can do a lot of the talking for you. This leaves you free to concentrate on getting good pictures. Your friend should try to put the locals at ease and distract their attention away from the camera. A friend can also help by holding equipment when you are changing films or swapping lenses. Or if you have to queue for tickets for excursions, an understanding partner can keep the place while you go to look for picture possibilities.

Above A long-focus (300mm) telephoto lens, by compressing foreground and background, makes an abstract pattern of these sun shelters on a German beach.

Don't 'steal' shots Show consideration for people who may object to being photographed if they think they look scruffy or dirty. In some countries there are those who believe that if you have a picture of them, you will hold power over them or even possess their soul. Don't be a tourist poking a camera at people as if they were animals in a zoo. Photographers who 'steal' shots in this way are not popular. Don't get in the way of what someone is doing, or that person may naturally become irritated. If in any doubt, ask permission first.

223

COMPOSITION AND ATMOSPHERE

Expose correctly Strong overhead sunlight creates harsh shadows. If someone is wearing a big hat, their face will be in a shadow and it will be difficult to pick up details of their features. It is also difficult to see detail in the faces of dark-skinned people. In a close-up picture of the face, over-expose the shot by one or two stops to bring out the features. Alternatively, place a large sheet of white card in such a position (out of shot) that it will reflect sun light back onto the person's face. Or ask the subject to move into the shade where the contrast between highlight and shadow will not be so extreme.

People and backgrounds Avoid confusing backgrounds. If you want the viewer's attention to be focused on one person or a group of people, separate them from their surroundings. You can do this either by using a telephoto lens to put the background out of focus, by positioning the people in front of a plain wall or hedge, or by crouching down so there is mostly sky behind them. Always bear in mind that, by including *some* of the background detail, you will help give the picture a sense of place; but this should not detract from the subject.

Landscape angle To avoid a 'flat' travel picture, have a person, river or road leading into a landscape to give it depth. To emphasise an interesting foreground use a wide angle lens and shoot from a low vantage point. Or, if you want to avoid an unsightly foreground, a telephoto lens will allow you to be selective about what you include. Guidelines such as 'Don't place the horizon across the middle of the frame' and 'Don't put the main subject in the centre of the picture' are only guidelines, *not* laws.

Framing A natural frame helps focus attention and lead the eye into the picture. An obvious choice is to use a tree, window or archway. Also look for more unusual 'frames' – your subject could be framed by the design painted on a famous building, or by a waterfall. But don't let the frame overpower the main subject.

Atmosphere Whatever the weather, keep your camera handy. Don't put it away just because the sun goes in. Interesting 'atmosphere' photographs can be taken in a tropical rainstorm, but shoot from shelter to keep your camera as dry as possible. Ominous storm clouds can turn a mundane looking landscape into a dramatic scene. Look out for a rainbow as the storm clears.

Lighting shift Throughout the day the light shifts. Be prepared to return to a scene at a time when the sun is lighting it most effectively. The low angle of the sun in the early morning and just before sunset generally gives the best results. This light is more flattering to both landscapes and people than the harsh mid-day sun. In the mountains, the early morning sun often glows pink on the snow for a few minutes. Be ready for it. And watch for shafts of sunlight shining through trees or windows.

Sunsets If you include the sun in the viewfinder frame, the intense light will give a very high meter reading, which would result in a very dark result. Over-expose the shot by one or two stops to record some detail in the sky and the landscape. Bracket your exposures to strengthen or weaken the colours. In the tropics the sun sets faster than in temperate latitudes, so you have to act quickly.

Night scenes Some of the best travel shots can be taken at night, particularly in bright neon-lit cities. Use a long exposure to record night time scenes successfully, as long as there is *some* light. Look for general street scenes, but look also for more close-up detail. Many cities have open street markets at night, selling food, trinkets, and so on. Always take your camera along – flash helps for poor light situations; or use a fast film (ISO 400 or faster) for candid shots.

By the sea Cameras can tolerate a certain amount of freshwater, but salt water is a killer and must be avoided. Wipe affected cameras with a lint cloth lightly soaked in WD40 or similar light oil. If you take a camera on a sandy beach, first grease the joints, mounts and hinges. Then tape over parts not in use, such as the sync. socket, motordrive terminal, and so on. Protect the camera in a bag. When changing films find a sheltered, shady spot. Store everything in plastic bags when not in use.

Hot climates If a camera is left in very hot direct sunlight, the glue holding the lens elements in place can melt. When you pick up the camera, the elements may be knocked out of place. If possible, store film in a fridge and remove it at least two hours before loading it into the camera. Insulating bags are available, into which you place freezer sachets to keep film and cameras cool. At the end of each day clean your equipment with a soft brush or cloth to remove sand and dust.

Cold climates If you are venturing to places with temperatures below $-32°C$ ($-25°F$), have your camera winterised. This involves changing the oil to a much finer grade. Store your gear in hermetically sealed metal cases and take lots of gaffer tape to seal all hinges and joints against fine snow. Where possible, keep cameras in air tight plastic bags with silica gel packets *before* coming indoors. This reduces the danger of condensation forming inside the camera.

GENERAL TIPS

Look after yourself *You* are the one who takes pictures. In hot climates, drink plenty of water, keep out of direct sunlight except for short periods and wear a hat and loose clothing. In cold climates dress accordingly – if you allow the core of your body to get cold, you would suffer from exposure and be out of action for several days. Avoid touching the frozen metal parts of the camera as bare skin will stick to them.

Buying film abroad Most countries in the western world have supplies of the most popular film types, but the film is often more expensive. If you use an unusual film, or are travelling to a remote area, it is safer and cheaper to take with you more film than you expect to use. Buying a film type you are not used to may produce disappointing results. If a small shop in an out-of-the-way village happens to stock the type of film you want, check the expiry date on the pack as the turnover of stock in this shop is probably very slow.

Processing abroad Unless you are going on an extended trip lasting several months, it is probably safer to bring all your film home with you and have it processed here. Having holiday snaps printed at a fast service kiosk in a resort area is quite different from entrusting transparencies to the international post.

Identify your pictures Always carry a notebook with you to jot down the details you are likely to forget, such as the names of towns and people. If you are travelling through several different places you will almost certainly forget where some of the shots were taken. Also, note interesting facts and figures which you can relate when you show the photographs. Take a few 'identification' establishing shots, such as the name of a town or national park on a signpost.

Selling holiday pictures Decide what sort of publications you wish to sell to – magazines, brochures, etc. Study carefully the types of pictures they use. Very few publications accept colour prints for reproduction, only slides. Telephone the picture editor or editor to make an appointment to show your pictures. He may ask you to send them, in which case use registered post. Select only your best photographs of the type used by that market. Put them in a plastic transparency sleeve so that 20 or more can be viewed at once. Caption the pictures with relevant details and enclose a brief covering letter and stamped self-addressed envelope for the return of your pictures.

SPORT & ACTION

SUPER TIPS BY EAMONN MCCABE

Freezing the action Use the highest shutter speed you can: it's better to use 1/500sec at f/2.8 than 1/250sec at f/4. The extra f-stop will not help to sharpen an out-of-focus photograph but the extra speed might help freeze the action. Action going across your field of view needs higher shutter speeds than action coming towards you.

Backgrounds In many ways the most important tip in sports photography is to make sure the background is as clear as possible. There is nothing worse than having a good photograph of, say, rugby or basketball, in which there is a tree or a concrete post coming out of somebody's head in the background. Avoid distracting signs and advertising boards. Try to get a plain background that will allow the viewer to concentrate on the action in your picture.

Peak of the action Most sports have moments in them when the players reach a peak of effort which makes for good photographs. A basketball player leaping to score, a boxer landing a knockout punch, a long jumper at the highest point over a sand pit. In football, never follow the ball but aim the camera where you expect the ball to drop. This will give you more time to focus and choose the right moment to shoot your picture.

Be aware Look for photographs as soon as you get to an event or training session. Players preparing, tense faces, managers giving orders, warm-up routines: such pictures often say more about a sport than an action photograph taken during the event itself. Also, pictures of joy or distress after a match or race can tell a great deal about a sport.

Length of lens Most amateur photographers' first attempts at sports photography suffer from the photographer not using a long enough lens. When starting out, a good rule is to use a longer lens than you first thought of for a particular shot. This has the effect of increasing the size of the image on the negative, which will give you more drama and make life easier when you come to print.

Film speed Sports photographers increase the speed of the film they are using in order to obtain usable negatives or transparencies from bad-light situations – such as floodlight football and boxing matches. A black and white film of ISO 400 can be pushed in processing to ISO 1600 without too much loss in quality. By so doing, the photographer will gain two stops in speed 1/250sec at f/2.8 instead of 1/60sec at f./2.8. This will help freeze the action – whereas a setting of 1/60sec could result in a blur and give an unusable result. Modern colour films can be uprated with very pleasing results.

Panning The trick with this technique is to pre-focus on a spot where you think your subject – a runner, racing car, horse or whatever – will pass; and to use a slow shutter speed, follow the action through the spot where you have focused, and let the shutter go while the subject passes that spot. The important thing to remember is to follow the subject smoothly all the way as it goes past you, and not to stop when you let the shutter go.

Zoom lens When shooting a sport such as rugby or horse racing, if you quickly zoom the lens in one direction you can achieve the effect of a reasonably sharp subject while everything else is a blur. By this means you create an impression of rapid movement which is particularly effective in colour photography.

Silhouettes By underexposing a group of runners or race horses and taking your light reading from the sky in the background, you can achieve a very striking photograph which concentrates on the silhouettes of the runners or horses against the sky rather than on expressions and effort. A yellow or red filter will increase the contrast between subject and background to give a very punchy result.

Knowing the sport The best sports to photograph in the beginning are the ones you know best. If you have a pretty good idea of what's going to happen next it gives you much more time to set yourself up for really effective action shots.

SUBJECTS

People in sport Sport is all about people. It's the people who drive racing cars, sit on the horses, and pedal the bicycles. Be alert to any development that may arise out of this, whether it's a head-to-head confrontation at a tennis match, or the grimly determined faces of the leading bunch in a marathon race. A violent tackle in a football match may lead to a sudden flare-up between the players. Be prepared to home in quickly on this.

Below Winners and losers: Jimmy Connors offers Ivan Lendl a consolatory pat after winning a tense rally during the men's singles semi-final, Wimbledon 1984.

Be prepared Before an action shot, do your homework. Check out locations, consider the best shooting positions. Check the weather and take enough film of the correct speed. For football pictures find out which is the stronger team – and head for the opposition's goal. Consider the lighting – try, for simplicity, to keep the sun behind the shoulders.

Be flexible However thorough your preparation, don't fall into the trap of thinking your photographic assignment will go like clockwork. During any sports event, there are so many possible incidents and developments that the photographer with a too rigid approach will miss the best shots. Be ready for controversy, look for the inevitable elation and dejection – if there's the chance of a good shot of the crowd or the team manager, be ready to turn away from the action. Always be prepared for the unexpected.

Winners Look for winning shots: the footballer in the act of scoring, the athlete breasting the finishing tape, the tennis player leaping the net, etc. Use a long lens to move in close and tight – it's the facial expression that can make or break a picture. Even down at the local park the expression of a winner can be just as interesting as that of a superstar in an international stadium.

Losers For every winner there are a hundred losers. Discretion is very important. It's an unwise photographer who goes too close to a sore, tensed-up, frustrated sportsman. Try to place the loser in the context of his particular sport. A tennis player who has lost is, for a very short while, isolated in his half of the court; try to portray that sense of isolation and despair. Losers are an intrinsic part of sport, but handle them tactfully.

Referees and managers Usually at the edge of sports action, referees and managers can become the main interest. Particularly in football and rugby, an over-zealous or officious referee is worth keeping an eye on. When a player is sent off, the display of the red card, the grim look from the referee, and the player's protests all add up to make a theatrical, even a comical shot. The team manager on the touch-line is also good material, whether he's laughing, crying or pulling his hair out.

Spectators Every major sporting event can attract its own particular type of spectators – the hat brigade at Ascot, strawberries and cream at Wimbledon, football supporters at an international match, etc. The techniques are simple – keep an eye open for the characters in the crowd who typify the event, and go for a picture sequence to help recreate the scene.

The start The peak of the action shots isn't always at the finish – the start can sometimes offer more. For a horse race or athletics sprint, look for pent-up energy on the competitors' faces. In a race let the starting gun fire and the athletes start to move out of their blocks before exposing. Catch them at full extension.

The finish Shooting the finish of an athletics race is all about timing and anticipation. At the precise moment when the winner crosses the line, he is likely to hold his arms aloft in victory. To record this successfully, pre-focus on the finish line and anticipate the exact moment when the victor crosses it. Wait too long and the shot can be missed. Just hope the winner doesn't keep his head down all the way.

Sprints The finish of a sprint race is particularly difficult because the competitors are in lanes. Unless there is a dead cert, the winner could emerge from any one of eight lanes. The best choice is a lens that isolates two or three runners. Keep an eye on the race to see which one is likeliest to win and concentrate on him or her.

GENERAL TIPS

Midway As well as the start and finish, the middle of a race can provide top shots. A group of middle

distance runners bunched together, jostling in a pack, works extremely well through a long lens which compresses them together as they approach the camera.

Eye level By far the most comfortable positions for shooting sport are standing and crouching/sitting. A camera case is very useful for support. You can sit on it – handy on a wet day – and, if you want a bit of extra height, it's ideal for standing on. Crouching down slightly is a simple way to emphasise action. A slightly high angle can portray the players against their pitch or court.

Below A low-angle approach emphasises the croquet player's intense concentration in McCabe's beautifully composed shot.

Worm's-eye view Adopt a very low viewpoint for an unusual angle. This often has to be deliberately set up, but that needn't detract from the action. A gymnast in a graceful pose, shot from a low angle, gives a dramatic effect. For this type of shot, a wide-angle lens is required. Avoid one that is too wide as this would distort the subject; a 35mm lens is ideal.

Bird's-eye view At the other extreme, a picture taken looking down onto the subject is effective. In a basket sport, such as netball, you might be able to set up a shot by climbing up the pole and shooting through the net at the players below. Court markings, as in netball, tennis, badminton, and so on, can add an attractive background pattern to overhead shots.

Fast frame For professionals, a fully fledged motor-drive is standard equipment, giving automatic film advance at five frames per second (fps). There are slightly lower models at three and a half frames, and also highly specialised ones giving 12 and even 14 fps.

Slower action These are basically slower motordrives, winding on the film at 2 fps. If you use the 'single frame' advance mode on the winder, film is wound on automatically, but you must press the shutter button for the next frame. With the winder set for continuous advance, the shutter fires automatically each time. Set for single-frame control: it allows you to fire exactly when *you* want to.

Sequences Fit an autowinder or motordrive for shooting sequences. A set of five or six pictures in a row can tell a story that a single shot can't. With a motordrive a 6 sec sequence will produce 30 pictures, so use a 36 exposure film. Follow important action but don't get carried away, otherwise you will have a lot of wasted film.

Indoor sports Shooting indoors presents a few specific problems. With relatively low light levels, requiring slow shutter speeds, it makes sense to use flash. But, more often than not, flash is banned at indoor sports events because it can distract competitors. Check beforehand whether you can use flash. Outdoor floodlit events present a similar problem. At these it is impossible to use flash usually because the subjects are too far away. In these cases, where fast film must be used, the photographer has to decide between daylight and tungsten film with colour.

Daylight or tungsten film? Before the sports event, try to find out what the lighting is; but be warned – there are even different qualities of floodlighting. If in doubt, it's probably best to opt for daylight film which gives a warm cast – more pleasing than the cold tungsten effect.

B&W or colour? Choosing between b&w and colour largely depends on personal preference and/or the final use of your pictures. Black-and-white is ideal for the photographer with a darkroom who may want to sell prints to the people being photographed or to newspapers or magazines. Colour prints are fine for showing around to friends. Colour slides can be projected or submitted to magazines for publication. Choose colour to show the brightly coloured competitors in action.

Fast or slow? Don't overlook the slower films, which can give much better results. The worst aspect of a bright sports picture against a clear sky is unsightly grain caused by a fast film. Best results are obtained by using slowish film – between ISO 50 and 100. The difference between shooting at maximum aperture on a 135mm f/2.8 lens and a 135mm f/4 lens is one f/stop. For similar exposures the 135mm f/2.8 photographer could use ISO 50 film – the other would need ISO 100.

All-rounder The best all-round film choice is ISO 200. This combines fine grain with a certain amount of speed. It is very useful for sports and action since spending the whole day outdoors might easily involve several changes in the weather. ISO 400 films are faster, but grain is more apparent. They come into their own on a typical, overcast winter day where fast shutter speeds are essential.

Floodlights When shooting under floodlights, films faster than ISO 400 are necessary. There are a range of ultra-fast films generally available, which will all give pretty good results in low light. If the light does get too low, try some creative shots using very slow shutter speeds for effect. The consequent blur of colour can be quite artistic – and it can certainly suggest energetic action.

LOCATIONS

All at sea Yachting, windsurfing and offshore powerboat racing all present one major problem – the action is usually too far away from the shore-based photographer. The best solution is to beg a ride on another boat to get in close. Don't get in the way of the competitors, hold the camera rock steady to negate the boat's motion, and take meter readings especially carefully – bright sky and sea can fool the camera meter.

Shoot wide Moving in close gives excellent shots of yachts. The billowing of the sail is exaggerated, creating a larger-than-life effect. At the other extreme, a row of masts taken through a long tele lens can be equally effective. Shots from the racing yacht itself are dynamic. The crew, busy in action, the surf pounding over the decks, a picture with part of the yacht in the foreground, are possibilities.

In the swim Swimming events usually take place in the calmer waters of a pool. Usually the key swimmers are in the centre lanes, requiring a 300mm tele to close in on the head and shoulders. Front crawl and backstroke are best taken from the side – make sure the swimmer turns his head towards the camera – while breast stroke and butterfly should be captured from the end, with the swimmer coming towards the camera. Remember to vary the approach and angle.

Diving in The start of a swimming race provides excellent opportunities. Shoot for a position slightly higher than the swimmer, and stand on a spot equivalent to a couple of metres into the first length. When the starter's gun fires, capture the swimmers in full extension as they reach for the water. A shutter speed of at least 1/500sec is needed. A shorter lens will capture all eight swimmers; a longer one isolates just a few, to give an unusual shot.

Below the water line Synchro-swimming provides the photographer with line and form in a graceful manner. A pair of smiling faces, with arms outstretched harmoniously, makes good material. But a more eyecatching view can be obtained from below the water line. Many pools have portholes for this, offering a fish's view of the proceedings. The portholes can also be used for shooting racing swimmers. The view from below can reveal much about swimming techniques.

Follow the action Many sports make photography easy because they take place in an arena. For marathons or similar long distance events be prepared to move with the action. Ride on the back of a friend's motorcycle for best shots.

On the road To get the best shots, go over the route yourself beforehand and select two or three vantage points. For a popular event, you will need to get to the best positions early. Try to get a shot, possibly looking downhill, which will allow the race leaders to be contrasted with the rest of the field further down the road. Once the field has gone past, it will be difficult to overtake them for another shot.

Marathons Shooting the big-city marathon races presents problems. With several thousand runners, it is impossible to photograph them more than once together, unless they are running several laps of a set course. Aim for interesting faces, particularly towards the end – the pain will be showing. In large towns, setting the runners against a famous building or bridge gives good perspective.

Silence For sports where silence is required of onlookers, you are up against it. That's why pictures of snooker players in competitive action are few and far between. It's a similar story with golf, although less extreme. On the tee or the putting green, the last thing a golfer wants is the click and whirr of a camera to distract him from his shot. You can't position yourself at a distance and use a tele lens – the crowds around the green would obscure your view. Take the picture just *after* the golfer has hit the ball.

Climb every mountain Good shots of rock climbers and mountaineers owe as much to physical fitness and skill as they do to photographic technique. Dispense with the camera bag – a back-pack is better, with copious pockets to hold equipment, and is essential if you, too, have to use a rope. Lightweight equipment is also better; a zoom lens is preferable to several different lenses, especially if you want to change focal length quickly.

Reflection Snowy mountain tops and ski-ing shots present problems with metering. The dazzling snow, especially on sunny days, fools the camera meter to give an under-exposed result. Most automatic cameras have a manual override facility, but this varies from one camera to the next. The best thing to do is to take a reading with the meter 'aimed' at the back of your hand; this gives a rough and ready exposure value for the scene as a whole. Metering the subject's face correctly is all-important – if it is too dark or too light, the shot loses impact.

Below A carefully chosen background is crucial to the clarity of this shot of a downhill ski racer. Originally on Kodachrome 64, the shot was taken with a 400mm telephoto lens and an exposure of 1/500 sec at f/4.

Haze Shooting high up in the mountains and by the sea can give a problem with ultraviolet haze, which is recorded on film like a blue mist. It is easily overcome by using a skylight UV filter on the front of the lens.

LENS AND SHUTTER

Freeze action With sports and other action shots, use a fast shutter speed to stop the movement. Some SLR cameras have a maximum shutter speed of 1/4000sec, but 1/1000sec is sufficient when shooting sideways at the action. If the action is head on, then 1/500sec or even 1/250sec will do.

Pan with action The problem with freezing the action using high shutter speeds is that the sense of movement is lost. A racing car, pin sharp against a sharp background, might just as well have been parked at the track-side – even though it may have been travelling at 150mph! So, when shooting from the side, track the subject with the camera, and use a relatively slow shutter speed (1/125sec) to record a sharp subject, with the background appearing as a mass of streaks.

Zooming the action This technique creates an unusual and eye-catching effect. With the zoom lens at its shortest focal length, and a slow shutter speed, pre-focus on a spot and wait for the subject to come into view. Then push the zoom to its maximum and, while you are doing this, take the shot. The main subject will be recorded with streaks of light shooting from it upwards and outwards.

Slow speeds for creativity Don't discount slow speeds for good action shots. Panning the action at very slow speeds creates off-beat effects. Athletes running round a track can be panned at 1/15sec or slower, at which speed their upper bodies will be recorded sharply while their legs will show a lot of movement and given an impression of speed. If you combine panning with zooming – the end result might not look much like sport – but it may be interestingly impressionistic.

Squeeze, don't jerk When shooting action photography, whether a fast or slow speed is used, try to keep the camera as steady as possible. Practise firing the shutter correctly – it can make the difference between a dramatic picture and the one that got away. Squeeze the shutter release and feel for the precise moment when it goes off. Repeat the action time and time again until it becomes second nature – a fraction of a second can make all the difference in action photography.

Steady does it When following high-speed action with long lenses, you must hold the camera steady. A tripod isn't much use because it is too cumbersome. A monopod (a one-legged support) is useful with long and heavy lenses and gives freedom of movement. Or you can use a rifle grip, which allows a degree of shoulder support. Otherwise, pull your elbows into the body, grip the lens tightly in the right hand and the camera firmly in the left for support.

Isolating detail When using a particular lens, aim to isolate significant detail. To avoid acres of wasted space in the picture, highlight the peak of the action. For these shots, a long lens is usually required. There are also times when you might want to relate this detail to the location, combining the action with a specific part of the background. In these cases a slightly shorter lens enables the photographer to record the main detail with a relevant backdrop for impact.

Longer than long Some sports must be tackled with extremely long lenses. Cricket is typical – with all the action in a small strip in the centre of the arena, you may find that the 'standard' lens needs to be nothing less than a 600mm telephoto. Shooting from the stands at a football match or an athletics meeting requires a lens of similar focal length. If you have only a short lens, shoot a wider expanse of the field, or wait until the action gets closer to your position.

Doubling up Use a ×2 teleconverter to 'double up'

the focal length of your lens: making an 80mm lens a 160mm, for instance. The problem with converters is the loss of light. While a 2× converter doubles focal length, it also lessens the amount of light reaching the film by the equivalent of two f/stops. Many professionals use a 1.4× converter, which makes a 600mm lens into an 840mm; the light loss with this is only 1 to 1½ f/stops.

Inexpensive telephotos Medium telephoto lenses range from 200 to 400mm. More importantly, they don't cost the earth. They are most useful when you can't get close to the action. To concentrate on football mid-field action, using a 300mm lens will allow you to follow the action and fill the frame satisfactorily. In athletics, the shot-putter doesn't want to be disturbed by the click of a shutter at a crucial moment: a 200mm lens will allow you to take the shot out of earshot.

Short stretch Lenses of 100 to 135mm are very useful – and don't overlook these settings if your zoom is 80-200mm. At a football match, this sort of length is ideal for goal-mouth action, allowing you to include strikers, goalkeeper and the goal without taking in the whole of the main stand as well. At many sports events it is possible to get close to the action, negating the need for a long lens.

Long but portable Mirror lenses are a cheap and portable alternative to telephotos. With a fixed aperture (usually f/5.6 for 300mm and f/8 for 500mm) they range from 300mm to 600mm or even 1000mm. The 300mm is only slightly longer than the typical 50mm standard lens and is easy to use. Taking up minimal space in the gadget bag, it is very useful at a sports event where a lot of walking is involved, and where tele lenses can become very tiring to use.

Wide impact Fit a wide-angle lens to create greater impact. Provided the action becomes very close you can emphasise the dramatic perspective a wide-angle creates. Wide-angle lenses distort the image, elongating those subjects towards the edges of the frame. In motorcycle scrambling and motorcross, for instance, where motorbikes fly through the air, careful positioning can ensure that the front wheel is towards the edge of the frame for best visual impact. But take care when going in close.

Ultra-wide effect There are occasions when a fish-eye lens or an ultra-wide-angle can be used to great effect. The pole vault is a difficult subject to capture on film. One way is to use a fish-eye lens, with its semi-circular view, from directly beneath the bar. From here you can include the landing mat, bar supports – and the vaulter right at the top. These specialised lenses can be used with great effect for one-off pictures; it's up to the photographer to visualise specific shots to get the most from them.

Compressed detail Exploit wide-angle and telephoto lenses for impact. With wide-angles, exploit their distorting effect and the ability to get in close. With telephotos, use their ability to isolate detail. Another quality of tele lenses is their ability to compress depth. If the subjects, say a racing car, are head-on and coming towards the photographer, using a long lens will 'compress' them, making them look much closer together than they really are. This adds drama and heightens tension in a shot.

PLANTS & GARDENS

SUPER TIPS BY HEATHER ANGEL

Creating depth A clump of flowers, a gate or an archway not only helps to provide foreground interest to a picture, but also invites the eye into the picture. Remember you see vistas in three dimensions, but a photograph is a two-dimensional image. Look carefully at the direction of the light, which can also help to create depth by casting strong shadows.

Below *Still water makes an attractive mirror image of the Music Temple in the gardens of West Wycombe Park.*

Appraise the background When taking any pictures of plants, but especially close-ups, always

look carefully at the background. Does it conflict with the foreground interest? Check that there are no unsightly vapour trails in the sky, hosepipes on a lawn, or rubbish in the background. A perfect bloom can be ruined by a tatty dead seed-head behind it, or even an out-of-focus blob of bright colour. Often only a small change of camera angle is needed to get a slightly different but greatly improved background.

A high viewpoint Look for a seat, a low wall or the top of a shed to gain an elevated view of a garden. A view from just a few feet above normal eye-level will provide a better perspective of a garden layout, while a first-floor window of a house overlooking a garden will give the next best thing to a bird's-eye view. A hill or a cliff top can offer a high-level view onto a stream, a lake or a coast line.

A low viewpoint Try crouching down to get a low-angle view of a large, tall flower or a spray of flowers or leaves against the sky. This will provide an uncluttered background which allows all attention to be focused on the subject itself. Statues can also be photographed in this way, with sky as backdrop.

Reflections in water Still water in a pond or lake reflects its surroundings like a mirror. Look for waterside trees, shrubs, 'temples' or statues which repeat themselves as upside-down images in calm water. A perfect reflection, however, is quickly destroyed by wind blowing across water or by a rising fish sending out ripples.

Perfect specimens It is not worth spending time and film taking pictures of flowers or fruits damaged by insects or frost. Always try to find perfect specimens which will be a joy to the beholder. Once a perfect flower is found, never delay taking it, for rain, frost or hailstones can ruin a beautiful bloom within minutes.

Backlighting enriches colours Red or yellow flowers or leaves look even more dramatic if they are lit from behind so that the colours appear to glow and stand out from their background. Look for red poppies in summer and deciduous leaves in autumn to photograph in this way.

Use a reflector Close-ups of flowers or fruits can sometimes be improved – especially if taken at a time of day when there are long shadows – by using a reflector to fill-in the shadows. Aluminium cooking foil wrapped around a piece of card makes an inexpensive reflector. Alternatively, there are neat circular reflectors available in white, silver or gold finish which collapse into a small pouch.

People convey scale If people are included in a picture they can give a clear indication of the size of a tree or of an architectural feature. When used in this way, people do not need to dominate the picture. Do make sure the colour of their clothing does not clash with any natural colours in the picture.

Taking sequences One of the easiest short-term photo sequences to take is of a large flower opening. An evening primrose flower will open in seconds, but most other flowers take several hours if not days to open. Sequences spanning an even longer time interval include before-and-after pictures of a new garden and also the same scene in different seasons. Remember to note the viewpoint and lens, and refer to the previous picture when taking the next one.

AROUND THE HOUSE

Garden view Wander around your garden with your camera, preferably on a fine day when the light is good. Don't take any pictures at first, but occasionally look through the camera viewfinder, assessing each part of the garden for possible pictures. Spring or summer, when flowers and shrubs are likely to look their best, may be the most suitable time for pictures. But don't rule out other times of year, especially if you have trees and shrubs with good autumn colour, or if you grow winter-flowering shrubs, or want to record seasonal changes in your garden.

Small areas Photographing a small garden may seem easy, but it can be a challenge to find the best viewpoint. Fit a wide-angle lens and shoot from a low viewpoint, perhaps with some colourful flowers in the foreground, to 'increase' the size of the garden visually. Or try a high vantage point, such as a bedroom window.

In perspective Try to give some scale to shots of the garden by including someone in the picture – perhaps digging or planting – or use familiar garden ornaments or furniture to add perspective.

Close-up Don't concentrate only on capturing a wide expanse of garden. Move in close and record small groups of flowers or plants. Even with simple cameras you can usually shoot as close as 1 metre (3ft) from the subject. The standard lens on an SLR can be focused even closer and you can add special close-up equipment (see 'Close-up detail' on page 000).

Houseplants Many houseplants make attractive subjects. Don't always photograph them where they are in the room. To shoot a small collection of plants, arrange them carefully on a table near a window, shooting from a side angle for best results.

Window boxes Whether or not you have a garden a window box full of flowers can make a pleasing picture. Try shooting the box on the window frame from indoors. Allow the shape of the window to dominate the foreground, with the view from the window slightly out of focus. Or photograph from the outside looking in, perhaps with someone at the window for extra interest.

OUT AND ABOUT

Get to know your area Wander around with your camera and see what sort of flowers and plants you come across in your neighbourhood. Aim to spend a whole day in a particular location – anything from 100 metres stretch of hedgerow to a tract of marsh or moorland – and see what varieties you find.

Local parks Try visiting your local park for shots of flowers and plants. Most parks are well stocked with interesting varieties, and when they are in bloom you can record a wide expanse of colour, often with an ornamental pond, trees and greensward.

Botanical gardens This type of garden offers one special advantage to the photographer – greenhouses full of rare and exotic plants. Look for strong shape or colour in the plants you photograph – ferns, palms and cacti all make interesting subjects. Try to choose a bright but slightly cloudy day for best light – you may find the greenhouse glass overhead acts as a useful natural diffuser for the light. If you come in from the cold, wait until your camera lens demists before taking pictures.

Woods and forests Gardens are not the only places offering good plant life – there is plenty to be found in wood and forest areas. Look for interesting plants in and around trees. Light can be a problem in heavily wooded areas, particularly when the trees are in leaf. Shoot in autumn when the foliage is less dense and the colours are more varied and interesting.

Ponds, lakes and rivers Look for interesting flower and plant life wherever there is water. Most ponds are quite still and you can record lilies and other surface plants quite easily. Use a polarising filter over the lens to minimise reflections. Seek out plants on the edge of a river or lake and use the passing water or wavelets as an effective background. Set the camera on a tripod and use a slow shutter speed (about 1/8sec) to record the movement of the river water as a blurred flow.

Underwater plants You don't have to be a sub-aqua diver to record underwater plants: you can shoot through the surface of the water. Place the camera face down into a glass bottomed box or small plastic fish tank. Pre-set the focusing to the approximate distance away from the plants and set for an automatic exposure. Make sure you work in clear water and avoid air bubbles on the camera container.

Urban plant life You will find many plants and flowers in built-up areas. You might come across an unexpected display of flowers in someone's window box or in a courtyard garden among tall concrete buildings. Even where plants have been covered by concrete paving, you may find some appearing between cracks, particularly in paving, and the sites of building ruins are invariably host to an abundance of wild flowers – sometimes including quite rare species.

LIGHTING

Seasonal changes A garden changes dramatically in the course of one year. Make a point of taking pictures during the different seasons, recording spring blooms, full colour in summer, the golds and browns of autumn, and the various winter-flowering plants. Choose the best four pictures from this seasonal change in light and colour and mount them together in a frame or album.

Weather dramas Changes in weather bring dramatic changes in light. Bright sunlight brings out the strongest colours in plants and flowers. Avoid windy days when shooting close-ups, otherwise the subject may be blown out of focus. Go out on rainy days: flowers bearing summer raindrops can look beautiful. Keep yourself and your camera dry by shooting from under an umbrella.

Snow-tinged Winter can be a good time for capturing unusual flower shots. Go out on a clear winter morning to a park or nearby wood and look for frost-tinged plants and shrubs. Look carefully for hints of colour, like evergreen plants, shrubs producing bright berries or winter flowers, and so on. A snow-laden holly bush with its bright berries looks delightfully seasonal at Christmas.

Light angle Consider the angle of the light when shooting outdoor plants. Avoid mid-day sun which casts 'flat' lighting. Early morning or late afternoon is the best time, when the sun is lower in the sky: side lighting reveals more of the shape and texture of the

249

flowers, and backlighting can illuminate petals.

Reflecting light With light coming from one direction you may have shadow areas in the subject which you want to 'fill in'. Use a piece of white card or similar to reflect light back onto the plant to produce more even lighting.

Adding flash You can add a bit of extra sparkle to flower shots by adding flash. Only a small amount of flash is required if you don't want to eliminate the effect of any natural daylight in the picture. First take a meter reading of the subject – this might be 1/125sec at f/11. If you have an automatic flash set it to two stops more than the meter reading – that is, f/5.6 – for a balanced daylight/flash exposure.

Shooting at night If you have to take pictures of plants or flowers at night, flash is the best light source. First shine a torch on the plant so that you can focus accurately; then set the flash to the appropriate setting for a correct exposure. Shooting at night has the advantage that you can eliminate any unattractive background details which would normally be visible in daylight.

In the studio When photographing flowers in a studio, choose a time when they are open and look their best. Arrange them in a vase and choose a plain-coloured background so that they stand out clearly. Try different lighting angles to reveal the shape and texture of the flowers. Flash is the best light source; lamps become very hot and may cause the flowers to wilt. Keep a fine-mist water sprayer handy for freshening the flowers.

In the greenhouse A greenhouse can be a natural outdoor studio. Set up the subject in the best lit part of the greenhouse, using daylight coming through the panes. You can shoot in direct sunlight, but you may need to soften the light by covering the glass with special diffusing material. Use white reflectors to fill-in any shadow details.

CLOSE DETAIL

Flower-heads If you own an SLR camera you won't have to buy special close-up equipment for more detailed shots. The standard 50mm lens on a 35mm SLR can usually focus down to about 0.45m (1ft), which is close enough to photograph a small bunch of flowers, or a large flower-head.

Real macro If you intend to do a lot of close-ups of flowers and plants, consider buying a macro lens instead of a normal standard lens. A macro lens gives a magnification of half life-size reproduction (life size is × 1). This is close enough for recording small flower heads, leaves in close up, and so on. As well as a standard 55mm macro you can buy longer 105 and 200mm versions for close up work from a distance.

Zoom macro If you can get hold of a zoom lens with a 'macro' facility you can focus more closely than with a conventional zoom (although not as close as with a real macro lens), and you will be able to photograph most of the parts of flowers and plants in reasonable detail.

Left Camellia flower. Such close-up shots require very careful focusing and preferably the use of a tripod.

Add a close-up lens Convert your standard lens for close-ups by adding a supplementary close-up lens. This looks like a filter and simply screws onto the front of the lens. Such supplementary lenses are available in different magnification strengths, depending on how close you want to photograph. Buy a variable close-up lens for a range of magnification strengths in one easy-to-use optic.

Extended close-up To avoid diminishing optical clarity, which is inevitable when you use a supplementary close up lens. Try a set of extension tubes or a bellows extension. Both these accessories fit between the camera body and the lens and allow a variable degree of magnification. A bellows extension can be adjusted to any magnification point within its range and is less restricting to use than tubes. Both types provide extremely close-up detail, but camera and subject must be kept perfectly still during focusing and exposure: the slightest movement will produce a blurred picture.

Close-up flash If the camera is very close to the flower or plant, as for a macro shot, the amount of light reading can be reduced. Usually the lens is too close for conventional on-camera flash to be effective – the light will pass over the subject instead of hitting it. For regular close-up lighting try a ring flash – a circular flash tube which fits around the camera lens and is powered by a separate battery pack.

Rigid support All macro photography calls for a firmly supported camera – slight movement can ruin a close up shot. You can use a good tripod or, when shooting indoors, try a small table-top tripod. This is ideal for photographing house plants or flowers on top of a table. Make sure you lock the adjustment controls on the tripod before each shot, otherwise the camera may slip out of focus.

THE SUBJECT

Finding suitable subjects Look through any book on flowers or plants and you will see there is an abundant choice of subject matter. Look in your own garden first – if you don't have the kind of species you would like to photograph, consider planting them for next year. Try some of the different locations mentioned earlier, photograph as many varieties as possible and see which ones make the most pleasing subjects to photograph.

Specific plants Set a theme for your plant photography by recording, say, the most attractive garden varieties of a particular species. Gardening books will help you to identify and locate various species and you can make a long-term project of building up a collection of pictures.

Access problems Some plants and flowers, particularly wild varieties, can be difficult to photograph because of their remote location. Be prepared to do a lot of walking or climbing to get access to less well known plants. A long telephoto or zoom lens will be handy for shooting species which are beyond normal range.

Scan low You can miss a great many smaller plants when walking around, so be prepared to scan a bit lower for hidden varieties. A long stick is useful for pushing aside grass and other cover to reveal small clumps of flowers. Lie down, with the camera supported by your elbows, for low close ups.

Perfect bloom Find out when flowers are likely to be in perfect bloom for pictures. In the open, this is likely to be for a certain short period in either spring or summer. Note down some possible dates, but remember that weather conditions can make a difference. With cut flowers, shoot after a day or so when they have had a chance to open up properly.

Mass of flowers When shooting a group of flowers, try a few different approaches. Fit a wide-angle lens to take in a wide area of flower bed – this will emphasise the shape and colour design. Or move in close to a single stem and let neighbouring flowers act as a colourful backdrop. With any group, try and focus on a central point so that most of the pictures will be sharp.

Time-lapse You can record a flower opening and closing over a period of time by using a time-lapse technique. Place the flower in front of a plain background and set a camera and flashgun on a tripod (the flash can be set at an angle to the camera if required). Then simply take a shot at regular intervals (say, every hour or two), either manually or by using a timing device. The result will be a series of pictures of the bloom opening and closing.

Trees It is easy to ignore trees when searching for subjects to photograph, but they can be very interesting. There are plenty of varieties to be found in parkland, open countryside, woodland, forest areas and special aboreta. Choose your viewpoint carefully and try picking out individual trees for pictures. Autumn is often the best time because the colours are more varied. A long lens helps to isolate tree detail from the background. Also, try looking upwards with a wide-angle to record a span of branches against a blue sky.

Leaves Move in close to photograph the leaves on a tree. Overhanging branches are easiest to shoot, otherwise some climbing will be necessary. Backlighting will reveal the shape, colour and texture of the leaves best. Look for different coloured leaves in autumn, not just on the branches, but on the ground after they have fallen.

Fungi There is a wide variety of fungi to be found in damp wooded areas. You will find them growing on and around trees – mushrooms and toadstools are examples. In these shaded areas there may be not enough available daylight, so be prepared to use flash. Angled lighting helps reveal the fungi's shape and detail.

Fruits and seeds Don't discard flowers after they

have wilted – their seeds and fruits can make pleasing pictures. Photograph them on the flower or when they have fallen to the ground. Look for fallen fruits in wooded areas – horse chestnuts on a bed of colourful autumn leaves, for instance.

Plants and insects Insects on plants and flowers add extra interest and scale to the picture. Close up equipment will be needed for most tiny insects, although you should be able to record, say, a bee or a ladybird on a flower head with a standard lens. Move in carefully so as not to frighten the insect away.

Keep a record Take a notebook with you when photographing plants and flowers and record what you have taken. When you take a lot of pictures of different species over a short period of time the notes will help you identify them after processing. Write down the film frame numbers (say, 1 to 36) and record the relevant botanical details (if known) next to each frame taken.

Good labelling Using your notes, lay out your pictures in the sequence taken and mark on them the names of each flower and plant. Keen horticulturalists will want to use the botanical names. Use small sticky labels for both slides and prints: do not write on the print itself or it may show through or become smudged if the paper is the conventional resin-coated type.

Blow-ups If you examine your pictures and find that the camera was not close enough to the main subject, remember it is possible to enlarge a certain section of the picture area at the printing stage. This can be done from either a slide or a negative. If it is a print, mark out the area you want enlarged and take the print and negative to the processor and ask for a sectional enlargement. With a slide, where there is no original print, draw a rough diagram showing the area of enlargement. There may be some loss of image quality, depending on how sharp and well-exposed the enlarged area is.

BUILDINGS

SUPER TIPS BY ADAM WOOLFITT

Allow enough time You won't get good pictures if you are running around trying to keep pace with a tour group or friends on a visit to some beautiful town or castle. Go alone or with another photographer.

Study your subject carefully Many buildings are not so wonderfully sited and finding a really good viewpoint is difficult and time-consuming. Both cities and landscapes can be cluttered up with electric wires, lamp-posts, and so on – which could ruin your shots.

Carry the right equipment On 35mm an 80-200mm zoom lens is excellent for details or longer shots of buildings within their landscape. A wide-angle lens (28mm or, better still, 24mm) is essential if you want to tackle architecture seriously.

Use your wide-angle with caution! If you point the camera upwards, parallel lines will converge; if you hold the camera level, you may have too much foreground. The solution to the problem is either to fill the foreground of the picture with things like flower-beds or water such as a pool or lake; or to invest (heavily) in a shift lens, which lets you frame the buildings without tilting the camera.

Learn about light If you want really good results you must learn to wait for suitable light and weather. Indeed, you may have to visit the location several times at different hours of the day and even in different seasons of the year before it all 'comes right'.

Choose an appropriate film Slower films (ISO 100) will generally give sharper results with less grain. When shooting slides indoors you may need an artificial-light film if most of the illumination comes from electric lights. Use only high-speed films (ISO 1200) when you have insufficient light to prevent camera or subject movement at your chosen f/stop.

Beware reflections! Flash pointed *straight* at flat shiny surfaces will bounce *straight* back, spoiling the pictures with flare or reflections. When shooting glass showcases or oil paintings, work from an angle; or, if you must shoot from directly in front, use a flash extension lead and place your light to one side of the reflecting surface.

Watch the contrast! Large rooms are much brighter near the windows. The most even light occurs at mid-day, when the summer sun is directly overhead and bounces light up onto the ceiling. Compose carefully, to exclude strongly lighted areas of floor, or windows showing the sky: these will be many times brighter than the rest of the scene and the film won't be able to handle it.

Hold the camera level You can obtain two-way spirit levels which fit into the accessory shoe for really accurate work. I prefer to use focusing screens with a fine etched cross-grid to help me align the verticals.

Always carry a folding mini-tripod If you get caught out, improvise! A pile of prayer books can level a camera in a cathedral; or a few coins will hold the lens level on a mantlepiece. I once slung my Nikon between two ski poles for a one-second exposure.

Paint a room If you like a challenge, try painting a large room with flashes. Shoot at night with a tripod and compose with the lights on. Use a flashgun with an 'open' flash facility and a quick re-cycle time. Turn off the lights, open the shutter on 'time' and then walk around lighting each area with individual flashes. Experiment with 5-8 flashes on ISO 100 film at f/5.6 before closing the shutter. With luck and a bit of practice you can light a very large area with a small flashgun in this way.

257

Above *Mellow, late-afternoon sunlight and shadow bring out the surface texture and shape of these Cotswold stone houses at Broadway.*

SUBJECTS

Exterior composition Every subject contains elements of good composition – the trick is to make them work photographically. These elements include line, shape, texture, volume, light and shade. Choose the ideal viewpoint and use shadows to emphasise line, depth, and mass in your composition, following the path of the sun. Think about the relationship between your subject and the surrounding space. Start with simple shapes, making them the centre of interest.

Viewpoint Determine your viewpoint by walking around the building to discover its interesting faces and surface details. Next, decide on distance based on foreground and background interest and choice of lens. Experiment by tilting the camera. If using a wide-angle lens, beware the distortion that occurs when the camera tilts off the horizontal. A pocket spirit-level to keep the camera level is one of the handiest accessories of the architectural photographer.

258

Urban buildings The disadvantage of cities is that they're busy, and offer less space and opportunity to frame buildings carefully. But you can get up high quite easily. Get to know a city on foot, noting the variety and contrast in architectural styles, and pay attention to how light and shadow make buildings and features prominent at different times of day.

Architecture in landscape Look for harmony and conflict between man-made structures and the natural world in the countryside. Hills and vistas of sky offer sweeping backgrounds, while animals, flowers and pathways provide varied foreground interest. Use a wide-angle lens to take advantage of every detail – but watch for intruding power lines or aircraft.

Timing On location many things can ruin picture-making. Increase your chances of success by timing your location shots. Get to know when a factory chimney expels smoke. Check local newspapers for events concerning buildings. For example, certain villages stage traditional 'ringing' ceremonies in which children join hands to encircle the church. Find out about the plans for and progress of restoration or demolition of major buildings and be ready to record any changes.

Picture ideas Once you've decided on a building to photograph, ask yourself if the subject suggests special treatment. Try the traditional approach to shooting a stately home or a ruined abbey, perhaps as a painter might have depicted them. For instance, pictures of buildings in the classical or Georgian style should emphasise the lines of perspective. Certain landmarks won't look impressive without their environs. Alternatively, single features can reveal much about a building – like the rose window or fan vaulting in a cathedral. Be aware of conventions – but try to avoid cliches.

TECHNIQUE
Direction of light Anticipating the angle of light

259

Above Careful attention to viewpoint and lighting helps to reveal the classical proportions and lines of perspective of Flintham Hall (Notts.)

saves time on location and offers compositional options. Find out which way a building faces, then draw a diagram with it relative to the four points of the compass. Trace the path of the sun, remembering the season: in midsummer it is at its highest, making very short shadows at mid-day; at about the turn of the year it is at its lowest, reaching scarcely half-way up the southern sky at noon. In the afternoon an east-facing façade will darken as the sun descends behind it, while façades facing west will be in shadow until afternoon. Avoid backlighting and low sunlight that casts your own shadow into view.

All-weather A serious architectural photographer will use the special advantages of seasonal weather. Dead leaves in a churchyard, snow melting on a cottage roof, lightning over a ruined building – conditions such as these imbue subjects with a special atmosphere. Capture an invisible breeze by means of the foliage of trees that surround a solid building: load the camera with film rated with the lowest ISO number, set it on a tripod, and keep the shutter open for several seconds, using a small aperture. In snow always select at least one stop more than the meter suggests. Under cloudless skies snow may reflect an excessively blue cast onto subjects – but this can be corrected by filtration.

At night Tall floodlit or interior-lit buildings make fascinating colour subjects. Pictures of buildings that are illuminated from below may appear too dark at the top, even when correctly exposed. Use a colour-correction filter to render fluorescent light correctly on colour film. Care is necessary with the unpredictable effects of long-duration exposures for night photography; a tripod and a steady surface are essential. Expose colour film for up to twice as long as the meter recommends and bracket your exposures. If your camera has a multiple-exposure facility try balancing interior lighting and any available twilight. Without moving the camera, make the initial exposure of the building and sky, calculated for at least three stops less than metered. Include the lights of moving traffic in the foreground to create a 'streaking' effect.

Changing tone Alter the balance of light and shade in b&w by using coloured filters. The rule is that any filter lightens the tone of a colour similar to it, while simultaneously darkening the opposite colour. Thus, a yellow filter darkens blue skies, but it lightens the colour of foliage; a blue filter darkens red brick, but lightens a cloudless sky.

Useful colour filters The most useful compensating filters for architectural work on colour film are the polariser and the 81A. A polariser darkens blue skies and eliminates reflections. The 81A 'warms' a blue cast or cool-looking subjects. Fit a graduated filter, available in various colours, to tint skies. For hazy effects use a soft-focus filter. The TTL meter in your SLR automatically compensates for filter exposure.

Film tolerance Colour and black-and-white negative films are more tolerant to exposure errors than transparency films. Experiment with colour infrared film to produce bizarre results.

Sharpness Fit the camera onto a solid tripod – preferably one with a built-in spirit level – and use a cable release to fire the shutter. If possible, use a small aperture for maximum depth of field. Avoid photographing in heavy wind or traffic which could vibrate the camera during exposure times of 1/60 sec and less. Telephoto lenses are most sensitive to shake. If you hand-hold the camera, support your body on a firm upright and hold your breath during exposure.

Buildings in focus Pictures of buildings demand sharpness from the foreground to the background, so wide-angle lenses are generally ideal. Within limits, a standard 35mm lens causes relatively little perspective distortion if it is tilted off a strictly horizontal position. Remember that the problem of sharp focus can be considerably eased if you use the smallest aperture possible, since it will provide the maximum depth of field.

Scale To judge architectural scale, just count the number of storeys in a building or compare the height of a steeple to the height of the walls. To show the scale of a building, try to include people or a familiar object such as a car. A photograph of a stately home implies that it is set in large grounds: but if a lesser dwelling has exotic surroundings they should be shown to indicate whether the house dominates the environment or is hidden.

Camera shift If you try to fit more of a building into frame by tilting the camera upwards, the verticals converge. Straighten verticals by elevating the camera position or by using an expensive shift (or perspective-correction) lens. These are made in 28mm and 35mm focal lengths and imitate the rising front effect of a large view camera. The lens moves upwards in its mount, but the film stays perpendicular to the building. Used horizontally the shift can correct a dramatically receding wall or remove an obstruction without the need to change viewpoint. Downward shift can be used with aerial viewpoints.

SPACE AND FORM

Panoramas Try a panoramic view to show a building in its environment. Set up a camera on a level tripod with a panhead, then decide where your panorama begins and ends. Pan the camera, take a sequence of views, letting each overlap slightly into the preceding picture. For continuity try to keep the sky and lighting even. Align the final prints in sequence, trim off the excess overlaps, and mount on stiff card.

Dominating foregrounds Ideally, foreground details direct the eye towards the main subject in a picture; but sometimes foreground objects dominate. Look for lines and patterns that draw attention to a building in mid-distance – paths, shadows and cobblestones, for example. Lenses of 28mm and wider make foreground objects loom relatively large, and some overlooked details can become unwelcome features in the finished print. On the other hand, you can use a macro or telephoto lens to focus on a foreground subject, such as a dew-spangled spider's web, with a modern building thrown out of focus providing the background.

Negative space In most architectural photographs background is negative space, surrounding the dominant shape of the subject. Telephoto lenses can create new relationships between objects miles apart by the effect of compressing perspective. A cemetary in the foreground can be made to dominate a power station in the distance, for example. *Never* let the background distract attention from the subject.

Rule of thirds The sky may occupy up to two thirds of an architectural photograph, so use its compositional possibilities to advantage; think of the superb cloudscapes in the paintings of Constable. The worst effects of dully overcast skies can be tempered by a warm graduated filter. A range of filters for black-and-white films can be used to darken skies.

Line and rhythm Straight lines dominate the world of architecture. Lines are crucial in composing an architectural photograph. They lead the eye to the centre of interest and they have symbolic meanings – the vertical lines in a church draw the eye heavenwards. Be sensitive to the rhythmic interplay of lines and surfaces and tones. Notice how the hard, severely functional lines of a modern building contrast with the more intricate lines and softly weathered stonework of old churches.

An eye for detail Architectural features such as brickwork, archways, gargoyles, inscriptions, and so

Right A stone arch makes a natural frame to ruins in the classical Roman city of Palmyra (Syria); side lighting picks out detail in the stonework.

on make fascinating pictures. The best light is angled sunlight because it throws textures into relief and exaggerates form. With colour film, use a polarising filter that deepens tonality and coarsens textures. In overcast conditions, and indoors, use an angled flashgun set at full power, but use a wide aperture to allow any available daylight to register in the picture.

Comparison and contrast In older cities different styles and types of architecture are lumped haphazardly together. You can point up this random collection of contrasting shapes by using a powerful telephoto lens; or you can create a sense of order from this chaos by, for instance, isolating a statue against the façade of a modern office block. See how you can compare and contrast old and new in the environment.

Macro architecture Use macro photography in architecture to photograph small models, or to record fine detail – inscriptions on brass plaques, for instance. With macro lenses and attachments you are hampered by a very shallow depth of field, so work methodically and take especial care with focusing.

Using people Don't make the buildings in your photographs look too 'antiseptic'. People at windows create interest and give a glimpse of life inside. To suggest scale shoot a window cleaner at work on a faceless skyscraper. A building is a very popular backdrop for portraits, either to show you've been somewhere, or as a meaningful part of a composition.

Exaggerate You can break the rules when photographing architecture. Make verticals converge dramatically by pointing the camera straight up at the roof. Use effects like a diffraction or a strong colour filter to create futuristic pictures. Compose with a zoom lens set to the maximum focal length then quickly switch to the minimum focal length while the shutter remains open for a 'zooming-out' effect. With colour film (slide) under-expose by half or one stop to saturate vivid colours (over-expose for print film).

LIGHT AND COLOUR

Architecture and fantasy Use architecture as one part of a double exposure, or a slide sandwich. To create an illusion of a lighted up building against a fantasy sky first take a photograph of a starlit sky, or a randomly perforated black card back lit. Then reload, ensuring that the film isn't cut off register, find a building surrounded by even black space (or shoot at night), and expose the roll again, bracketing exposures throughout. To make slide sandwiches put two thinly exposed transparencies together in the same slide mount and project for effect.

Creative reflection Use reflective surfaces to emphasise symmetry in architecture, or to introduce objects into the composition that lie outside the frame. Some modern architecture with mirrored façades reflects surrounding skies and buildings. Be careful that the amount of light from the reflected image isn't greater or less than that of the background. Water makes an interesting foreground to architecture. An exposure time of several seconds records motion on the water and reproduces an exotic reflection of the sharply defined building.

Useful shadow Shadows can be used to hide unwanted details. If a background is so obtrusive that it threatens to overwhelm the picture subject, observe it at different times to see if shadows will obscure it or soften its effect. If there's a broken window pane in a house you want to photograph, wait for side lighting to put it in shadow. Visit a location at various times of day and in different light.

Interior design Interiors of buildings can contain interesting architectural details, such as staircases, vaulting, woodcarving, stained glass (see page 268), and objects of furniture. All such things can be used to convey atmosphere or set a mood.

Available interior light With black and white film you can mix daylight and electric lamplight. Balancing these is more difficult with colour film; try to match your daylight or tungsten type film with the predominant light source, and ensure that colour casts from unbalanced light sources don't affect the film colour. Fit a colour-correction filter to convert tungsten film for use in daylight, and vice versa. Soften direct window light with a shade or curtains. The best-lit façade usually faces north, lit from a south-facing window.

Additional interior lighting Lighten shadows in large interiors with flash or tungsten lamps. To 'paint' shadow details set the camera on a tripod with a small aperture, and during a time exposure fill shadows with a repeatedly discharged flashgun, or 'paiting' with lamplight. Keep moving to avoid leaving a 'ghost' image. Watch for reflective surfaces and roomlights that may 'burn out' picture areas. Use angled flash to define low relief details such as wall plaques.

Left Carefully placed lighting at floor level effectively illuminates this stalactite-work ornamentation in the Alhambra palace, Granada (Spain).

Interior composition Locate a point of interest around which to compose. Draw the viewer's eye in by keeping well-lit areas near the centre of the picture, and allow shadows to deepen towards the edge of frame. If strong contrasts arise expose for lighter shadows, then bracket. Err on the side of over-exposure. Always watch out for your own image in mirrors, glossy walls, windows, glazed doors, and other reflective surfaces. Keep the foreground in proportion, elevating the camera to reduce it if necessary.

Stained glass To photograph stained-glass windows, bright overcast daylight behind the window is ideal. Take your meter reading from a piece of glass of average tone and density for an overall exposure. Be careful not to aim the camera upwards to create converging verticals. A very large window may be recorded in sections then reconstructed in prints joined together.

All-white subjects The most difficult interior subjects are white within white spaces. Use flash to create shadow edges and make contrast between foreground and background. To create definition around a white doorway bounce flash from a white ceiling to cause a soft shadow on the walls beyond. Direct flash makes harsh shadows. Light any white object against white to create shadow definition, white evenly illuminating the background one or two stops lighter.

Experiment Photographing architecture is challenging and unpredictable, even to professionals. Never be afraid to experiment – failed attempts merely cost you some film – which can be a bargain if a lesson is learnt. Explore different compositional ideas, or even design your own interiors with fabrics, cushions, carpets, etc. Look at how the glossy magazines handle interiors.

WILDLIFE

SUPER TIPS BY STEPHEN DALTON

Welfare of subject The most important thing to remember when photographing wildlife is to place the welfare of the animal before the photograph. Avoid subjecting any creature to more stress than is absolutely necessary. Birds are particularly prone, if frightened, to desert their nests and young, so nest photography should never be attempted by anyone who is not familiar with the techniques involved or the idiosyncracies of the species. Flash photography may also frighten many animals.

Know your subject Whenever possible become familiar with the animal you are working with by reading about and observing its habits before using your camera. Understanding and anticipating the behaviour of the animal is one of the secrets to successful wildlife photography, and is much more useful than an encyclopaedic knowledge of photographic techniques.

Below Electronic flash and a shutter speed of 1/2500 sec combined to capture this shot of a brown rat leaping from a dustbin.

Interest Pictures of animals *doing* something are more interesting than straight portraits. Try to show action of some sort – running, flying, jumping, feeding, fighting, courtship or play. Equally worth capturing on film are the less active aspects of nature such as camouflage, warning coloration, or some behavioural trait. If you have to make do with a portrait, make it a good one by clever use of lighting and composition.

Near or far Getting close to your subject with a medium focal-length lens, perhaps by using a hide or stalking, generally produces technically better results than by employing massive telephoto lenses. Watching animals from close quarters is certainly more exciting than viewing from afar. If you are able to get very close to your subject without distressing it, a wide-angle shot may be most effective to show both the animal and its habitat.

Composition Become aware of lines and shapes in the picture area, making them work for you to improve picture design. Avoid cluttered and confusing backgrounds; sometimes these are difficult to get away from in nature. Whenever possible move around your subject to find the best viewpoint. The key to good composition is simplicity.

Natural lighting Study the effects of lighting and notice how it can totally change the mood of a scene. Back or side lighting is nearly always far more attractive than flat lighting when the sun is behind the camera. Early morning is a wonderful time for nature photography. Texture is enhanced by the oblique direction of light, sunlit objects have a warm glow, and often the shadows are touched with blue. Fog, mist and dew add exciting possibilities for early morning shots. It is also the best time to see many animals.

Flash pitfalls Electronic flash is a very convenient way of providing portable light, and within limits it arrests both subject movements and camera shake.

However unless used with discretion flash can produce ghastly results. The main aim should be to try to make the animal look as though it is lit with natural light. Avoid the flat lifeless effect of having the main light anywhere near the lens axis – keep it well to one side and use fill-in whenever possible. Also, unless the animal is nocturnal, avoid jet-black backgrounds (remember that light intensity falls off with the square of the distance).

In the studio There are times when animals are best photographed indoors rather than in the wild. Some insects and cold-blooded creatures, for example, are more easily handled in the studio, and are perfectly happy in captivity. In such cases, though, a thorough knowledge of the subject is vital, for not only does its natural habitat have to be reconstructed on the table-top, but the captive has to look at home within it. Do not forget to release the creature exactly where you found it as soon as possible.

Close-up Modern macro lenses make it easy to focus close-up to insects and other small creatures. As with

Below In this shot of a desert locust taking to the air, electronic flash enabled Stephen Dalton to use an aperture of f/16. The large depth of field available at this aperture, and a shutter speed of 1/2500 sec, secured a pin-sharp image.

telephoto lenses, the extra magnification increases the risks of camera shake, particularly at small apertures, so it is sensible to use some form of camera support. Flash eliminates this problem but requires sensitive handling – remember to avoid black backgrounds, flat lighting and large areas of shadows.

High-speed photography So called 'computer' flash guns can be used to reduce or arrest the image movement of rapidly moving animals such as flying insects and birds. Choose a flash unit which can be manually switched down to low power – the lower the power the higher the speed. By selecting 1/8 or 1/16 power, a speed of 1/5,000-1/10,000sec may be obtained, but bear in mind that the light output is reduced proportionately. Thus it will be necessary to enlarge the lens aperture by several stops or to use a faster film than normally.

Capturing the right moment As it is difficult or often impossible to gauge the exact moment for firing the camera, an optical trigger is best employed, so that the animal itself fires the camera shutter when it breaks the light beam. There are a number of such units on the market. Remember that camera shutters take between 1/10-1/20 second to open and that this long delay has to be taken into account when setting up the beam and photo-cell, otherwise the creature may be completely out of focus or out of the picture. The delay can be eliminated by using open flash, but this technique can be used only when the ambient light level is very subdued.

GARDEN WILDLIFE

Birds Look out for birds visiting your garden, particularly during the winter months when there is less food about. Set up a cat-proof bird table with scraps of food and nut dispensers hanging on it for the birds to peck at. You can then photograph them at eye level from a discreet distance, using a telephoto or zoom lens in the 80-200mm range to catch close up detail. Shoot from behind a house window or through a hole cut in a nearby shed.

Birds in flight Photographing birds in mid-air requires fast reflexes. First, take a light reading from the sky and pre-set the exposure for one stop more than indicated (to capture detail in the bird). Pre-focus the lens (usually at infinity) and use as fast a shutter speed as possible (about 1/500sec) to 'freeze' the motion of the bird's wings.

Small pond If you have a small pond in your back garden this can be a natural habitat for certain types of wildlife. Watch for small insects as well as for toads and other aquatic animals. In many cases, special equipment will be needed to take pictures: include a close-up lens, extension tubes or bellows extension; and a low-level tripod will also be useful.

Small insects Find small insects to photograph on garden flowers and plants, as well as under top layers of soil. Work with close-up equipment in good light, or use flash to add extra detail.

ZOOS AND PARKS

Zoo photography You can photograph a wide variety of animals on a one-day visit to the zoo. Most

Below Regular 'patrons' of nut-baskets, great tits make an excellent subject for wildlife photographs. This shot, originally on ISO 64 colour film, was taken with an exposure of 1/2500 at f/11.

zoos permit photographers to take pictures of the animals. Choose a day when the zoo may not have many visitors, perhaps in mid-week, so you can wander around with your camera without being jostled.

Restrictions Look out for notices which restrict the use of photography – they are important for your safety as well as for the well-being of the zoo residents. Don't use flash where this is forbidden – you may frighten the animals. And don't set up a tripod where it is likely to obstruct the public walkways.

Open spaces Some of the larger zoo animals – bears, lions, tigers, etc – are allowed to roam around in large open pits so that visitors can look down at them without bars to obstruct the view. You'll need a long lens (up to 200mm or more) to get in close enough to record the animals' heads. When they are moving around, a zoom will allow you to frame the pictures more exactly.

In cages When photographing caged animals, you can practically eliminate the bars by making sure the subject is a reasonable distance away from them. Use a long lens (over 80mm) and select a wide aperture (around f/5.6 or wider) so that, with the lens focused on the subject, the depth of field will be limited enough to throw the cage bars out of focus.

Through glass When you take pictures of subjects behind glass, make sure the glass is reasonably clear. Watch out for reflections, particularly from angled glass which can pick up details of any overhead lights. Use a polarising filter over the lens to reduce reflection. If flash is permitted, shoot from an angle (not straight on) or hold the flashgun off-camera to avoid the light reflecting back into the camera lens.

Difficult lighting Inside animal houses you may come across a variety of lighting problems. If the light level is low, you may need flash. If this isn't permitted, a fast film (ISO 400 or faster) will be needed; you may not be able to use a tripod for long exposures with slower film. If fluorescent lighting is in use it may produce a green colour cast in ordinary daylight-balanced colour film. If permitted, use flash to overcome this, or fit an FL-D conversion filter.

Activity time Keep a look out for the most interesting pictures at feeding times. Monkeys and seals, in particular, have a lot of fun when feeding and you may get shots of the keepers involved with the activity too. Elephants being bathed can also yield some good shots, from the subjects as well as from the crowd.

FIELD WORK

Safari parks In most safari parks you are restricted to viewing, and photographing, the animals from the safety of your car. *Never open the windows to take pictures if this is prohibited.* Use a long lens and press it up against the window glass to minimise reflection; it helps if you have cleaned the car windows before setting out.

In the countryside If you want camouflage but don't want to go to the trouble of building your own hide, try using a net covered in leaves, branches and other natural materials. Lie down and drape the net over you, leaving space to point the camera through. Or hide behind a tree tying one side of the net to the trunk and draping the rest over your head. A small folding seat aids comfort. Put black tape over any shiny metallic parts of your cameras and lenses.

Permanent hide If you are really enthusiastic you may wish to construct your own permanent hide. You can buy metal-framed hides with spy-holes for photography, or you can build your own from natural materials (wooden stakes, covered in netting and branches).

Mobile hide Use your car as a mobile hide. Park near to woodland or other wildlife areas and shoot through an open window, resting the camera on the window frame. Use a special window clamp to support the camera if needed. A tent draped with camouflage can easily be moved into position and allows extra room and comfort for the photographer.

Planning a field trip Choose your location carefully. Study large-scale Ordnance Survey maps and if necessary visit the spot without your camera to familiarise yourself with the terrain. Make a list of what equipment is needed, particularly lenses. Read about the subjects you intend to photograph – knowledge of their behaviour at various times of the year will help you time your trip for best results.

Legal aspects Before you go out into the field to take pictures, consider the legal aspects. Is the land open to the public? Is photography permitted? Do any conservation laws forbid photography of certain species? Remember that many of these restrictions protect the wildlife you are trying to photograph. Don't break the law just to get a few pictures.

Field accessories Keep accessories to a minimum on a field trip, especially if you are likely to have to do a lot of walking or climbing to the location. Too much heavy equipment will be a hindrance rather than a help. Restrict lenses to two or three – a wide-angle, a medium range zoom, and a long telephoto are sufficient to cover most wildlife. A few filters can be helpful, such as a polariser, skylight, and possibly one special-effect such as a graduated filter. A tripod and cable release are essential. For photographing birds and other shy animals, binoculars are a must.

Stalking animals To avoid setting up a special hide, try stalking animals. Before your trip study the habits of the animals you wish to photograph and when you are likely to capture the most interesting activity; dawn and sunset are often best times. Good stalkers should know where to find the animals in the first place. Approach animals cautiously and be ready to shoot them on the move.

Long wait Even with the best preparation you can spend many unproductive hours waiting to catch a good shot of your photographic 'prey'. Wildlife can be unpredictable, so you need a lot of patience and determination. Be sure to take a supply of food and drink to help you pass the hours.

HIDDEN CAMERA

Arrive early If the 'early bird catches the worm', the early photographer certainly has more chance of catching the best pictures. If you arrive in the field early and set up before your subject is likely to appear, there is a better chance of your not being noticed. Once settled, stay where you are and wait for the subject(s) to turn up.

Baiting Animals and birds are attracted by food. If you can lay down some food as bait at a reasonable distance from the camera, there is likely to be some activity to photograph before long. Learn as much as you can about animal and bird feeding habits, and choose the bait most likely to attract those you wish to photograph.

Remote control This allows you to take pictures when you are some distance from the camera. Place a camera fitted with an autowinder or motordrive onto a tripod and connect a long air-release to the shutter button. Squeeze the pump on the other end of the release each time you want to take a shot; then the film will be automatically advanced, ready for the next exposure.

Infrared beam You can also fire the camera from a distance by using an infrared remote-control unit. Fit the receiver to the camera's shutter release button and hide within firing range of the camera, using the hand-held infrared control unit to trigger it for each shot. Or you can set up an infrared beam emitter and receiver in the path of the camera. When the subject breaks the beam the circuit automatically triggers the camera: the photographer doesn't even have to be there!

Flash throw When using flash – for photographing in low light or at night – you may need a flashgun with a good range for distant subjects. Choose a unit with a 'zoom head' which extends the light beam into a longer, narrower beam when using long lens.

Infrared film Use infrared film to photograph wildlife at night. An infrared flashgun emits light which is invisible to the naked eye – but the effects can be seen on infrared film.

SPECIAL LOCATIONS

Mountains There are plenty of opportunities for capturing wildlife in mountain areas. You can find mountain goats, sheep and other wild animals even in remote areas. Use a long-focal-length lens to insolate the subject, particularly when stalking. A skylight filter should be taken to reduce the effects of shooting animals at altitude. Take the minimum of equipment in a back pack with a waterproof cover.

Extreme cold In snow covered regions the extreme cold and harshness of the conditions can offer the wildlife photographer the greatest challenge. Camouflage is difficult in snow, so photograph your subjects behind a small white screen with a hole cut in it for the camera lens. To capture animal detail in snow over-expose by at least a couple of f/stops. Seal the camera with tape to keep out cold.

In the heat In the extreme heat in some countries, particularly those with desert areas, wildlife photography presents many problems. Because of the heat you may be able to shoot only in the very early morning and just before sunset. In any case, most animal activity takes place at these times, and the light will be low enough to reveal interesting textures. Keep equipment and film in a 'cool' box or use an aluminium case to reflect heat; never use a black case, which will absorb heat.

Rain forests Many of the great tropical rain forest areas support an incredible abundance of bird, reptile and insect life. Light levels tend to be low in dense forest, so look for clearings or river banks. Humidity can harm film and equipment so keep them in a case with a good seal. Place silica gel inside the case to absorb moisture.

Sea and seashore Look for interesting sea life near the shore. Seagulls are prominent on most shorelines and often fly and settle in groups. Look for marine creatures such as crabs in rock pools.

Underground Visit underground caves for interesting forms of wildlife. Inhabitants can include bats, cave shrimps, salamanders and insects. Most caves are dark places and unless you are working in the natural light of a cave entrance, use flash.

STUDIO WILDLIFE

Special set It can be far easier to photograph small animals, especially insects, in a studio set-up. Build a special set from natural materials (branches, leaves, foliage, etc) on top of a large table. Surround the borders of the set so that the subject(s) can't run away. Flash is the quickest and most effective light source.

In flight Use a covered tank to record insects in flight. A glass panel over the top of the tank will allow light from the flash to pass through. An infrared triggering device should be used to capture the subject as it passes in front of the camera: when the subject breaks the beam the exposure will be made automatically. Once set up the photographer can leave the insect to photograph itself.

Photomicrography Insects and other small forms can make fascinating images when photographed under a microscope. You can fit most SLR cameras to a microscope using a simple adapter. Place the subject on a glass and, using a strong light, focus through the viewfinder. For best colour quality, change the lamp for a flashgun when ready to shoot. Experiment with exposure for best results.

INDEX

ACKNOWLEDGEMENTS

The publishers thank the following for providing pictures in this book:

Colour Section
Heather Angel/ Biofotos VIII-IX, 244, 251; Stephen Dalton/ NHPA XII-XIII, 269, 271, 273; Lichfield 96, 124, 133, II-III, 210, 213; Eamonn McCabe/ The Observer 109, VI-VII, 230, 233, 234, 249; Adam Woolfitt/Susan Griggs Agency X-XI, 258, 260, 264, 267; George Wright IV-V, 217, 223.

Black-and-White Photographs
Michael Busselle 99; Greg Evans 155; John Freeman 122, 141; Chris Haigh XV below left; M A Hollis 153; S Harrison 144; David Rosen 94, 95; Sigurd Thorgiersson XVI above; Timothy Woodcock 119, 126, 143, XIV, XV above and below right, XVI below.

Drawings
Kuo Kang Chen 7, 23, 31, 33, 39, 41, 42, 43, 47, 58, 63, 67, 73, 76, 78, 80, 82, 85, 88, 102, 105, 135, 149, 157, 165, 166, 169, 173, 175, 177, 181, 183, 186, 187, 195, 207, 290; Stan North 9, 17, 21, 24, 30.